Things are in the saddle,
And ride mankind.

Ralph Waldo Emerson
Ode Inscribed to W.H. Channing

The New Global Investors

ROBERT A. G. **MONKS**

THE New Global Investors

Investors

HOW SHAREOWNERS CAN UNLOCK SUSTAINABLE PROSPERITY WORLDWIDE

CAPSTONE

First published 2001 by
Capstone Publishing Limited (A Wiley Company)
8 Newtec Place
Magdalen Road
Oxford OX4 1RE
United Kingdom
http://www.capstoneideas.com

CIP catalogue records for this book are available from the British Library and the US Library of Congress

ISBN 1-84112-109-6

Typeset in 11/14 pt Bembo by
Sparks Computer Solutions Ltd, Oxford, UK
http://www.sparks.co.uk
Printed and bound by
TJ International Ltd, Padstow, Cornwall

This book is printed on acid-free paper

To Peter F. Drucker

Contents

Acknowledgements   xi
Introduction and Summary   1

1 Adaptability: *Corporations Can Change*   9
2 The Promise: *Institutions Arise to Encourage the Expression of Genius*   20
3 The Problem: *Corporate Hegemony Threatens a Free Society*   42
4 The Solution: *The New Global Investors*   79
5 A Fiduciary Framework: *A Setting for Investments*   111
6 The Language of Accountability: *How to Depict True Corporate Value* 145

Conclusion – Where We Are and Where We are Heading:
How to Restore Authentic Corporate Ownership   175

Appendix I: Brightline®   191
Appendix II: Stone & Webster Employee/Beneficiary Remedies   199
Index   213

Acknowledgements

I acknowledge with thanks my debt to Peter Drucker to whom this book is dedicated. It might well be said that all writing on corporate governance is but a footnote to the oeuvres of Peter Drucker. Specifically, this book came out of a luncheon with Peter in Claremont, CA in July 1998, during which he generously reviewed my work to date and said: "Don't you see that governance is best understood as a subset of investment?" Once he pointed it out, I did see it and this book is the result.

I received much appreciated help from four unidentified readers and Kirsten Sandberg of the Harvard Business School Press. Alex Lajoux's erudition and style grace every page. Barbara Sleasman, the finest professional I have ever met, has made the production of the book a joy – for me! Mark Allin and Richard Burton of Capstone have over many years supported my writings. Richard has particularly contributed to this book with important editorial suggestions.

Many people have read drafts and made helpful suggestions. In particular, George Herrick, Alastair Ross Goobey and Allen Sykes made detailed and valuable suggestions. I am particularly grateful to Allen Sykes for pointing out that government inaction in enforcing the trust laws has created a barrier to effective corporate governance that can only be removed by suitable remedial government action.

I am drawing conclusions from 25 years of experience with corporate governance and this book is informed by the involvement of many partners and colleagues. All will understand that the desire to leave no one out precludes a long list and that from the beginning Nell Minow has improved all that I have tried to do.

Robert A.G. Monks
Cape Elizabeth, Maine
December 2000

Introduction and Summary

Investment is the process of foregoing immediate expenditures in order to build a more prosperous future. What kind of future are we now building? In this realm, the past is truly prologue. To predict what is ahead, we need to look in the rear-view mirror.

For most of recorded history, all of the energy of all the inhabitants on earth was needed for procreation, shelter, food and protection. People lived short, brutish lives and world population was stagnant. Not many centuries ago, humankind finally began to achieve a surplus – something more than the necessities for survival. Artificial institutions slowly evolved to provide goods more efficiently than individuals working alone. People in effect "invested" their own resources in the institutions in exchange for needed services.

In its earliest manifestations, investment was transcendent – an activity pursued by large, societal institutions such as the family, the Church, or the emerging nation-state, for purposes collectively determined.

Religion satisfied human need for a purpose in life. In exchange, the universal Church required that surpluses belonged to God, of whose wishes the Church was the exclusive interpreter. After the first millennium, the Church in the West faced dissent, and in mid-millennium, schism. The Church required the force of the state to maintain its position. For this the state exacted a price, most famously paid by Henry VIII's confiscation of monastery lands in the United Kingdom. Monarchies were always short of cash – palaces and wars are expensive – so they authorized the mobilization of energy in corporate form so as to generate a wider base for taxation. The price for this was a new "estate" – one rivaling government and the Church in power.

The rise of the corporation gave rise to a new ethos: investment by individuals or groups for *their own economic ends* (or the ends of the beneficiaries they represent). At first suspect, such investment has gradually attained moral and legal acceptance – and indeed, social enthusiasm.

The right of the individual to make fruitful investments is a cornerstone of modern liberty. This book builds on that cornerstone to present a modern history of investment. Our story begins with the first East India Trading companies, and moves in leaps and bounds to the current era. We shall see at the conclusion of this book that something is amiss. Rather than freeing human genius, the modern corporation, in many instances, is holding it captive. In the words of Ralph Waldo Emerson, quoted in the flyleaf of this book, "Things are in the saddle and ride mankind."

Reviewing the sweep of history for the past 400 years, we can see a dramatic shift in the meaning of private investment. At first in the modern era, investment was a combination of human endeavor and negotiable instruments – sweat and equity. These two were closely affiliated. This affiliation split asunder, however, with the rise of the large publicly held corporation in the twentieth century. This development differentiated – and, more important, divided – the worlds of ownership and management.

Limited liability, combined with scattered holdings, gave investors new freedom, while management remained anchored in responsibility. This splitting of the corporate atom would have disastrous effects.

For many years in this century, ownership of shares was widely dispersed. Shareholders were faceless – often unknowable to managers. Indeed, corporate managements routinely paid advisors to discover the beneficial owners of shares traded through stock brokerage firms.

There arose a class of *rentier* – passive, indeed parasitic, owners with no connection to the management of the ventures they backed, and no desire to forge one. Their reasoning seemed flawless: "If I have two choices – one is to do nothing and collect 'x,' the other is to involve myself in the venture and still collect 'x' – I will elect to do nothing every time."

The passive owner's lack of involvement created management hegemony. This is a problem Nell Minow and I introduced in our first book, *Power and Accountability*, and described at greater length in subsequent titles, *Corporate Governance*, *Watching the Watchers*, and *The Emperor's Nightingale*. It is also a problem with which I personally have wrestled for most of my working life.

(I will appear on occasion in this book as many of its conclusions are based on my personal experience in this field.[1])

For the past century, including the decades of my working life, corporate power has evolved in many of the same directions as Church and state power before it. Many of the factors that diminished the power and legitimacy of Church and state as the controllers of humankind's surplus are beginning to be manifest in the Global Corporation.

From society's perspective, the splitting of the corporate atom has engendered grievous loss. Enterprise was allowed to grow based on a self-regulating relationship to society and the environment – Adam Smith's "invisible hand." The melting away of shareholder responsibility with the proliferation of numerous owners has left society the poorer. As skyrocketing CEO salaries show, resources are enriching corporate leaders rather than providing returns to owners – and thus society.

Fortunately, however, following a curious concatenation of events, ownership has – after a long hiatus – regained its "face." Today, as in the early part of this century, there are relatively few, easily identifiable "owners" of all of the publicly traded corporations in the world. To be sure, they are not managers, as in the past. They are, rather, the trustees for giant pension funds and mutual funds. These trustees can and indeed must exercise the legendary ownership role once fulfilled by powerful, yet accountable, managers. I call these trustees Global Investors – using the term "investor" in its fullest sense to imply responsible ownership.

This book will unfold as follows:

Introduction and Summary
1   Adaptability: Corporations Can Change
2   The Promise: Institutions Arise to Encourage the Expression of Genius
3   The Problem: How Corporate Hegemony Threatens a Free Society
4   The Solution: The New Global Investors
5   A Fiduciary Framework: A Setting for Investment
6   The Language of Accountability: How to Depict True Corporate Value
    Conclusion: Where We Are and Where We Are Heading: How to Restore Authentic Corporate Ownership

Chapter 1 begins our book *in medias res* – in the middle of the current era. It shows how today even the most tradition bound and lethargic corporate enterprise is susceptible of transformative change.[2] Corporations are adaptable. Corporations need not be dominated by bureaucratic imperatives. They are capable of flexibility and responsiveness. This can be seen in the recent history of Westinghouse/CBS/Viacom. Under the leadership of a gifted new chief executive officer, Westinghouse transmogrified out of its original business, location, name, and even its existence as an independent company. The personal agent of this change, himself, ultimately had to acquiesce in his own removal. All of this was accomplished in response to the imperative for maximizing returns to shareholders.

How can these returns be maximized? Corporations are by their nature successful in proportion to their speed and effectiveness in change. There can be no single code that will define appropriate corporate governance – performance must be the ongoing tension between managers and owners as proxies for society. This is indeed the very essence of investment.

Chapter 2 introduces the concept of "investment" from an historical perspective. We argue that the corporation is the optimal structure for the fulfillment of human genius and the creation of wealth, alleviation of sickness, and understanding of the world. Tracing a course through religious texts, we illumine the conclusion that ownership without responsibility has never been ethically acceptable in the Western world. No one intended the modern corporation to function without owners. This is the unintended consequence of many unrelated developments. High taxation of inheritance compelled founding families to sell controlling blocks of stock. The families needed to transfer shares easily, which militated against any hint of encumbering ownership. Without informed and effectively involved owners, it seems probable that corporations inevitably will take on a bureaucratic cast, threatening both their own and society's healthy survival.

Chapter 3 attempts a "tour d'horizon" of the harmful impact of corporations on current American life. We are informed by the lyric voice of Carolyn Chute of the fate of the class of Maine people who have been left out – maybe left behind – by the corporate world. No attempt is made to balance corporate virtues against the shortcomings enumerated in this chapter.

Corporate financial contributions have raised the costs of political campaigning and lobbying to levels where individual participation is virtually irrelevant. The institutions relate to each other.

The real "smoking gun" is CEO pay. While the amounts – beyond any comparative in time, place, or enterprise – are staggering enough to belong to the Schlesinger taxonomy, the real problem is the fact that CEOs, by controlling their boards, set their own pay. This conflict of interest signals that the corruption of the corporate system is at hand. We compare this development with the evolution of power over centuries in churches and nation states. When the objective of an institution becomes and is perceived as the enrichment or glorification of its leaders, decline of the institution will follow. How (and how much) the principals (or owners) of these pay their agents (or managers) says a lot about how these institutions are run and for what purpose. It is impossible for an outsider to evaluate the performance of a board of directors. Through the incentive systems created for principal executives, boards manifest what they think is important. If there is no effective control in this realm, one must ponder whether there is any effective limit to corporate management power over the whole range of matters that affect us all.

Chapter 4 identifies and labels a class of the institutions who collectively are the largest owners of modern corporations. These GIs ("Global Investors") are the public and private pension funds of the US, UK, Netherlands, Canada, Australia, and Japan.[3] Through extrapolating the specific holding of a number of the largest pension schemes, we conclude that the level of ownership in virtually *all* publicly voted companies in the world is large enough to permit the effective involvement of owners in the governance of those corporations. This involvement will have beneficial results for society.

Pension funds are distinctive trusts. In contrast with mutual funds, insurance companies, and even foundations and endowments, pension funds have identifiable beneficiaries – typically individuals who will retire in 20 years with adequate resources and with the intention to live with dignity in a safe, clean, and civil world. Because the human objects of the trusts have harmonious and definable characteristics, the trustees can administer trust assets – portfolio holdings in many companies – in a way that furthers these objectives.

Chapter 5 provides a framework for fiduciaries – a scaffolding they can use to rise above a terrible paradox of our times. Note well a quarter century of proof that:

1   activism adds to value and improves corporations; and

2 government-created trustees – pension funds, mutual funds, and banks – decline to take advantage of this fact. (They are very much like the legendary economist refusing to bend down to pick up the $20 bill from the sidewalk because it is impossible that it would be there.)

Institutional investors – most of them trusts – hold a majority of ownership of US and UK companies, yet there is little evidence of shareholder activism in most of them. Although prominent investors like Warren Buffett, Carl Icahn and Martin Ebner have demonstrated that shareholder activism can enrich its practitioners, and while corporate "governance" has supposedly improved as a result of such efforts, nothing much has changed as a result. Neither the private pension funds (excepting the College Retirement Equities Fund [CREF] and Hermes) nor the "great and the good" (in the form of foundations and university trustees) have joined this beneficial movement. What kind of revolution is this in which the natural leaders refuse to participate? While the letter and the spirit of the law both require fiduciaries to act exclusively for the benefit of plan participants, the reality is that beneficiaries have a right without a remedy. No "rational" plan participant can afford to bring a case. Even if such a participant could surmount the economic inefficiencies they would be stopped by the burden of proof. This is a situation where government has – inadvertently, to be sure – fouled the market for corporate governance. Lawmakers have taken ownership away from individuals and put it in the hands of trustees, passing trust laws to support this new status. Unfortunately, however, government has failed to enforce those laws and has failed to make suitable provision for individuals to enforce. Only the faintest glimmer of hope can be seen in the Stone & Webster case – now under litigation.

Chapter 6 offers guidance to corporations interested in developing such a language – the chapter describes the efforts that are currently underway to help measure and report their impact on society. This ranges from the enormous commitment of a company like Shell, which has employees and customers all over the world, to focused pressure groups (such as INFACT, which is comprised of a few dedicated individuals). The Coalition for Environmentally Responsible Economies (CERES), arising out of Exxon's Valdez oil spill, has provided leadership for the creation of universal environmental standards under the Global Reporting Initiative (GRI) – much as the accounting profession has created the Financial Accounting Standards Board (FASB).

The communications technologies of this new era permit dissemination of information freely and immediately. While there will never be – and should never be – a single, static code for conduct, there are certain principles that should inform the entire corporate community – principles such as disclosure, legal compliance, and restraint with government. The evolution of these governing principles provides a convenient "handle" for the involvement of owners. Owners cannot manage and should not manage. They should, however, provide and monitor performance guidance on core principles.

Option-based compensation – referred to in Chapter 3 – inclines recipients toward values that are relatively short-term – five years or so. Some leading corporations like Ford have created incentives for executives' performance that are tied to certain measurements other than stock price. Ford wants to encourage a culture of "customer concern" with the thought that such encourages long-term enterprise value. Ford's owners are conspicuously involved in management. Can Ford be a model for others?

We conclude with a summary of where we are and what we might do to progress. It boils down to the question of government's willingness to cure the unintended consequences of its successful retirement policy. The cure will have broad implications. Once the duties of a pension trustee are codified, they will be found applicable to other fiduciary institutions.

Endnotes

1   For more on my personal experiences, see Hilary Rosenberg's fine biography, *Traitor to His Class* (New York: John Wiley & Sons, 1999).

2   IBM, like Westinghouse, reached into the McKinsey Alumni Association to find a change-agent CEO. Appropriate leadership can be found.

3   These are the only countries with pension systems that are substantially funded.

Chapter 1

Adaptability

Corporations Can Change

The forces of globalization have substantially accelerated convergence towards the publicly held corporate form. The availability of information – instantaneous, free, and universal – has brought the reality of change to everyone everywhere.

Yet all businesses, once successful, develop an aversion to change. This fact is abundantly clear in the story of Stone & Webster, recounted in Chapter 5 of this book. As this appalling case shows, it is so hard to achieve sustainable profitability that managers have an overwhelming temptation to lock in place all the rules – including the rules that govern their pension funds. This is why the large corporations are, if the truth be known, so very much in favor of complicated regulatory structures. As entrenched players, they know the rules; new entrants have a steep learning curve to climb if they are going to compete.

When corporations want to change, they can do so very effectively. But *change must be led by someone who is willing to accommodate societal concerns*. Is it the "board of directors?" Is it the "philosopher king" CEO? In my view and experience, the answer is no. The answer, instead, lies in corporate shareowners. It is difficult to imagine any constituent having the independence, the motivation, the knowledge and the power of these investors, especially today with their new global reach.

It is this capacity to respond to change that distinguishes the publicly owned corporation from other business organizational forms. The first corporations, including notably the East India Company, were created by government to serve a particular public objective. They were instruments of the state. This tradition lingers in many countries, most notably in post-World War II Japan. The difficulty lies in the inability of the state, or – for that matter, anyone – to know enough in order to proscribe a continually healthy and profitable course for an enterprise. Could the most elite Japanese or French civil servant have anticipated so violent a necessary change and have proscribed such an effective response as Microsoft's in 1995, when Bill Gates bet on the Internet?

Again and again this unique energy of the private corporation is evidenced through experience. With all their flaws, corporations are better than the alternative: state-owned enterprises. Why? Because corporations, if owned by shareholders, are highly adaptive. State-owned corporations run without market pressures are far less adaptive. The best they can do is phase out when the public no longer needs them.

How very different from the typical state-run company is the splendid example of Westinghouse Corporation, which has used its relatively high level of freedom, energy, and resources to maximize shareholder value, converting from a diversified technology firm with $11 stock to a television and radio company with $45 stock – and changing its name twice in the process. What explains the change? The engine was a set of managers and importantly, owners, committed to optimizing shareholder value.

We deliberately selected a company involved in communications technology. Technology advances emanate directly from an environment of freedom. The liberation ratio = freedom + genius/constraints. When the liberation ratio declines, pressures build to create new institutions. Technology provides a phenomenon new in the planet's experience to this time: Information can be available to everyone, everywhere, at the same time and free. CBS has been an exemplary part of this change – and all because its leader understood and shared the goals of his company's owners.

The WX/CBS/Viacom story

WX, as it appeared on the New York Stock Exchange ticker, was an institution – cited for excellence since its founding in 1886. In that year, George Westinghouse developed the technology that found practical uses for alternating current, successfully competing against the advocates of direct current – among them his contemporary, Thomas Edison.

His company has since achieved an enviable list of firsts: the first tungsten lamp, the first commercial radio station, the first television camera, the first atomic engine for the Nautilus submarine, and the camera that broadcast man's first steps on the moon. In 1900 George Westinghouse introduced the slogan, "The Name of Westinghouse is a guarantee." Today we say, "You can be sure ... if it is Westinghouse." However you say it, Westinghouse has been known for innovation, for quality, and for technology designed to improve the welfare of mankind. The Westinghouse Science Honors Institute (for promising high school students) is still one of the most respected programs in a culture keen to the possibilities of technology.

Let us look more closely at the history of Westinghouse to see the important role played by investors in changing the company over time. While the company has been one of the most prestigious in the land (one of the Dow Jones 30) for most of the twentieth century, it has not been free from problems. History records that George Westinghouse lost control of his company in a financial panic in 1907. Along with its long-time rival – The General Electric Company – Westinghouse was convicted of a price-fixing felony in the so-called "electric company conspiracy" of the late 1950s. In the 1960s, the company virtually went bankrupt on account of promises to purchase uranium at a fixed price in a market that fell precipitously. The courts were persuaded to extend the ancient doctrine of "force majeure" in order – one suspects – to save a great corporation.

The comfortable prosperity of companies like Westinghouse – coddled by oligopoly and US world dominion following victory in war – became sorely threatened in the 1970s with the abandonment of the gold standard and the reality of foreign competition in domestic markets. The great General Electric was driven out of computers, driven out of making television sets, and driven out of nuclear power generation. Westinghouse diversified with a vengeance into activities spread across the commercial spectrum, from low-income housing to resort development in 135 divisions with marginal profitability and no organizing theme.

Its belated entry into the finance field in the late 1980s was a disaster, the extent of which was amplified by appalling board misjudgments and incompetent top management. In 1987 Westinghouse Credit Corporation accounted for 16 percent of the entire corporate profit with a return on equity above 20 percent. An incentive compensation scheme that rewarded increments to return on equity without any consideration of debt led to the situation described by Peter Nulty in *Fortune* magazine as "shoveling the loans out the door with the speed and abandon of a go-go S&L into high-risk, high-return investments,"[1] such as shopping centers, junk bonds, and leveraged buyout (LBO) financing. Because short-term earnings increased and the public failed to notice the build-up of debt, WX stock actually went up in 1989.

The last Westinghouse CEO to be a national figure was Douglas Danforth. When he retired, the board was unable to agree on a successor. Directors split 5–5 between longtime staff person John Marous, age 63, and the younger Paul Lego, with a career as an operating executive. No Solomon emerged to resolve this deadlock, so they divided the baby: Marous was to be CEO for two years and Lego was committed as his successor. Marous was in charge of the Credit Corporation; Lego oversaw the rest. By the time Lego took over in 1990, long-term debt had escalated to $5.2 billion, the company had an operating loss of $844 million, and $3.5 billion of WX's assets were classified for "restructuring."[2] By the close of 1991, fully 67.3 percent of WX's assets ($6.52 billion) were considered bad. *Business Week* commented that only the fall 1991 negotiation of a new line of credit kept Westinghouse from filing in bankruptcy.[3] I made note in my journal of a meeting during this troubled era.

> *"A meeting with Paul Lego on October 22, 1992, was almost surreal. He was literally the only executive present on the top floor of the Westinghouse building in downtown Pittsburgh. We had a spaghetti luncheon, prepared by his closest colleagues in the company, Tony and Eileen Massaro, in the empty executive dining room. The formal meeting started with (I clocked it) a 25 minute unprompted monologue in the style of the Rime of the Ancient Mariner. Each verse of the lengthy rhyme ended with the refrain 'It ain't my fault.' Paul was at the same time genuinely in love with Westinghouse, bursting with pride to be its head, furious about his colleagues' ineptness – 'They took my cash flow and put it into that bottomless pit,' and unconscious as to the imminence of corporate death."*

In late October, Lego had to issue a statement saying the company was not contemplating a bankruptcy filing. In November, the company announced that it was getting out of the financial services business and would henceforth concentrate on its historic leadership positions in transport, temperature control and broadcasting markets, as well as on three technology-based businesses: electronic systems, environmental systems and power systems. As I noted in my journal, "This isn't the end of it. Somewhere in that big company, there is a small company trying to get out."[4]

In December, WX adopted a whole range of governance amendments in a belated effort to appeal to institutional shareholders.

In January, Lego departed.

On April 28, 1993, I spoke at the annual meeting in Minneapolis, citing an editorial I had published simultaneously in the *Wall Street Journal*:

> *"[Westinghouse] is a company all but ruined by mismanagement and neglect. The mismanagement was the fault of the chief executive officers; the neglect was the fault of the board. The CEO resigned after four months; the directors are still there. That is the problem … Unfortunately [under American law] shareholders can't 'fire' the board; the law permits only a symbolic withholding of approval. In withholding my approval, I am casting a vote of no confidence."*

On July 1, Michael H. Jordan, a consultant with McKinsey, was named the new chairman and CEO of Westinghouse, the first from outside the company in 64 years. Jordan indicated early on that he was going to do what had to be done and very sensibly declined to talk with anyone for six months. His "coming out party" was held before a packed crowd in the big ballroom of Donald Trump's flagship hotel, The Grand Hyatt Hotel on 42nd Street in Manhattan on January 11, 1994. The speech from this calm Yale/Princeton alumnus gave the candor that one expects from a hustle-hardened consultant. His message: "No quick solutions, no easy answers, patience, better execution, and maybe we can get the results that GE gets from comparable businesses."

More journal entries follow:

> *"Undated (April 1995) – Torrential rain on the windows of Michael Jordan's hotel room in Orlando, Florida, provided atmosphere for two hours of intricate chasing after possibilities for WX. How much time will the market give him to change the company culture? He thinks that tightening up will produce substantially improved earnings, but he doesn't sound confident that it will be enough. It boils down to the old Maine joke – 'There is no way to get there from here.' The core businesses don't have the scope or the margins to carry a major enterprise. The only asset with value appeal is broadcasting. Nobody can believe the*

company's accounts – too many changes. Michael won't quit his outside boards, but concedes that his own is mediocre.

"September 12, 1995 – Pittsburgh headquarters – after 15 months, WX is still trying to get a handle on the problems and develop new opportunities. Power generation business is dead, so the firm is pursuing niche markets – long shots like nuclear power in China – with Jordan's personal time. You can count the improvements, but there does not appear enough progress to change the basically negative momentum. New directors are being sought – but Jordan will not cut down his own outside commitments – he listens well and describes suggestions as 'interesting.' Finally, I ask – 'interesting means yes, interesting means no?' He doesn't miss a beat – 'Interesting means I am not going to be bullied.' Only one discordant note – an utterly random 'I don't need this job.' This is an energy that will work out its own solution. Will the 1994 results confirm the present direction?"

Jordan had induced Fred Reynolds, a personable and insightful financial maven, with whom he had worked at Pepsi Cola, to join WX as CFO. Together, Reynolds and Jordan reviewed the portfolio of businesses and found that they were not as badly run as originally feared. Their ability to understand the interrelationship between the cash flow and the liabilities of the disparate entities and to articulate it with confidence to lenders and investors provided the element of credibility that a decade of incompetence had eroded.

Plainly, Jordan's intent at the time of his first annual report was to save the Westinghouse franchise – sell off what had to go in order to pay down debts, improve operations, and restore financial discipline and systemic coherence (over one hundred different accounting systems) to headquarters. Transformation could be neither large nor quick enough to attract capital competitively.

A pattern began to emerge. Westinghouse divisions had not kept up with worldwide developments and either were not large enough to form the core of a continuing enterprise – power generation business, for example – or were dominant in an anecdotal market – refrigerated transportation. Again and again, the conclusion was forced that the only business susceptible of being favorably valued in the marketplace was broadcasting. Traditionalists would continue to advise that broadcasting be sold and the proceeds used to free up the industrial units that were the traditional soul of the enterprise. Jordan and Reynolds, the outsiders, came rather quickly to a contrary conclusion – they should use broadcasting as the base on which to build a modern communications empire.

Such a decision is the genius of the corporate mode. The corporate institution exists in order to create long-term value for its owners. There is no "bill of rights" guaranteeing right to life for particular industrial units or right to location for particular communities or right to employment of specific individuals. The corporate energy is the search for competitive investment of capital. This undiluted focus accounts for the worldwide dominance of the corporate form over partnerships, co-operatives, mutual enterprises, and government-owned or dominated companies. The deployment of financial and personnel resources in the focused pursuit of an identifiable objective results in creation of values that ultimately enrich all constituencies – what Jordan's old firm McKinsey & Company calls the "virtuous circle of shareholder value."[5]

On August 1, 1995, WX announced the acquisition of CBS for $5.4 billion. The market had expected this, and WX stock rose barely ten percent. Where is the money coming from – J P Morgan, where else, and – down the line – from the continuing disposition of industrial businesses. The price appeared "full," but only because the market had savagely written down the management of the selling Tisches.

> "Westinghouse was still recuperating from a string of massive losses, and banks were clamoring for debt repayment. Cash flow was stretched thin. Fronting costs on expensive power-generating projects overseas drained a large and growing chunk of working capital 'Westinghouse could barely buy lunch, much less CBS,' says a securities analyst who recommends the stock today.[6]
>
> "To work, it would require that everything fall neatly into place; Westinghouse must get financing to do the deal, it must sell off assets at a good enough price to pay down all or most of that new debt, and it must in the end turn out to be good at the broadcast game. It's asking a lot, but if it does work, what a change. Instead of a crummy bunch of low-margin businesses, you have a hot, high margin company with room to grow.[7]

This announcement coalesced all of the fear and suspicion of traditional Westinghouse – employees and deserted community. Had Michael Jordan ever moved to Pittsburgh? Did he own a house there? One Westinghouse employee stood up during a meeting after the announcement and accused Mr. Jordan's team of "leaving for New York on a luxury liner and leaving the rest of us behind on a leaky barge."[8] Westinghouse's decade-long failure to keep up with the worldwide competitive trends compelled the conclusion that the businesses being sold are more valuable to other enterprises than to a US company increasingly focused on broadcasting. Reynolds got fine prices for the businesses:

- 1994 – Distribution and Controls to Eaton – $1.1 billion
- 1995 – Real Estate Development
- 1996 – Knoll group to Warburg Pincus – $565 million
- 1996 – Defense Electronics to Northrup Grumman – $3 billion
- 1997 – Thermo King to Ingersoll Rand – $2.56 billion
- 1998 – Power Generation to Siemens – $1.53 billion

All of these units are performing well in their new incarnations. Jobs have been added, not lost. The same suppliers and employees are for the most part grinding, polishing, and welding for the same customers just as they ever did. But there are new owners now, and more profits for them, who have paid handsomely for the opportunity.

Meanwhile, Westinghouse was making substantial acquisitions in the communications area. It acquired the leading independent radio operator, Infinity Broadcasting, for $4.9 billion, and announced the acquisition of two major cable TV stations, The Nashville Network and Country Music Television. And in the same year – 1997 – it announced that CBS would be "spun off" into a separate company from the surviving Westinghouse industrial companies. In fact, this never worked out as the dispositions continued and viability of the remaining assets became doubtful.

Jordan announced that as of December 1, 1997, Westinghouse would become a media firm known only as CBS Corporation. What was left of the industrial assets were to be sold in pieces. Headquarters will move to New York City, the stock ticker WX and the 111-year-old name Westinghouse would vanish from the face of the earth. On March 22, 1999, the new Westinghouse Electric Company, a combination of three enterprises in the nuclear and environmental fields, was born as the subsidiary of Morrison Knudsen Corporation and British Nuclear Fuel Laboratories.

Progress at CBS was not immediate. In acquiring Infinity, the new venture also acquired its largest shareholder and a legendary media value enhancer – Mel Karmazin. Karmazin successfully became part and then leader of the enterprise, beating out first CBS's Peter Lund to become chief executive of CBS's television station group, and then Michael Jordan himself at the end of 1998 to become CEO of CBS, itself. An energetic and optimistic man, Karmazin in 1999 merged CBS into Viacom and became CEO in waiting for the mantle to pass from the 77-year-old Sumner Redstone, who owns an even larger stake in the combined enterprise than he does and who shows Armand Hammer-like tenacity in holding onto life and his job.

In May 2000, despite considerable public opposition, the merger became legally effective and George Westinghouse's legacy became part of the Redstone–Karmazin empire.

Michael Jordan's five years with Westinghouse provide unique insight into the character of capitalism at the end of the twentieth century. As one observer wrote, "He's very capable, but he's not a charismatic-type figure. He's got a game plan and strategy and tries to carry it out, but I would describe it as more leading by doing: this is what I am doing – come and follow me."[9] His education at the principal meritocratic East Coast institutions provided comfort in dealing with financial institutions and engineering expertise to inform his judgments in weighing values at a traditional technology company like Westinghouse.

The McKinsey legacy

The ubiquity of McKinsey & Co. has been widely observed. It becomes clear in hindsight that the legendary Marvin Bower, past managing director of the consulting firm, was able to communicate insight into the process of value adding that has made so many of his alumni into successful CEOs in world class companies. Between Pepsico (where he did not become CEO) and the investment firm of Clayton, Dubilier & Rice, Jordan had the opportunity to meet this generation's business leaders, to become a director of several companies, and to earn significant amounts of money long before deciding to take on the ultimate challenge of "turning around" Westinghouse (in the style of his former McKinsey colleagues Lou Gerstner at IBM and Phil Purcell at Dean Witter, now Morgan Stanley). While he was not conspicuously undercompensated for his time at Westinghouse, it is probable that Jordan has not in recent decades otherwise worked so hard and so long for so little.

What emerges is the human incarnation of capitalist energy – a corporate leader convinced that resources must be committed in the direction of earning the best competitive return, possessed of superior analytic skills, not pressed by time or personal need, willing to reverse direction in the face of evidence, and willing to be abused personally for not pleasing all of the people all of the time. And crowning this portrait was Jordan's willingness to leave – without public rancor – a position of power that he was entitled to keep indefinitely.

Michael Jordan manifested the strategies necessary to enhance ownership value and was endlessly patient and purposeful in taking the chances necessary to achieve his goal. This corporate leader found an enterprise firmly anchored in the past and barely out of the clutches of bankruptcy. Patiently but surely, he tested several solutions, and ended up with one that changed the ownership and management of virtually all of the assets he inherited. In the process, he created highly competitive value for the company's investors. He did so with the active support of investors whose investments spanned the globe. This is the nature of the publicly held corporation – US style – at the end of the twentieth century. (See Fig. 1.1.)

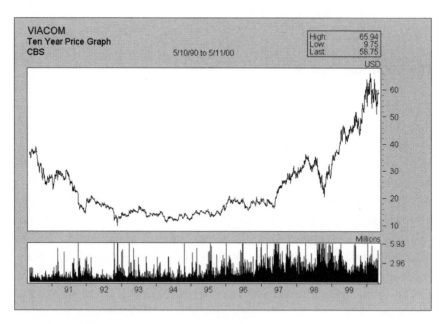

Fig. 1.1 Viacom Corp. – ten-year price graph.

Endnotes

1   Peter Nulty, *Fortune*, November 4, 1991, pp. 93–99.

2   Westinghouse, *Annual Report*, 1990, pp. 2, 21–24.

3   *Business Week*, March 8, 1993, p. 69, as cited in James P. Hawley & Andrew T. Williams, *The Westinghouse Corporation and Institutional Activism* (a research proposal), October 4, 1994.

4   Nell Minow, "Westinghouse Decides to Retrench, but CEO Remains under Fire," *Wall Street Journal*, November 24, 1992, p. A5.

5   *McKinsey Quarterly* 1997, 2, pp. 156–167.

6   S.L. Mintz, "Why Westinghouse Thinks Buying CBS will Solve its Operational Woes," *CFO*, April 1996, p. 29.

7   Jay Palmer, "Strategy Switch? Westinghouse's Sudden Interest in CBS May Reflect Radical Plan in the Making," *Barron's*, July 24, 1995, p. 12, quoting author.

8   Timothy Aeppel, "How Westinghouse's Famous Name Simply Faded Away – Media-Struck CEO Didn't Follow Through on Promise to Keep Industrial Lines," *Wall Street Journal*, November 20, 1997, p. B6.

9   Lisa Green, "Jordan's Strategy Faces Major Test," *USA Today*, August 2, 1995, p. 3B.

Chapter 2

The Promise

Institutions Arise to Encourage
the Expression of Genius

The corporation has emerged in the later decades of the twentieth century as the premier institution for the identification, cultivation, and realization of genius – and for the conversion of that genius into value. Innovation has generated vast new wealth. The availability of information, patient investment capital, and supportive legal and ethical systems provides an atmosphere conducive to creativity. The explosion of new research and new products across virtually the entire spectrum of business life has transformed human conduct and, in most instances, improved the quality of life for all.

As always, however, progress has exacted a price. Concomitant with all these improvements in productivity, however, has been the centralization of power. The modern Global Corporation, not unlike Church and state before it, can be a force for weal or woe. The answer to this question lies in the hands of the owners. The failure of members and citizens to force effective reforms from within the Church and state has sharply eroded the significance of those institutions, which might well have perished were it not for reformers. Would the Catholic Church have reclaimed its vitality had there been no Jesuits? Can the investor behave in a more enlightened manner and preserve the vitality of the corporate institution?

History yields some answers in particular, The Parable of the Talents, as told in Matthew 25: 14–46, King James Translation, which begins as follows:

"Thou oughtest therefore to have put my money to the exchangers, and then at my coming I would have received mine own with usury. Take therefore the talent from him, and give it unto him which hath ten talents. For unto every one that hath shall be given, and he shall have abundance: but from him that hath not shall be taken away even that which he hath." [1]

In the year 1611, readers of the English language encountered these words for the first time in their own idiom – during a time the financial world was changing forever, for reasons well explained in this parable.

At one level, the meaning of the parable, attributed by the Gospel writer Matthew to Jesus, was time-honored and universal: those who have gifts of any kind should invest them. If they do, those gifts will multiply, and that multiplicity will in turn be rewarded; while an opposite progression into poverty will befall those who do not invest in such an active manner.

At another level, however, the statement was and still is entirely radical – a concept so stunning that even today most listeners refuse to hear it. The message that came through to the ordinary citizen for the first time just 400 years ago was this: *active financial investment is imperative for human welfare.*

The seed of this idea is bearing fruit today. To understand this multiplying effect, consider that in 2000, the world's stock of liquid financial assets was seven times larger than it was in 1980 (See Fig. 2.1) – and geometrically

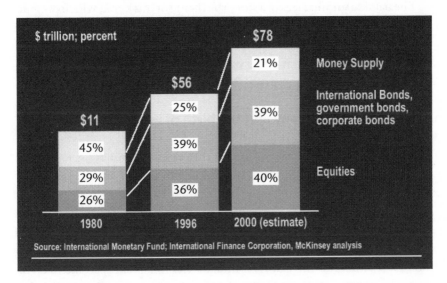

Fig. 2.1 By 2000, the world's stock of liquid financial assets will be seven times larger than it was in 1980. (Source: *McKinsey Quarterly*, 99–4, p. 75.)

larger than it was in the years when the Parable of the Talents was spoken, written, and variously translated.

How did this stupendous growth evolve over the space of 20 years – or 2000 years? In the past several centuries, millions of sermons have been preached on the Parable of the Talents, including sermons from my father, a man of the Episcopal cloth. And many books, including business books, have quoted this ancient story. But to my knowledge, no one has ever focused on the unmistakably *financial* content of this parable.

Yet in my view, it is the financial point of this passage that demands the most attention. The parable speaks not only of talents, as in human capabilities; it also talks about those talents as *expressed economically through investment*. The parable in fact prophetically captures the essence of an economic era that began to take hold in England at precisely the time these words were being translated by King James' 47 paid scribes.

The synchronicity is strong. Whatever one's view of the individual allegedly speaking these words – Divine Son of God or purely human – few would deny the cultural weight of these words. And their meaning is clear. A figure no less important than Jesus, one deified by Christians, and recognized as historically significant by adherents to all other major faiths, was urging humankind to make *active use of its financial wealth – in a word, to invest*.

The parable summarizes in a story the theme of this book, which presents a theory and history of investment in the modern age – an age that dawned in England, with the birth of the East India Company in 1600, just as the King James translation was underway.

The East India Company and the birth of economic modernity

The English East India Company came into existence just as the long reign of Queen Elizabeth I of England was coming to an end (she died in 1603). This event marked a turning point in economic time. The Tudor monarchs had accomplished much in bringing their country to the forefront from the point of view of wealth, effective government, and foreign adventure. King Henry VIII had enriched the monarchy and its noble allies by confiscating the vast resources of the Catholic monasteries. Sir Francis Drake had circumnavigated the globe and led the effective resistance to the Spanish Armada in 1588. The merchant classes in London had effectively organized internal trade and had accumulated substantial savings for investment. Yet there was much more to come.

Above all, it was on British soil under the Tudor watch that one of the earliest events in modern corporate history would unfold: the creation of the East India Company. This single event would make England the center of gravity for modern investment.

To be sure, the Spaniards and the Portuguese enjoyed a substantial head start in navigation and the generation of wealth from foreign colonies – so much so that Pope Clement VIII saw fit to give them half the world. He mediated on Spain's behalf in the Franco-Spanish War in 1598, and, in the process, reserved unto Spanish powers a large portion of Christendom beyond Europe. The Dutch, too, were a force to reckon with. They had been most enterprising in finding commercial opportunities neglected by the Iberians. Indeed, it was the success of the Dutch expeditions that broke all the political obstructions to the creation of the East India Company in England on the last day of the old century.

The British had been slow to organize their own East India Company, but concern about Dutch advancement sparked action. As John Keay observes in his history of the English East India Company:

> *"The final straw came with the news that the Dutch were now seeking to augment their eastern fleets by purchasing English shipping. Arguing that the national interest was at stake, in July 1599 – just two months after ships of the second Dutch fleet began returning with packed holds – a petition was ready for Queen Elizabeth's perusal."*[2]

And so it was the British who, through this petition and its aftermath, would jump first into economic modernity. They were latecomers to be sure only recently emerging from feudal primitivism, and one of the last in Europe to catch the spirit of the Renaissance that rose early from the south. Yet in this case, the last would come first.

During the first 60 years of its existence across the reigns of the Tudor and Stuart dynasties, the East India Company would help shape the economic future of Europe and the new Americas. Responding to internal rhythms, the young firm made manifest a genetic code for successful commercial organization.

A particular genius

The specific organizational properties of the East India Company, as a quintessential early corporation, are well known. Among them are limited liability and centralized management by those with a personal interest in the venture – both points to be discussed in greater detail later in this chapter and in this book.

Yet the *most important* aspect of the East India Company's impact on England and the world over the next centuries is rarely discussed. It was the genius of the English to discover that *wealth generation requires a sharing of power and role between government and commerce.* There is a rich significance to this fact – one that will be explored throughout this book.

Perhaps starting as early as the Magna Carta in 1215, the English monarchy understood well the advantages of permitting – even encouraging – other, nonmonarchial sources of power and wealth. These sources could be independent without being threatening, the British rulers realized. Indeed, the monarchs reasoned, such powers could be complementary.

The generation of successful commercial enterprises – ranging from trade guilds to nascent companies such as East India – created a new and vibrant source of wealth for the state. In England, rulers grabbed for that brass ring at every turn. Indeed, Prince Charles, heir to the throne, personally invested £6000 in East India stock for himself.[3]

By contrast, rulers in other nations felt threatened by such developments and inhibited them – to their detriment. Despite their need for funds to support their high standards of living and to pay for their wars, many monarchs outside of England continued to dominate the commercial life of the nation – with baleful results. Not so for the English, and this was their unique genius. (What we call genius may have had elements of luck about it, but that is the nature of history.)

The significance of monopoly rights

The critical element in the entire life of the East India Company was its receipt *of monopoly rights* granted by King James I, Queen Elizabeth's famed successor. King James declared that trade to the East would be conducted by only one company: this one. This declaration was, in itself, a curious conceit analogous to the Pope's above-mentioned division of the unknown world. The sovereign was divvying up a world in which he had no ownership rights. Indeed, he knew that the Spanish, the Portuguese and the Dutch all had competing claims. Yet his act had an undeniable brilliance.

King James was asserting that a monarchy (and by implication any state) can advance its own legitimate interests through the *creation and licensing of an independent entity*. This was an utterly new idea. It would become another important element in the corporate genetic code – as would the converse idea: that corporations do not have natural rights (monopoly rights or others); only rights conferred to them by the state.

The state wanted to use corporate power, not surrender to it. We note from the earliest days that certain powers were denied the company. For example, court minutes of the chartering of the East India Company specifically deny the "right to grant commissions empowering the use of martial law."[4] While the East India Company from its earliest days was an expression of English power, the political authorities were always striving to limit the scope of its functioning, even at eight thousand miles remove. It is this same joinder of political and economic interests that characterizes the modern corporation, with the state retaining the ultimate authority to define corporate scope.

Much of world economic history in the last four centuries can be explained from this careful symbiosis of state and commerce – especially when read in light of the famed Parable of the Talents. The generation and expansion of business revenues and profits would provide constantly self-replenishing sources of financing for royal and state purposes. This provided a boost to the economy far stronger than any that taxation could achieve.

The English seem uniquely to have understood the compound interest that accrues to faithful investment, as in Matthew's parable. There is a natural limit to taxation as a means of generating revenue, but there is virtually *no limit to the wealth that can be created through the unshackling of human genius.*

A popular investment target

In a few pages, we will begin following the East India Company's legacy through later years and into our own era. But first, let us take a closer look at its genesis – starting with its all-important progenitors: the world's first modern investors.

There was no shortage of subscribers to the new East India Company. This much is clear from the *Calendar of State Papers Colonial – East India Series* (1513–1616).[5] These official chartering papers state that on December 31,

1599, "a privilege for fifteen years [was] granted by Her Majesty to certain adventurers for the discovery of the trade for the East Indies." Among these "adventurers" – surely an apt description of the world's first equity investors – was George, Earl of Cumberland, along with 215 knights, aldermen, and merchants. Sir Thomas Smythe, alderman, was elected to be the first governor, and no less than 24 committees were elected annually to see to the business of the corporation.

Famously, the adventurers had petitioned the Privy Council (on September 25, 1599), for the privilege of doing business in incorporated form "for that the trade of the Indias, being so faire removed from hence, cannot be traded but in a joint and a unyted stock."[6]

The Queen retained authority to terminate the venture after two years. If she failed to do so, the charter would automatically be extended a second 15-year term. The charter confirmed all "privileges and immunities" normally granted by the monarch, and then added some new ones, including:

> *"authority to fortify and plant in any of their settlements, to transport thither colonists, and to carry out the ammunition and stores free of customs; no East India goods to be entered in the custom house without the knowledge of the Company; [and] power to appoint Presidents on shore and captains at sea to govern the people under their respective commands …"*[7]

The company enjoyed great success in its earliest voyages, which were financed on an individual basis, with overlap into future voyages. Thus even in its infancy the company was more than a gambling slip (a gamble that the ship would accomplish its commercial goals of the moment). Rather, the young company showed many of the signs of the modern corporation – signs that would become clearer in the "Cromwell charter" of 1657. At that point, the company became a genuine joint-stock endeavor, receiving continuous, unlimited investment without reference to individual voyages, and valuing and trading stocks at its headquarters in Leadenhall Street, London.

Long-term investing: a new mindset

Attention to organizational structure and leadership brought early success. It is virtually impossible to translate the financial returns into meaningful statistics, but the balance of opinion confirms 87½ percent return on the first voyage, disaster on the second, and sustained rate of return above 10 percent over time.

In the first six decades of the company's life, the investors' mindsets evolved from a project-by-project, quick-buck mentality into something far more beneficial to themselves and to society.

The conversion was gradual – a phenomenon noticed by K. N. Choudhuri, principal modern historian of the East India Company. In recounting the company's heyday (1620–1640), he notes:

> *"The principal weakness of the Company stemmed from the fact that a large number of its shareholders were unable to shake off the idea of making a quick profit on the East India trade, an expectation that was not only encouraged by the result of the early separate voyages but was also in line with the 17th century practice of a quick turn over of capital."*[8]

But this flaw was not permanent – much less fatal. Investors' short-term mentality began to lengthen as they faced the realities of doing business in a remote location. The company needed to establish (in Choudhuri's words) a "semi-political, semi-military function in non European countries."[9] This need in turn generated a new concept in modern finance: the concept of a *long-term commitment* to a commercial mode. Investors would give capital not just for a single voyage or set of voyages, but to the *enterprise itself.* Their funds would be continuously committed to the business and would be perpetually at risk.

In order to attract investment on these terms, company founders needed to make provisions for liquidity. In the Cromwell Charter, "the Stock was not to be wound up like its predecessors, but at the end of the first seven years (and every third year after) a valuation was to be made and any adventurer wishing to withdraw was to be paid out on the basis thereof and others admitted in his place."[10]

A lasting energy

No historian has actually seen the original copy of the new charter. Small wonder: we must remember that all during the early years of the East India Company, England was convulsed with violence. Beheadings, exhumations, and other acts of rebellion were commonplace in an era that saw the end of the Tudors, the accession of the Stuarts, the agony of the Long Parliament, civil war, the Protectorate of Oliver Cromwell, and, following Cromwell's death, the Restoration of the Stuarts.

Remarkably, the company emerged from these political cauldrons with its powers not only confirmed but enhanced. This must tell us something about the firm grip this little shipping business had on conventional life during its time. Clearly, this fledgling enterprise had a kind of energy that could transcend the most violent of traditional upheavals – an energy for investment that could transform government from the convenience of sovereigns to the obligation to encourage and protect the capacity for profitable investment by energetic citizens.

The East India Company was the seed; the modern corporation, the flower. With the charter, the DNA was in place, with all its inevitable logic.

400 years: the East India legacy

Today, 400 years after the birth of the East India Company, thanks to the willingness of investors to truly invest in commercial enterprise – and not merely bury their money in the earth, in mattresses, or in public sector debt – we have arrived at an historical turning point. Consider very simply the story of Bill Gates. The institutional ingenuity of investment has evolved to a point at which one man without the need of educational credentialing, and solely through the application, investment, and reinvestment of the fruits of his own genius – with some help from outside equity investors – has been able to create within 25 years the largest company in the world, and to make himself its richest inhabitant.

The origins of investment

How did the modern economic world move from the Earl of Cumberland and his 215 associates, each with their bag of gold, to the power of a Bill Gates and the public and private funds that have invested in and out of Microsoft during the latter part of this century?

The origins lie deep in the history of humankind, beginning with our very human need to strive. The need to believe that there is purpose to life encourages effort. The products of this effort must be protected against violence – one might even say against human nature itself. Of all the products borne of human effort, perhaps the most lasting are *the institutions we have created to encourage the capacity of individuals to fulfill their creative potential through investment.*

One such institution is organized religion. Human beliefs created various religions, including Judaism and its offshoots, Islam and Christianity. All three of these major religions warn against usurious lending, but leave the door open for investment.

Judaism, Islam, Christianity, and investment

The so-called Old Testament of the Bible (sacred scripture, as quoted from the King James version) clearly sets down the ground rules for lending.

> *"If thou lend money to any of my people that is poor by thee, thou shalt not be to him as an usurer, neither shalt thou lay upon him usury. If thou at all take thy neighbour's raiment to pledge, thou shalt deliver it unto him by that the sun goeth down. For that is his covering only, it is his raiment for his skin: wherein shall he sleep? And it shall come to pass, when he crieth unto me, that I will hear; for I am gracious." (Exodus 22: 25–27).*

And further,

> *"And if thy brother be waxen poor, and fallen in decay with thee; then thou shalt relieve him: yea, though he be a stranger, or a sojourner; that he may live with thee. Take thou no usury of him, or increase ... Thou shalt not give him thy money upon usury, nor lend him thy victuals for increase." (Leviticus 25:35–37)*

Israel condemned usury (the charging of interest on a loan) because it led to poverty and certain forms of slavery. Even with the introduction of a market economy, the Torah provided strict laws on surety, such as prohibiting the taking of collateral if it were to destroy a person's access to livelihood.

Importantly, however, as Judaism evolved, it did not prohibit the transfer of money into enterprise. Indeed, one might well speculate that the elaborate rules of financial sacrifice set forth in Judaism, particularly throughout Leviticus, were precursors of the notions of investment.

Investment, as defined in the opening of this book, is the *process of forego-ing immediate expenditures in order to build a more prosperous future.* In this sense, it is very closely analogous to the material goods (such as valuable livestock) and time (Sabbath days) that Jews were required to give to the Lord (using the King James term). In Leviticus the Lord speaking to Moses, sets forth elaborate commandments for bringing offerings to the temple. It also con-tains the famous command to leave some of the field threshings for the poor in the community. Those who make such sacrifices (in a very real sense, long-term investments) will experience prosperity:

> *"If ye walk in my statutes, and keep my commandments, and do them; Then I will give you rain in due season, and the land shall yield her increase, and the trees of the field shall yield their fruit.*
> *"And your threshing shall reach unto the vintage, and the vintage shall reach unto the sowing time: and ye shall eat your bread to the full, and dwell in your land safely … And ye shall eat old store and bring forth the new because of the old." (Leviticus 26: 3–10)*

To be sure, the connection between investment and abundance is not as direct as in the more modern Parable of the Talents. The equivalence, how-ever, is clear: what you give up (invest) now, if you bear in mind the public welfare, will return to you multiplied many times over. The spirit of long-term investment seems to help, not hinder, economic effort.

Islamic business ethics also regard profitable lending with suspicion, based on the sayings of the Holy Qu'ran regarding usury:

> *2:275 –* "God destroys usury, and increases charity."
> *2.278 –* "O you who believe! Be careful of your duty towards God and relinquish what remains of usury if you are believers."
> *3:130 –* "O you who believe! Do not consume usury making it double and redouble, and be careful of your duty to God so that you may be successful."
> *30:39 –* "And what ever is taken in usury so that it increases in the prop-erty of men, it shall not increase him with God; and whatever is given in char-ity, desiring the Intimate Knowledge of God – these it is that will be returned manifold."

The notion of Islamic charity, like the notion of the sacrifices required of the Jews, leads to a notion of financial abundance. The Qu'ranic verses set forth above constitute the basis of a code of behavior for Islamic banking.

Investment requires the participation and involvement of the client. Once the investment is made on behalf of the client, the bank acts as custodian and is responsible for overlooking all managerial decisions as well as maintaining control over all financial accounts. Funds remaining dormant may not be invested in interest accounts. The Islamic bank views investment as a combination of personal involvement and the commitment of resources. Accordingly, the bank's compensation is in the form of carried interests in the various projects.

In an ideal Islamic bank, the administrators must formulate policies that protect both the material and spiritual interest of their clients, as well as dealing equitably and compassionately with those whom they have entered into contractual agreement. This latter concept – albeit a foreign one in today's business practices – is an essential element in the good health and harmony with society.

Eventually, through the growth of an investment culture in the late twentieth century, both the Old Testament and Qu'ranic notions of sacrifice and charity would find a parallel in the broader movement of global investment. As we shall see later in this book, true investment, divorced from any ties to the usury that expects fixed short-term interests, can take on the multiplying properties of sacrifice and charity.[11]

Christianity and investment

If Judaic and Islamic traditions lay a philosophical groundwork favoring an investment mentality, Christianity appears to build the actual path to its expression. From early days to present times, this particular faith seems the most hospitable to investment. Catholic Christianity, for example, has officially endorsed the dignity of this human activity.

In his encyclical *Centissimus Annus*, published in 1991, Pope John Paul II, responding to controversies over collective versus private wealth, asserted the intrinsic value of ownership, which "morally justifies itself in the creation, at the proper time and in the proper way, of opportunities for work and human growth for all," calling work and growth the "universal destination of material wealth."[12] Ethicist Marcy Murninghan writing about the "covenant" that business must make with society, notes that these words "could well be interpreted as one call of the covenant, offering access to a better life to those traditionally excluded from economic enterprise."[13]

In the pre-millennial frenzy of the late twentieth century, the *Wall Street Journal* ran a series of articles on the past 1,000 years. One of these articles highlighted the role of organized religion in creating the climate necessary for free enterprise and thus investment.

> *"It was the Church more than any other agency... that put in place what [Max] Weber called the preconditions of capitalism: the rule of law and a bureaucracy for resolving disputes rationally; a specialized and mobile labor force; the institutional permanence that allows for transgenerational investment and sustained intellectual and physical efforts, together with the accumulation of long-term capital; and a zest for discovery, enterprise, wealth creation, and new undertakings."[14]*

How true this is. Ever since the emergence of humankind, collective energies – at first in small units, and then gradually larger ones – have transformed the circumstances of existence, event by event. Consider the spread of Judaism from a tiny band of relatives to virtually every nation in the world. Note the growth of Christianity from a Jewish fringe group to a major world faith. Contemplate the amazing spread of Islam in the years following the death of Mohammed across the entire landmass from New Guinea to France in a single century (eighth century) – and its tremendous expansion in the few years since. All these movements show the vitality of religious belief – and in particular, beliefs about the property of investment.

We have seen a parallel between ideas in these religions and the idea of investment. But how actually did the world move from economic primitivism into the modern age of investment? Let us review the history.

During the 1000 years between 500 and 1500 – a period some call the "Dark" and "Middle" ages – the western world was dominated by an all-powerful Church. This entity was considered to be the unique interpreter of God's will on earth, and as such entitled to collect and redistribute the full usufruct of humanity's efforts. Gradually, over the next 500 years, the idea of temporal power emerged, and the emperors and kings – once powerful only through military might – evolved into legitimate rulers of nation states. The Church had to accommodate itself to civil power. This was clear from Martin Luther's statement about the religion of German states: "Eius regio, cuius religio." ("Religion is what the ruler believes.") Religion was a function of civil leadership. Some centuries later, Otto van Bismarck put it even more clearly: "How many troops does the Pope have?"

As Church and state fought for control over the wealth created in society, individual enterprises gradually assumed unignorable significance. Although they rendered unto Caesar and God, merchants were free at last of the arbitrary power of pope and prince. Thus they were able to coordinate the work of many people and to bring the fruits of this collective effort to the public good as well as their own profit.

Business needed an environment of safety – a way of accumulating wealth without the threat of confiscation, a safe harbor from regal and clerical arbitrariety. This right had to be spelled out in writing. Sir William Blackstone, eighteenth century jurist, records the grant of a corporate charter to the City of London, which granted that city immunity from regal expropriation.

The City realized full well that it would have to pay taxes – and even to provide bodies to defend the civil state, but the other end of the bargain was worth it. In return for its obeisance to the sovereign, the City could generate wealth in confidence.

The medieval law against perpetuities

At that time, as today, religions appeared to be suspicious about passive investments. As mentioned earlier, prophetic voices had railed out against any system that yielded returns without reference to the human involvement in the transaction. Divine purpose, these voices inveighed, would be violated when burdensome interest was paid on money loaned. Divine approval, it seems, was only available when investment is commingled with human effort. While wealth arising out of the association of man with property was a reflection of the transcendent glory of God – and shone all the brighter when invested in larger causes – wealth derived from property selfishly hoarded was an offense to the Almighty.

Abhorrence of unproductive property was articulated in the middle ages in Western Europe through the "law against perpetuities" limiting the amount of time that property could be withdrawn in trust out of the normal workings of commerce. Concern over the dead hand of perpetual ownership found expression in the "mortmain" laws found in various times throughout Europe. The feudal law of *manus mortua* decreed that serfs would have no power of testamentary decree to charity. If they died without heirs, their property would revert to their feudal lord. Later, the concept found a more benign expression in laws forbidding impersonal ownership – such as ownership of property by an absentee landlord.[15]

Such latter concepts made a fundamental distinction between property in the grip of passive or deceased owners, versus property growing fruitful through attentive investment – an idea that would grow in meaning throughout the evolution of the corporate form.

The phases of corporate evolution

The first phase of corporate evolution, lasting well into the Middle Ages, viewed passive ownership with suspicion. Thinkers of this age believed that institutions organized purely for business or financial purposes were morally inferior to institutions operating with larger social interests in sight. While the commercial class was valued for the revenues it generated, it was clearly inferior to the noble or priestly class. Disconnected from family and Church, commercial enterprises represented a departure from nature and spirituality. They seemed to take wealth out of the community rather than using it to enhance community. The accumulation of wealth without consideration of its use or need was seen as a process of wealth-chasing and therefore demeaning. The prevailing belief was that the accumulation of wealth should be something that helped achieve loftier goals, such as fulfilling the spiritual or material needs of human community.[16]

Yet during this time, as mentioned, the world's great religions set forth a compelling paradigm of long-term investment to a heavenly kingdom. This idea would eventually flower into modern notions of investment – and a second phase of corporate evolution.

The second phase of corporate evolution occurred in Europe during the sixteenth, seventeenth, and eighteenth centuries as an essential component of World exploration and the beginnings of trade. The central precept of all early corporations was that even though they were chartered as private entities and possessed special privileges and monopoly rights, they were still expected to carry out activities with a public purpose. This dual expectation, that private and public interests were joined at the yoke of privilege, became firmly lodged within English law.

Religion, country, investment – gospel, glory, and gold – each of these phenomena was intangible, abstract, and capable of meeting the most basic needs and desires of human kind. These institutions, as the title of this chapter states, arose in order to encourage the expression of human genius. My earliest memories as a student at Harvard College were of the words inscribed over the lecture hall "Man is the measure of all things." This focus on the perspective of the individual and its "divine" integrity are part of the legacy left by the Puritan founders of the New England colonies – a legacy eventually embraced by much of the modern world. In this last segment of our opening chapter, let us reflect on that genius and the institutions that empower it.

The ultimate meaning of investment

Paul Gauguin, famed runaway from the Parisian *beaux arts* establishment, inscribed three questions in the corner of his magnificent painting of "Man in Natural Paradise" now hanging in the Boston Museum of Fine Arts. "From whence do we come, who are we, and where are we going?"

In a world where the volume of known information is so large as to defy measure, it is noteworthy that never has anyone provided a satisfactory answer to any one of these three questions – not Gauguin's idyllic natives, not Albert Einstein, not the cumulative wisdom of all who ever lived. But despite our inability to provide answers, we will forever be asking these same questions – and exploring possible answers with every fiber of our beings.

Human beings have always possessed the traits crucial to survival. Among these are energy, imagination, and the willingness to take risks. While it is plain that our time on earth is lonely and filled with uncertainty, we humans have been able to devise solutions that improve the circumstances under which we must exist. Over time, we collectively have conjured up a panoply of myths that address our two most fundamental challenges – sanity and survival – and have provided a basis for the conviction that life is worth living and that individual effort has meaning.

So what do these philosophical reflections have to do with the history of modern investment? In a word, everything. To offer access to a better life, we as a society must encourage the creation of channels for human genius, and the best way to do this is through productive long-term investment. Such a channel, if protected from certain common perils (to be discussed in the next chapter), can create sustained prosperity – an economic version of the paradisiacal scenes immortalized by Gauguin.

Society in the free economic world has already come a long way in this regard. In the past 100 years in the US, characterized largely by free markets, humankind has seen great increases in prosperity. The Cato Institute recently summarized these in a document entitled, "The Greatest Century that Ever Was." Authors Stephen Moore and Julian Simon note that during the twentieth century, life expectancy increased by 30 years, infant mortality rates fell tenfold, agricultural productivity rose nearly tenfold, income rose from $4800 to $31,500, and average real wages (adjusted for inflation) increased from $3.45 an hour to $12.50, and household assets in real (1998) dollars increased from $6 trillion in 1945 to $41 trillion in 1998.[17] They also cite many more indicators of increased prosperity, as shown in Table 2.1.

Clearly, an extraordinary boon befell us in the twentieth century, at least in the United States. Moore and Simon attribute this boon to free markets. In a sense, they are right. But let us look deeper. Is the cause really free markets, or is it the phenomenon of active, responsible, long-term investment – the turning of five talents into 10 through astute investing? Based on my experience and observations as an active participant in capital markets during my twentieth century lifetime, investment, not merely freedom, is the cause of our great national prosperity. All over the world there has been wonder that major American corporations could "downsize," dramatically laying off tens and even hundreds of thousands of workers, while at the same time national unemployment levels dropped. The explanation is that large venture capital investments in new ventures have been creating an estimated 500,000 high-quality new jobs every year.

The nature of investment

Investment does not exist in the sense of being tangible. Rather, it represents agreement among individuals as to how contributions of different kinds of goods and services are to be managed and valued.

In recent history, investment was represented by the manual entries into books of account. Today it is probably only a few keystrokes recorded in electronic memories. Whatever the mode of record, all individuals are disposed to treat these recordings as a legitimate allocation of resources.

Table 2.1 Twenty-five wonderful trends of the twentieth century.

Trend	1900–1920	1995–98
Life expectancy (years)	47	77
Infant mortality (deaths per 1000 live births)	100	7
Deaths from infectious diseases (per 100,000 population)	700	50
Heart disease (age-adjusted deaths per 100,000 population)	307 (1950)	126
Per capita GDP (1998 dollars)	$4800	$31,500
Manufacturing wage (1998 dollars)	$3.40	$12.50
Household assets (trillions of 1998 dollars)	$6 (1945)	$41
Poverty rate (percent of US households)	40	13
Length of workweek (hours)	50	35
Agricultural workers (percent of workforce)	35	2.5
TV ownership (percent of US households)	0	98
Homeownership (percent of US households)	46	66
Electrification (percent of US households)	8	99
Telephone calls (annual per capita calls)	40	2300
Cars for transportation (percent of US households)	1	91
Patents granted	25,000	150,000
High school completion (percent of adults)	22	88
Accidental deaths (per 100,000 population)	88	34
Wheat price (per bushel in hours of work)	4.1	0.2
Bachelor's degrees awarded to women (percent of degrees)	34	55
Black income (annual per capita, 1997 dollars)	$1200	$12,400
Resident US population (millions)	76	265
Air pollution (lead, micrograms per 100 cubic meters of air)	135 (1977)	4
Computer speed (millions of instructions per second)	0.02 (1976)	700
Computer ownership (percent of US households)	1 (1980)	44

Source: *The Greatest Century that Ever was: 25 Miraculous Trends of the Past 100 Years*, Stephen Moore and Julian L. Simon, (Washington, DC: The Cato Institute, December 15, 1999). Policy paper No. 364, p. 6, Table 1.

Investment property is the cornerstone of civilization. Humankind has devised legal systems to protect it: philosophers proclaim its indispensability to individual freedom, police systems and courts have been created to enforce its ownership rights, and armies have been formed and deployed to protect its overseas manifestations.

Most people in today's world consider the purchase and sale of securities in various public markets to be "investments." But are they? These actions may well constitute an investment for the individual but they have little impact on the company whose shares are traded, much less on society. Yet they should have such an impact, in both spheres.

Stephen Timms, Minister for Pensions under Prime Minister Tony Blair of the United Kingdom, recently spoke at a meeting of PIRC about modern notions of investment:

> *"In Wesley's words, penned some 250 years ago, we are told that we are 'placed here (on earth) not as proprietors, but as stewards. We are entrusted for a season with goods of various kinds; but the sole property of them does not rest with us.'*
>
> *"Central to his message is the idea of stewardship: that everything we gain or are given is only conditionally ours. We are not the absolute owners of our wealth; rather we are custodians or stewards. This is a way of thinking that has become more familiar to us in recent years: we recognise that our children and grandchildren will have to deal with the environmental problems we leave them, and we have already begun to address the damage we have done…*
>
> *"Money can be a force for good. The gaining of money is good, provided it is carried out with due regard to the rights and well-being of others. And just as individuals can gain and amass wealth, so can companies and institutions. What is important is that the money so gained is used rightly."*[18]

Investment energy

Investment energy differs significantly from that of religion and nationalism due largely to the advent of technology. Today, information is universal, instantaneous, and free. It is possible for people all over the world to be in direct communication. While investment across every nation of the world is now not only possible but commonplace among the largest institutional investors, the impact of investment is also susceptible of being evaluated and understood on a global basis.

The possibility of investment within an holistic ethic tends to hasten the decline in importance of both the nation state and secular religion. As one observer has opined, "Today nation-states' traditional responsibilities are being 'unbundled' by a combination of forces. The rise of the multinational corporations and global markets limit their economic influence. Cyberspace and the Internet belong to no one."[19] Peter Drucker sees us heading into a period of time that he calls "the new pluralism."[20] We are moving from a century-long period dominated by government, to a century in which commerce will reign. What will that mean for humanity?

It can mean increased prosperity, if we heed the clear call of the wisdom of centuries. Leaders of *all* institutions must take leadership responsibility for the fruits of their investments. They each must lead their own institutions and lead them to better performance. This requires single-minded concentration by all. All members of each institution need to take community responsibility beyond their own walls, and that includes investors. In the next two chapters, we will explore the implications of this imperative – the ultimate legacy of the Parable of the Talents, and the final harbor of the East India Company's first voyage into modernity.

Endnotes

1   *"For the kingdom of heaven is as a man travelling into a far country, who called his own servants, and delivered unto them his goods. And unto one he gave five talents, to another two, and to another one; to every man according to his several ability; and straightway took his journey. Then he that had received the five talents went and traded with the same, and made them other five talents.*

"And likewise he that had received two, he also gained other two. But he that had received one went and digged in the earth, and hid his lord's money.

"After a long time the lord of those servants cometh, and reckoneth with them.

"And so he that had received five talents came and brought other five talents, saying, "Lord, thou deliveredst unto me five talents: behold, I have gained beside them five talents more." His lord said to him, "Well done, thou good and faithful servant: thou hast been faithful over a few things, I will make thee ruler over many things: enter thou into the joy of thy lord." He also that had received two talents came and said, "Lord, thou deliveredst unto me two talents: behold, I have gained two other talents beside them". His Lord said unto him," Well done, good and faithful servant; thou hast been faithful over a few things, I will make thee ruler over many things: enter thou into the joy of thy lord." Then he which had received the one talent came and said, "Lord, I knew thee that thou art an hard man, reaping where thou has not sown, and gathering where thou has not strawed: And I was afraid, and went and hid thy talent in the earth: lo, thou has

that is thine". His lord answered and said unto him, "Thou wicked and slothful servant, thou knewest that I reap where I sowed not, and gather where I have not strawed: Thou oughtest therefore to have put my money to the exchangers, and then at my coming I would have received mine own with usury. Take therefore the talent from him, and give it unto him which hath ten talents. For unto every one that hath shall be given, and he shall have abundance: but from him that hath not shall be taken away even that which he hath. And cast ye the unprofitable servant into outer darkness: there shall be weeping and gnashing of teeth."

The Parable of the Talents, as told in
Matthew 25: 14–46, King James Translation

2   John Keay, *The Honourable Company: A History of the English East India Company* (New York: HarperCollins, 1991), p. 13.

3   Philip Lawson, *The East India Company: A History* (New York: Addison Wesley, 1997), p.30.

4   Ed Sainsbury, *A Calendar of the Court Minutes of the East India Company, 1655–1659* (Oxford, 1916), p. xviii.

5   Ed Sainsbury, *Calendar of State Papers Colonial – East India Series, 1513–1616* (London, 1862) p. 115, reported as #281.

6   William Foster, *The East India Company*, Vol. 1 (Rutledge, 1933) p.147.

7   Ed Sainsbury, *A Calendar of the Court Minutes of the East India Company, 1655–1659* (Oxford, 1916), p. xvii.

8   K.N. Chaudhuri, *The English East India Company – The Study of an Early Joint-Stock Company, 1600–1640* (Frank Cass, 1965), p. 56.

9   *Ibid.*, p. 26.

10   Ed Sainsbury, *A Calendar of the Court Minutes of the East India Company, 1655–1659* (Oxford, 1916), p. xix.

11   Khosrow Djahanbani, private communication to Robert A.G. Monks, May 26, 1998.

12   Quoted verbatim in Marcy Murninghan, *Corporate Civic Responsibility and the Ownership Agenda: Investing in the Public Good*, (Boston, MA: McCormack Institute, 1993), p. 9.

13   *Ibid.*, p. 39.

14   Michael Novak, "How Christianity Created Capitalism," *Wall Street Journal*, December 27, 1999, p. 8.

15   Linguists may be amused at the variety of spellings acceptable for this term in the medieval English. *Mortmain* was the most common, but also current were *mortemain* (conforming to the French), *mortmaine* (completely wrong, but used nonetheless, and, in Chaucerian style, these

other variations: *mortmayne, mortemayn, mortemayne, morttmayne.* For a history of the etymology of this term, see the *Oxford English Dictionary* (Oxford: England, 1971 [or any year]), at mortmain.

16 Murninghan, *op. cit. supra*, p. 59.

17 Stephen Moore and Julian Simon, *The Greatest Century That Ever Was: 25 Miraculous Trends of the Past 100 Years* (Washington, DC: The Cato Institute, 1999). Income is measured as real per capita gross domestic product adjusted for inflation. Wages are also adjusted for inflation. Stephen Moore is director of fiscal studies at Cato. Julian Simon, who passed away before this paper was published, was a professor of business administration at the University of Maryland, and a senior fellow at the Cato Institute.

18 Speech by Stephen Timms MP at the PIRC Corporate Responsibility Conference, February 11, 1999.

19 Paul Lewis, "As Nations Shed Roles, Is Medieval the Future?," *New York Times*, January 2, 1999.

20 Peter F. Drucker, "The New Pluralism," *Leader to Leader*, 14, Fall 1999, p.18.

Chapter 3

The Problem

Corporate Hegemony Threatens a Free Society

In its few centuries of existence, the modern corporation has empowered individual genius and bestowed great social benefits. Yet the modern corporation has also done social harm. Therefore, no history of modern investment would be complete without a direct reckoning with the dark side of corporate history.

In his famed *Wealth of Nations* (1776), Adam Smith set forth the clear purpose of modern corporations. They enable pursuit of private interest creating an "invisible hand" that works for the public good. Despite his generally favorable view of the private sector, Smith identified four threats posed by the corporate form as it was evolving in his era. Writing about "joint stock companies," Smith expressed concerns about their unlimited life, unlimited size, unlimited power, and unlimited license.[1]

Four threats posed by modern corporations

Today Smith's concerns about lack of limits on corporations appear to be borne out.

- Corporations have a potentially infinite *lifespan* cut off only by bankruptcy, merger, or reorganization and sometimes not even then. Early corporate charters permitted corporations to operate according to stated missions, expressed as socially useful purposes. If corporations failed to follow those purposes, their charters could be revoked. That notion is long gone. A corporation may change every single thing about itself, yet still be chartered to operate. Bankruptcy no longer means going out of business. Rather, it means a chance to reorganize – and persist.

- Corporations also have seemingly limitless *size,* with each new mega-merger larger than the last. In 1989, the world gasped at the sheer size of Kohlburg Kravis Roberts' $25 billion buyout offer for RJR Reynolds. At the time, it was by far the largest price any company had ever fetched. Just 10 years later, Exxon paid $79 billion for Mobil – three times that old record, without sparking any discussion of gigantism. And in early 2000, two pharmaceutical firms paid $161 billion to buy two firms again, without provoking commentary.[2] The merger of Mannesmann and Vodafone created a company worth in excess of £225 billion. Yet as many corporate critics have noted, this amount of money is many times the gross domestic product of entire nations and even some continents. By anybody's standards, corporations are thought properly to cut a wide swath across society.

- As for *power,* examples are legion. Corporations have political action committees (PACs) that make contributions to candidates for elected office, creating conflicts of interest for the legislators they support and have made "soft dollar" contributions on such a scale as virtually to eliminate participation by individuals.

- And finally, there is *unlimited license* – the ultimate fruit of the other three main corporate traits. Of all the threats posed by a large, modern corporation, this one is the most troubling.

The social downside of unlimited license

License means the freedom to do what one wishes. As every schoolchild knows, freedom and responsibility go hand in hand. Therefore, in every culture, there is an effort to instill an internal sense of values – one that can go beyond the letter of laws. Why? Because human laws, by their very collective nature, suffer from a paradox: they will always be oppressive yet inadequate. This is, was, and always will be true of every set of laws enacted from the Hammurabi Code in the twenty-first century BC to the statutes of every nation in the twenty-first century AD – and before and after these arbitrary points in time.

In the case of individual human beings, responsibility picks up where the laws leave off. The faculty of human conscience, combined with ethical precepts, enables most individuals to dedicate their individual genius to the good of society. To a great degree, the corporate structure can lend greater life, size, power, and license to this good purpose.

But these same four traits can cause harm as well. That is, the corporate *structure itself* can encourage and empower *irresponsible* actions, problems made all the worse through corporate hegemony.

A panorama of change

It would be overly ambitious for me, a mere student of history (albeit a life-long student) to pretend to present a complete "history" of the corporate form in the years since Adam Smith. This is a task best left to professional historians, and I commend them to it. I will, however, report here as a kind of "financial journalist" some reflections – both original and derivative – about these years.

Royal issuance of corporate charters, mentioned in Chapter 2, established a pattern that would last until the late nineteenth century. Business enterprises were literally creatures of the state in those years. As such, corporate activities were, by definition, in the public interest. By the beginning of the nineteenth century in the United States this sovereign power had transferred to the state legislatures. Oftentimes, the granting of corporate status was conjoined – as in the case of the East India Company – with the conferral of a monopoly franchise such as sole right to build a ferry, a bridge, or a canal. This development converted the largely theoretical question of chartering into a highly practical struggle for gain. Monied and powerful applicants for charters corrupted the government process.

By the 1840s, "reform" resulted in corporation laws, which permitted use of that form by anyone as a matter of right. No one noticed that the connection with public interest had been severed. Slowly but surely, for much of the balance of the century, corporations moved away at restrictions on capital, longevity, and purpose. Corporation lawyers earned their keep by devising techniques to avoid these restrictions, and state governments competed to pass laws with progressively diminishing limitations on corporate functioning, in order to attract the lucrative business of legal domiciling. Substantive limitations on corporate functioning ceased to be an integral part of the grant of the franchise. By the end of the century corporations were free of restraints imposed by their charters. Control from within the corporate structure itself was a matter of the past.

The federal government responded decisively to the problems of burgeoning corporate power. Early in the twentieth century the US federal government enacted far-reaching laws seeking to prohibit monopoly and unfair competition. Following the financial binge of the 1920s, the federal government focused reform on specific markets. Over a ten-year period, comprehensive legislation regulating the issuance and trading of securities, the functioning of investment companies, and the abolition of public utility holding companies was enacted. In the 1960s and 1970s federal legislation was enacted respecting fairness in hiring practices, limitations on environmental impact, campaign finance reform, and prohibition against bribery. Over the past two decades, the US Congress has spent a good deal of its legislative time refining those statutes.

This pattern of "external" regulation of corporations has been only a mixed success. While the creation of normative standards is necessary in a federalist country and a pluralist world, the realities of bureaucratic implementation are daunting. It has been said that America at the end of the twentieth century was a country where "you either obey the law or hire a lawyer, and you either pay taxes or hire an accountant." The inherent weakness of government in trying to regulate one of its largest sources of revenue is evidenced by the growth in both lobbying and campaign financing by corporations. Government efforts at "reform" of these processes range from the ludicrous – lawyers weren't "lobbyists," for example – to the genuinely tragic escalation of campaign costs to the level where non-corporate involvement is virtually irrelevant.

The asymmetry between corporate and state power has been exacerbated by the globalization of business enterprise. Corporations can choose any domicile in any country and will, predictably, choose the least confining one. As a result legal restraint on corporate functioning worldwide is becoming less effective. The century-end burst of antitrust initiatives in the case of Microsoft seems to belong more to the American pattern of distrust of the big (i.e. Milken in the 1980s) than to a resurgence of corporate regulation. Increasingly, international institutions – the Organization for Economic Cooperation and Development (OECD) and the World Bank – have developed international codes of governance best practice. The importance of these is not so much in the substance (although the OECD's antibribery code has been adopted by many countries), but in a growing conviction that minimum governance standards are essential. Leadership in this field belongs to the United Kingdom, where the work of Sir Adrian Cadbury has sparked worldwide scholarship, concern, and change. I have been both witness and participant in the extensive reexamination of the role of corporations in society that have been taking place in the United Kingdom for most of the decade of the nineties. As a consultant to the reworking of the Company's Act by the Department of Trade and Industry, and as a frequent speaker to interested groups, I have been deeply impressed by the intellectual discipline and determination of Britons from all parts of the political spectrum to find a way of accommodating corporate energy to the public good. This brings the circle full cycle and back to the effort to contain corporate power from "inside."

Arthur Schlesinger, Jr, has identified a cyclical pattern in American history of roughly thirty years duration during which national concern swings back and forth between selfishness and generosity – between fixation over personal enrichment and a more spacious commitment to national and international values. So, during the last century, we had:

- The greed of the "robber barons," followed by antitrust legislation and World War I.
- The "Roaring Twenties" followed by Depression and rebuilding through government help.
- World War II and the prosperity of the 1950s, followed by the protests of the 1960s and reforms of the 1970s (notably the Foreign Corrupt Practices Act and the conviction of prominent individuals for illegal campaign contributions).
- The zeal for reform and evidence of corporate misconduct uncovered in the 1970s ultimately led to the introduction of comprehensive reform bills in both Houses of Congress during the second session of the 96th Congress: "Protection of Shareholders' Rights Act of 1980," introduced by Senator Howard Metzenbaum, and "Corporate Democracy Act of 1980," introduced by Congressman Benjamin Rosenthal. Unfortunately, national attention and energies shifted, and neither bill was reported out of Committee.[3]
- The Wall Street Boom and "trickle-down" economics of the 1980s and 1990s followed by the current period of anti-corporate protest.

The problem: corporate hegemony

Many of the ills of modern life – nonsustainable levels of personal and institutional debt, toxic air and water, workplace injury, loss of livelihoods for communities, and political bribery, to name a few – all these can be traced to the corporate lack of responsibility to one or more constituencies.

Corporations do not create these results intentionally. No corporation wants to cause poverty, pollution, disability, unemployment, and corruption. Rather, corporations want to make profits. But in the pursuit of profits, corporations may find that antisocial behavior pays. As a practicing lawyer, I was profoundly disappointed with how much of our energies went into obviating the law's spirit while ensuring that our clients literally complied with its words to the letter. An example was the work we did on behalf of a client having a near monopoly in the abrasives business. Junior lawyers reviewed the files and removed documents which had any air of "anti competitiveness" about them. These were turned over to the senior partner as part of a program with the Orwellian title of "The Records Retention Program." The short-term economic gains from some bad behavior (such as paying less than a living wage) are often higher than the cost of refraining from them. Either the odds of getting caught are low, the fine is less important than the profits from bad behavior, or a combination of the two. Therefore, to achieve profits in the short term, corporations exact a "social price."

A high social price

This social price is high, and rising. At the turn of the new millennium, a number of groups expressed their resentments against international trade and financial organizations and, in direct association with these, multinational corporations.

- In December 1999, talks of the World Trade Organization "collapsed in a cloud of tear gas in Seattle," as an AP newswire recently reminisced. Representatives of the 117 nations subscribing to WTO free trade principles had to go home, their work undone, because of street protests by a variety of groups.

- In April 2000, these same groups, now loosely affiliated in an umbrella group called the "Mobilization for Global Justice," reconvened for more activity, this time targeting the World Bank and the International Monetary Fund. Groups present for the April demonstrations included the American Federation of International Labor – Congress of Industrial Organizations (AFL-CIO), as well as environmental groups such as Friends of the Earth, and small political groups, such as Forum of Indian Leftists.
- In the fall of 2000, further and more expansive protests took place at the annual meetings of the World Bank and the International Monetary Fund in Prague.
- Throughout 2000, a group called the Jubilee 2000 Coalition has called for "cancellation of the debt of the world's poorest countries by the year 2000 under a fair and transparent process."[4]

Although these groups focus first and foremost against international trade and financial organizations, they all cast some blame on the "multinational corporation" – a term that appears on many a protest poster in their mass rallies.

These protesters, and other corporate critics in recent times, see corporations as entities that yield a great deal of power, and use this power as a free license to perpetuate themselves and their managers, rather than to enrich society.

Concern has spread from capitalism's traditional opponents to its most reliable supporters. *Forbes* magazine's cover story starts:

> *"Anticapitalist demonstrations have always been a part of the life of this country. But, until recently, they've been pretty much confined to college campuses, where such protests are a perennial rite of passage. These days, though, resentment against US corporations, and the drug industry in particular, has boiled over into the American mainstream. The drug industry's prices are high, its profit margins are fat. Those profits are at risk. We're not talking about fringe politicians or Naderites as the enemies of profits. We're talking about Republicans."*[5]

Business Week lectures to the Roundtable: "The business elite ought to take more responsibility for the impact of their global operations on workers, communities, and the environment."[6] And it devotes a cover story to a burning economic question: "Global Capitalism: Can It Be Made to Work Better?"[7]

The Financial Times writes about "Unpopular Capitalism" and cautions: "As long as the demands of the public and capital markets are in conflict, politicians will conclude that anti-business populism promises electoral dividends. The message for big [read global] business is hardly reassuring."[8]

Four propositions

As we look back at the East India Corporation, we might well ask: How did this happen? Here is the logic of the corporate "DNA" strands that brought us to our present state.

- *Proposition 1. Limited liability encourages investment.* Perhaps the most famous trait of the corporation is the limited liability it offers its owners. This trait has caused the corporate form to proliferate greatly in the past 400 years. It must foreclose any effort to impose obligation or responsibility on to individual "owners." In any given year, tax officials in nations around the world receive returns from thousands or, in the case of large developed countries such as the US, millions of corporations – many of them new and small. In one advertisement, a single US attorney claims to have helped set up "110,000 corporations in the past 22 years."[9]
- *Proposition 2. The opportunity for profit encourages externalization of risk and responsibility.* As it goes through life, a corporation takes many actions that have many potential consequences. Rather than suffering the consequences themselves, corporations have shifted them onto the buying and taxpaying public. Generally accepted accounting principles in the US (and similar systems worldwide) have enabled them to do this. Later on in this book, readers will encounter the language of accountability, with solutions to this self-perpetuating problem.
- *Proposition 3. Distant externalities, lacking the scrutiny of any government, permit antisocial corporate behavior in pursuit of profit.* These externalities may be 8000 miles away – the distance spanned by the East India Company – or merely eight – the number of miles that might separate an absentee landlord from a rental property inhabited by low-income renters. In either case, the pursuit of profit may encourage behavior that benefits the corporation at the expense of some of its constituencies.

- *Proposition 4. Aggression invites corrective action.* Justice has a way of making itself felt sooner or later, and corporate aggression is generally curbed in the end. Unfortunately the normal savior is the government, to the woe of taxpayers.

Now, 400 years later, we are living with the legacy of that logic. The costs that would be externalized by the young company could be a metaphor for the attacks on the environment, workplace safety, governmental functioning, and the whole panoply of modern complaints we hear (and sometimes lodge) today.

Brandeis' warning

Supreme Court Justice Louis D. Brandeis offers wisdom in this regard. In his court decisions and congressional testimony, he warned that a corporation, unconstrained by chartering law, would develop along the lines of the Church and the nation state into a menace that would undermine the critical elements of a free society. Here are some of his strongest words:

> *"The prevalence of the corporation in America has led men of this generation to act, at times, as if the privilege of doing business in corporate form were inherent in the citizen, and has led them to accept the evils attendant upon the free and unrestricted use of the corporate mechanism as if these evils were the inescapable price of civilized life, and hence, to be borne with resignation.*
>
> *"Throughout the greater part of our history, a different view prevailed. Although the value of this instrumentality in commerce and industry was fully recognized, incorporation for business was commonly denied long after it had been freely granted for religious, educational, and charitable purposes. It was denied because of fear. Fear of encroachment upon the liberties and opportunities of the individual. Fear of the subjugation of labor to capital. Fear of monopoly. Fear that the absorption of capital by corporations, and their perpetual life, might bring evils similar to those that attended mortmain.*
>
> ***"There was a sense of some insidious menace inherent in large aggregations of capital, particularly when held by corporations.*** *So at first the corporate privilege was granted sparingly; and only when the grant seemed necessary in order for the community to gain some specific benefit otherwise unattainable. The later enactment of general corporation laws does not signify that*

the apprehension of corporate domination had been overcome."[10] *(Emphasis added.)*

New voices of protest

Today, apprehension over large corporations continues. A Country Western song entitled "God Bless the Little Man" paints a picture of small towns closed down because of large shopping centers, and independent stores closed because of pressures from larger chains. The central figure, a store-owner, operated independently "'til the big money shut him down." Any listener whose life has spanned more than 20 years, and who has some experience with suburban and exurban areas can empathize with the imagery – and perhaps with the experience itself.

The anti-corporate movement: some points of friction

- *Artistic control.* Rock musicians, independent filmmakers, and other artists are rebelling against control by big media and retail companies.
- *Brands.* In-your-face marketing campaigns have sparked antibrand attitudes among students.
- *CEO pay.* Nearly three-fourths of Americans see executive pay packages as excessive.
- *Commercialism in schools.* Parent groups have mounted battles in hundreds of communities against advertising in the public schools.
- *Consumerism.* Anger and frustration are mounting over high gasoline and drug prices, poor airline service, and HMOs that override doctors' decisions. The latest fiasco: faulty auto tires.
- *Frankenfoods.* Europeans' skepticism about genetically modified food is taking hold in the US, making targets of companies such as Monsanto.
- *Globalization.* Environmentalists, students, and unionists charge that global trade and economic bodies operate in the interests of multinational companies.
- *Politics.* Public revulsion over the corporate bankrolling of politicians has energized campaign-finance reform activists.

- *Sweatshops.* Anti-sweatshop groups have sprung up on college campuses; they routinely picket clothing manufacturers, toy makers, and retailers.
- *Urban sprawl.* Groups in more than 100 cities have blocked big-box super-stores by Wal-Mart and other chains.
- *Wages.* Some 56% of workers feel they are underpaid, especially as wages since 1992 have topped inflation by 7.6%, while productivity is up 17.9%.

Business Week, September 11, 2000
http://www.businessweek.com/2000.htm

Let us listen at some length to the rage of Carolyn Chute who speaks for the "underclass" of one of America's poorest states – Maine. Chute speaks of citizens whose ancestors have been in the staff of Maine since the European settlement. These people feel "left behind" in the national progress and prosperity. Their inherited skills – attuned to needs for food, shelter, and sustenance – have been rendered irrelevant by what Chute calls corporatization. Slowly but surely, those living in a traditional way grow impoverished in spirit as well as pocket book. The gap between haves and have-nots widens – with cruel results.

I see this all around me as a resident in Maine. My family has maintained an island farm in the poorest town of the poorest county of the state since the beginning of the 19th century. I myself have driven to every town in Maine over the last 30 years of active involvement in politics. From this vantage point, I have witnessed first hand the worsening fate of those living on the margin of a corporatist economy. Even as that economy generates tremendous wealth for many, it has also created poverty for some, as natural resources – wood and fish – have disappeared or become less competitive.

Chute is right. When profits, determined in the conventional narrow way, provide the sole informing energy for corporate management, there is a heavy social cost.

As Chute writes:

"(To the tune of "This Land is Your Land ...")
This land is NAFTA's!
This land is GATT'S land!
These owners tell us
To just keep moving!
Forget our families!

Forget our hometown!
Just shut up and buy, buy, buy!"

Chute has recently written *Snow Man*,[11] which in some 250 pages is the
outline of a much longer work in process fulminating against the damage
caused to ordinary citizens by the corporate world. She maintains an active correspondence with the Second Maine Militia and answers letters as
"Revolutionary Abby." A comprehensive bill of indictment emerges as well
as a sense of what is wrong and what should be done to cure it.

> *"Also imagine corporations limited in size, limited in life, limited in rights (very*
> *limited), limited in power (like NO POWER)… just back-and-forth healthy*
> *business. Business should not be about power. It should only be BUSINESS.*
> *No representation in our government for business. Only human beings should*
> *have representation. No Constitutional human rights to corporations what-so-*
> *ever. No corporation in our government – lobbies or campaigns. Campaigns*
> *redesigned so that they do not COST MONEY, especially through media,*
> *THE PEOPLE'S AIRWAVES. Corporations will not be allowed to have*
> *sneaky little seminars with our educators, judges, legislative advisors, governors,*
> *and mediafolk … No more trying to do this MIND CONTROL thing, the*
> *PR to get us to think of corporations as Heavenly Fathers, etc. Charters should*
> *be written with conditions and limits and then REVOKED when these rules*
> *are broken. Now THIS would be Free Enterprise!"*

Chute is neither wrong nor alone in decrying lobbies. Indulgent talk of
the "best government that business can buy" is the staple of American history, but the twenty-first century has created the worst government in this
way, by removing the individual from involvement with the public agenda.
More than one voice has protested this development. As Jacques Barzun
notes in his tour de force, *From Dawn to Decadence*:

> *"Originally, the national interest was to be determined by each member indi-*
> *vidually, and his view determined his party allegiance and his vote. But now a*
> *committee chairman weighed the arguments of the lobbyists and bargained with*
> *other chairmen to secure in advance the vote of the chamber. True, group interests*
> *had always been influential; but when lobbies became part of the machinery, the*
> *aim was to seek a balance of many competing groups instead of ascertaining the*

needs of the nation's large constituencies land, commerce, finance, empire and the poor."[12]

The fallacy of corporate citizenship

Chute makes a valid point. Corporate citizenship is a grave fallacy. The Founding fathers of the American Republic did not contemplate that corporations would be citizens. Indeed, the word "corporation" is not mentioned in the Constitution. The notion that corporations would be entitled to constitutional protections, such as the right to participate in the electoral process through expenditure of funds, entered the nation's law through a circuitous route. It appears in a single, unargued sentence in *Santa Clara County v. Southern Pacific Railroad Company*, the 1886 case relating to the voting rights of freed slaves. The court asserted that each legal person, including corporations, has the right to one vote. Error has followed error and the US Supreme Court in a series of recent decisions – notably *Buckley v. Valeo* 424 US 1 (1976) and *First National Bank of Boston v. Belotti* 435 US 765 (1978) – has apparently set in concrete the status of corporations as citizens.

In the *Buckley* case, the Supreme Court ruled that the First Amendment of the Constitution of the United States protects the spending of corporate political action committees as a type of free speech.

In the *Belotti* case, decided 5 to 4, the court validated the right of the First National Bank of Boston to advertise in opposition to an income tax referendum in Massachusetts.

A contemporaneous article in the *Atlantic Monthly* noted:

> *"In some quarters this and other related court decisions were perceived as unleashing the mighty economic power of big corporations to influence public opinion unfairly. In fact, in writing for the minority, Justice Byron White saw the majority opinion as opening the door to corporate domination of 'not only the economy, but also the very heart of our democracy, the electoral process.'[13] But Justice Lewis Powell, Jr., for the majority, said, 'The inherent worth of the speech in terms of its capacity for informing the public does not depend upon the identity of its source, whether corporation, association, union or individual.' And Chief Justice Warren Burger, in a separate opinion, added that 'media conglomerates' pose 'a much more realistic threat to valid [political] interests' than other corporations."*

Chief Justice Rehnquist, dissenting in the same case, stated that "... the blessing of potentially perpetual life and limited liability ... poses special dangers in the political sphere."

These dissenting voices echo earlier cautions. In *Railroad Co. v. Collins* 40 GA 582, the court stated:

> *"All experience has shown that large accumulations of property in hands likely to keep it intact for a long period are dangerous to the public weal. Having perpetual succession, any kind of corporation has peculiar facilities for such accumulations, and most governments have found it necessary to exercise caution in their grants of corporate charters. Even religious corporations, professing and in the main, truly, nothing but the general good, have proven obnoxious to this objection, so that in England it was long ago found necessary to restrict them in their powers of acquiring real estate. Freed, as such bodies are, from the surebounds – the grave – to the schemes of individuals they are able to add field to field, and power to power, until they become entirely too strong for that society which is made up of those whose plans are limited by a single life."*

By permitting corporations to participate in politics although not to vote, the Supreme Court has importantly changed the polity. The question isn't the amount of money. Ross Perot is personally in a position, as is Malcolm Forbes and Nelson Rockefeller before him, to invest as much money in election efforts as any corporation or, indeed, as all corporations cumulatively.

The question is the identity of the source and the capacity of individuals to have representation of their interests. Put another way – whose country is it? Does it belong purely to flesh-and-blood individuals, rich and poor – or does it belong to corporations as well?

Concern is not uniquely the province of political extremists. Consider the admonition of lawyer–author Scott Turow:

> *"But my view is that* Buckley *may well come to be regarded as a sort of twentieth century stepchild to* Dred Scott, *the case that held that the property rights of Southern slaveholders in their slaves had to recognized in the North.*
>
> *"To our eyes,* Buckley *appears far less iniquitous. But as in* Dred Scott, *the Court used formalistic reasoning to find constitutional protection for economic interests at the cost of fundamental notions of equality. We can only hope that the long-run damage to the Republic is not as severe."*[14]

What is the long-run damage to any nation that allows corporations to have many of the same rights as citizens? And how precisely do these rights operate to the public detriment? In order to consider these questions, we turn to consideration of a particular industry: tobacco.

The tobacco industry: a case in point

The intense confrontation between the US tobacco industry and the whole spectrum of federal and state legislative, executive, administrative, and judicial systems provides an important lesson. It clearly illustrates the corporate tendency to influence – even to dominate – the creation of public consensus that is ultimately the basis for law. Indeed, the tobacco drama suggests the most serious of problems: an industry with enough power and skill to co-opt the political process.

The tobacco industry in the US has long been welcomed into corporate citizenship. But in recent decades, the American public began to focus on tobacco's health effects. Rumors of unspecified risks evolved into well-documented reports of deaths – half a million fellow citizens dying of tobacco-related causes every year.

In recent years, there has been a barrage of lawsuits and proposed new laws in this industry. A close look at the turmoil surrounding this change exposes the fundamental chasm that can separate the culture of commerce from concerns about the public good.

In light of these legal issues, it is not surprising that the board of RJR Nabisco, the country's largest tobacco company, hired a lawyer as its CEO: Steve Goldstone, formerly of Davis, Polk & Wardwell LLP.

In a *New York Times Magazine* cover story, Goldstone set forth a concise version of his responsibilities when dismissing the moralism of industry critics:

> *"I know these guys like to put this in moral terms, but if they can't convince Congress to ban this product, **we don't have any choice but to sell it**. As far as I am concerned, the day after any bill passes, we'll be selling cigarettes."*[15]
> *(Emphasis added.)*

In Goldstone's view, if a certain behavior is legal, it is acceptable, end of story: It is inappropriate to probe any further. "I have no moral view of this business," Goldstone told a *New York Times* reporter. "I view it as a legal business. You shouldn't be drawing a moral judgment about a business our country says is perfectly legal and is taxed like crazy by it."[16]

The legislative background

While Goldstone's statement that he as a businessman is obligated to sell cigarettes unless their sale is made illegal has surface credibility, it rings hollow when one considers the extent of his power to determine what the law is. Not only does Big Tobacco participate largely in the conventional electoral process, but it also commits defining resources for creating the public opinion that underlies popular consensus.

Goldstone made his telling comment, by happenstance, in the context of an unexpected tobacco industry success in defeating an ambitious anti-tobacco bill. The measure would have increased the price of cigarettes by $1.10 a pack in taxes, creating government revenue to be spent on smoking-related health research and services, and an anti-smoking advertising campaign. This initially popular bill was killed by a $40 million advertising campaign – large even by American standards – that managed to persuade voters that the bill was about boosting tax revenues and expanding bureaucracy rather than on curbing smoking among the young.[17]

Money and persistence are the ultimate Washington weapon. The *Wall Street Journal* chronicles how it works:

> "On the day the Senate killed comprehensive tobacco legislation, Sen. Mitch McConnell stood up at a closed-door meeting of Republican senators to deliver good news: The tobacco industry would mount a television ad campaign to support those who voted to knock off the bill. Such ads, Mr. McConnell says now, 'would be generally helpful to people who decided to kill this bill as a big tax increase on working Americans.'"[18]

How could any group of corporations turn the tide of history so handily? The tobacco industry is a master at the process, using a surefire combination of tactics.

One tactic is an inspired program of charitable contributions to high visibility activities. Take for example Philip Morris, which has tried to associate itself "at every opportunity with positive social values, institutions and ideas," according to Richard Kluger's portrait of the company in *Ashes to Ashes*. "If it behaved like a sterling corporate citizen," Philip Morris reasoned, "people would overlook the unfortunate tendency of the core product to shorten life expectancy."[19]

You can't fool all the people all the time. "I don't want to live in peace with these guys," declared Dr Kessler, former head of the US Food and Drug Administration, in an interview with the *New York Times*. "If they cared at all for the public health, they wouldn't be in this business in the first place. All this talk about it being a legal business is euphemism. They sell a deadly, addictive product. There's no reason to allow them to conduct business as usual."[20]

Talk of legalism and showy charity are not the only tactics up the sleeve of big cigarette companies. Other tactics for winning friends and influencing people include:

- soft money contributions ($13,972,640 from January through June 1997, mostly to the Republican party);[21]
- large campaign contributions to key legislators; and
- huge retainers to former leaders-turned-lobbyists.

This last ploy is bread and butter for Verner-Liipfert, Bernhard, McPherson and Hand, Chartered, Washington, DC, a law firm that exemplifies Washington's famous "revolving door." This power brokering law firm employs former majority leaders from both sides of the Senate aisle: Democrat George Mitchell and Republican Robert Dole. In the months leading up to the legislative victory, Verner-Liipfert collected over $10.2 million in lobbying fees from the tobacco industry, prompting one observer to note that, "last week, the industry got its money's worth."[22]

A victory like this makes influence peddling worthwhile, despite the seeming apostasy of "bought" supporters in the short term. To be sure, legislators may accept pro-tobacco money with one hand, and then vote against tobacco with the other. Over time, however, the hands do move in sync.

Former House Majority Leader Newt Gingrich once boldly declared, "I don't care how much they gave in the past, or how much they will give in the future. The cigarette makers do not deserve our protection."[23] But at just the time Gingrich was reading today's polls, his Senate colleague Mitch

McConnell, Chairman of the Republican Senate Campaign Committee, was preparing tomorrow's – and clearly, in this instance, the effort paid off.

Not surprisingly, given the way the corporate–government partnership has evolved, tobacco company CEOs like Goldstone see their jobs as creating a receptive environment for their companies through public relations, lobbying, and financing the election of favorable officials – apparently without financial, governance or ethical restraint – and in maximizing its immediate profits.

Even this, admittedly legalistic and narrow, approach is not problem free. The "market" simply will not attach a multiple to earnings from tobacco sources that is competitive. This is why the tobacco industry embarked on its apparent misguided efforts for settlement with the State Attorney Generals. In Goldstone's words:

> *"The opportunity was so unique – I was able to go to the board, to the shareholders and to the employees who own stock and say What is the point of producing earnings if nobody puts a value on them? We're getting Pyrrhic victories in these cases, because nobody is putting a value on our earnings. Call it Coke envy: the tobacco companies are revenue machines, and yet the stock market fearing the instability of endless litigation is not embracing them as they do other consumer products giants like Coca-Cola ..."*[24]

Goldstone the manager cannot be content simply with producing great earnings; he has to concern himself with the multiple placed on those earnings in the market place to produce value for his shareholders. This is where the two components of governance – legitimacy and competitiveness – converge. *The market place appears to penalize companies whose functioning affronts societal standards.* This raises the cost of capital and tends to make those companies uncompetitive. We will consider this phenomenon at length in Appendix I.

Strategic mistake

It would appear as if the managements of US tobacco companies have made a strategic mistake in choosing to risk their owners' values on an income stream deemed suspect by the public and politicians. The oldest US tobacco company – American Tobacco – some ten years ago diversified its operations out of domestic tobacco, changing its name first to American Brands and then to Fortune Brands.

Legal battles

In the 1990s, the tobacco industry successfully resisted a proposed federal law that would have included substantive regulatory requirements. Instead, they settled for the morass of litigation and laws pending in the various states. At other times, they have championed federal laws over state laws – a switching back and forth they use to suit their purposes.

In 1982, the US Supreme Court declared in *Edgar v. Mite Corp.*, 457 US 624 (1982), that an Illinois antitakeover law was in conflict with federal law, which permitted hostile takeovers. For the next several years, lobbyists tried unsuccessfully to persuade the Congress to pass laws prohibiting hostile takeovers, but in the end, they did not need too. The Supreme Court, in *CTS Corp. v. Dynamics Corp. of America*, 481 US 69 (1987), reversed its decision in *Edgar v. Mite*, and affirmed the right of states to pass antitakeover laws.

At that point the corporations headed to the state houses. This same tendency in the tobacco situation takes the "law" from the relatively public limelight of Washington, DC, to the rather murky, usually unenforced and ineffective, disclosure requirements of the state capitals. "While it is no secret that lobbyists in Albany use expense accounts to garner support, the practice has largely escaped scrutiny because state lawmakers have declined to require disclosure of all gifts."[25] While lawyers are usually included in the most recent federal requirements to disclose lobbying expenses, the pattern in the state houses is different. Listen to Raymond Harding:

> *"In an interview Harding said he did legal work for Philip Morris, not lobbying. He said that he had spoken to government officials on behalf of Philip Morris, but only in the context of legal matters, not legislative or administrative ones. 'I give them legal advice about dealing with various government organizations', Harding said. 'I never lobbied for them.'"*[26]

As Florida, Minnesota, Mississippi, and Texas reached settlement, the attorney generals of several key states tried to salvage some sort of master agreement. Eventually, the 46 state attorney generals agreed to drop pending lawsuits in return for payments of $206 billion. Add in the other four states, and the total bill for the Big Four tobacco companies rose to $246 billion, to be paid over the next 25 years. Meanwhile the federal government has re-opened litigation. The price of a pack of cigarettes has gone up, and tobacco companies are now acting as *de facto* tax collectors. Predictably, their profits will go up – in the short term.

The public would not be wrong to conclude that politics and therefore law itself is a game – a very expensive and complicated game. Indeed, one rock song by Sting, "If I Ever Lose My Faith in You," laments that our politicians "… all seem like game show hosts to me." Like most games, it is won by those with the best advisors and the most patience.

What is disturbing is the tobacco industry's ability to claim on the one hand that it acts in the open and simply does what is legal, while on the other hand spending vast amounts on advertising to change the forum where the "law" is decided. This presents the most difficult facet of the multi-faceted problem of corporate legal compliance.

The Report of the Committee of Experts on Tobacco Industry Documents (July 2000), published by the World Health Organization, is the most comprehensive and credible analysis of the world-wide efforts of the industry to dominate institutions supposedly in the position to monitor its functioning. The report states:

> *"Evidence from tobacco industry documents reveals that tobacco companies have operated for many years with the deliberate purpose of subverting the efforts of the World Health Organization (WHO) to control tobacco use. The attempted subversion has been elaborate, well financed, sophisticated, and usually invisible."*

Are corporate managers obligated to follow the route of the US tobacco industry and simply drive the determinations to a forum they can secretly dominate? It is plain that this is not a decision that an individual CEO can make. The profit-maximizing role will be interpreted as requiring the CEO to take every step that can be described as legal (even if nobody would consider it within the spirit of the law) until and unless those for whom he works direct otherwise. Will the board of directors do that? We have already witnessed the pressures they confront in the low value that the stock market places on their equity. Twice in the past three years, this opportunity to buy low sell high has attracted the attention of the investor Carl Icahn, one of the few individuals with the experience, the money and the chutz-pah, to be able to mount a credible claim to taking over the company.

Who, then, is to decide what are the appropriate benchmarks to govern corporate conduct in availing itself of different legal systems? While we are focusing largely on questions involved in the US federal system, their present scope is Global, as was made clear in the widely applauded sale of its tobacco interests by Sarah Lee. Revolutionary Abby knows where this leads:

> *"We are here to insist that DEFENSE must be the PEOPLE. We are here to insist that the great Industrial Centralized Power Gorgon is not just about a bunch of guys in suits behind closed doors having martinis with our Senators, judges, the Pres. and his Cabinet (yes, all presidents, not just this or that one) … we are saying that the terrifying tyrannical creature is not just this behind closed doors, it's about all the public institutions erected in the service of this monster …*
>
> *"We are here to ask you to join us in challenging the corporate-owned government to ask if BY WHAT AUTHORITY do they strain and divide and trick and exploit the American people and people of other countries? If the Constitution says WE, the People, then having given the Corporation human rights was an act of treason by a high court in 1886, all those that have assured human rights to any corporation since then have also committed TREASON."*

We need to consider the legitimacy of Abby's rage. Does the corporate system constitute such a menace to the survival of a free society that we need respond to a state of emergency? Is the inevitable effect of Globalization going to be the exacerbation of the problems which inflame Abby? Can a profitable economic system – to say nothing of a free society – long endure this pervasive sense of oppression?

A final quote from Revolutionary Abby:

> *"For over a hundred years, Big Money, Bankers and Trusts and Foundation and Corporations have all been pouring their resources into ingenious PR (Public Relations) to get us all to THINK Corporate. Before TV. Long before TV. They have been pumping up the Corporate Values for a long, long, time."*

Table 3.1 Corporate values vs. values of common sense and common decency.

Corporate values	Values of common sense and common decency
Type A	**Type B**
Success!	Neighborliness
Performance, top speed, high volume	Compassion
Winners and Losers	Trust
Upward Mobility	Quality of work
Inequality	Responsibility to others
Bettering one's self	Equality
Competition	Patience
Honors for some	Questioning wrongs, challenging wrongs
Let the weak ones fall by the wayside; they deserve it. They were given every opportunity. They just didn't try hard enough	He ain't heavy; he's my brother
It's their fault, punish them	Cooperation
Obedience to the "inevitable"	Not feeling guilty about a day off
Isolation	Respect for the planet
Distrust	Trust your senses
Watch your back. It's a jungle	Fairness
Be hard	Prudence
Believe *only* the experts	Honesty
Be assertive.	Hopes and dreams
Only bullies win	Honor for all

Exerpt from Caroline Chute's undated brochure

Media companies

Earlier, we quoted Justice Warren Burger in the *Belotti* case, when he noted that "media conglomerates" pose "a much more realistic threat to valid [political] interests" than other corporations. This may be true – but the threat itself is an outgrowth of the corporate form.

The pattern of communications companies assembling worldwide into conglomerate form is now established. There are virtually no radio, television, or newspapers that are not part of multi-industry, multi-national companies. The organs of communication are now governed by the same profit maximization rules as other businesses. We will not pause to opine on the ethical, informational, and aesthetic differences between national television like BBC and network television, or between Rupert Murdoch's Page 3 topless photo in the *Sun*. The communications industry has unique and essential properties in a free society – the capacity to frame the agenda and to mobilize discussion of critical issues. Every organ of communication will reflect its owners' predisposition, whether it is the Soviet newspaper *Pravda* or the Sulzburgers' *New York Times*. Communications companies uniquely possess the power to direct and control public dialogue on issues that importantly affect themselves.

The recent history of US federal legislation affecting the right to use the broadcast spectrum compels the conclusion that the present balance of power, the dynamics underlying our society, produces unacceptable results. Former majority leader Bob Dole has probably accepted more campaign and charitable contributions than any other American currently active. "TV broadcasters have rightly kept a watchful eye on a bloated government. Whether it was $600 toilet seats or $2000 coffee pots, they have always helped us quickly identify waste. But they have been strangely silent on this issue … When it comes to billion dollar giveaways to them 'mum' is the word."[27] The communications media have successfully thwarted all efforts to solve the "campaign finance" problem through offering free or reduced price Television time to candidates. Even Senator John McCain (R-AZ), whose courage is legendary, withdrew the proposal for free television from his campaign reform proposal. At the time of the inconclusive November 2000 elections in the United States, one commentator declared an unlikely victor: "This year's presidential race may be too close to call, but one clear winner has already emerged: local TV stations. Local broadcasters are reaping the bounty from the most expensive election cycle in history. Armed with unrestricted "soft money," political parties and special interest groups have joined presidential candidates in an $850 million TV-ad battle to woo narrowly targeted groups of voters. *What's more, the scramble for air time in certain media markets has sent ad rates soaring."* (Emphasis added.) They even raised the rates for public service![28]

Our concern is specifically focused on the importance of communications in a free society. As Dean Alger notes in *Megamedia*:

> *"If the public has reason to doubt the independence and integrity of new operations, a vital part of democracy is damaged. It is equally vital for democracy to have a truly diverse set of media sources present in the public arena, a variety of alternative information and perspectives representing a real competition of approaches to news definition and thoughts on the direction in which our society*

should head. The continuing advance of megamedia and their increasing domi-nation of the prime mass media spell a profound constriction of that diversity and a severe diminution of the marketplace of ideas, and thus a danger to de-mocracy."[29]

The media – television, print, radio – is increasingly consolidating world-wide into a few huge corporations. The major US television networks are all subsidiaries of conglomerates – General Electric, Disney, Viacom. This expands largely the scope of subjects that will not be covered for public scrutiny. A chilling example comes from Jane Meyer, writing for *The New Yorker*, one of the few publications today not owned by a major conglomer-ate.

"When a producer at '20/20' considered doing a piece on executive compensa-tion, two people familiar with the deliberations say, the idea was dropped be-cause no one wanted to draw attention to the extraordinarily rich pay package of Disney's chairman, Michael Eisner … Another producer for the network, who asked not to be named, says that the news division's need to steer clear of Disney comes up all the time."[30]

Emergence of the publicly owned corporation as the dominant mode for investment

The publicly traded corporation has become recognized as the optimal mode for investment. Much of the explanation for this lies in its character-istics:

- Corporations can be organized by anyone for any purpose anywhere with virtually no minimum requirements. This makes the corporate form available to all who seek the opportunity to convert their genius, energy and good fortune into marketable wealth.
- A corporation with publicly traded stock permits an optimal division of specialties. Those capable of providing ideas, energy and manage-ment can be rewarded alongside those whose contribution is limited to money.
- Investors are safe in limiting the extent of their liability to the amount that they invest in the corporate enterprise.

- Once money is invested as part of the equity of a corporation, management can employ that money however it wishes to achieve its objectives without fear that the money will be removed.
- The investor in a publicly traded stock has the ability to dispose of his holding at will. Thus long-term capital for the enterprise is a short-term commitment for the capital provider.
- Corporations are creatures of the state and are, therefore, in theory, subject ultimately to the state's determination of limits on its operation, as dictated by the public interest.

Corporate self-financing

The large publicly held corporation has certain attributes that importantly affect its behavior. Mature corporations are largely self-financing. The corporate system as a whole withdraws more equity capital from the market than it raises. Buybacks are more frequent and, in the aggregate, bigger than initial public offerings.

In most recent times, corporate values are unaffected by the payment of dividends. Corporations with the same level of earnings are valued the same whether or not they distribute a portion of those earnings to shareholders. Nor are corporations dependent on banks for financing. The sale of certificates of deposit in the market place gives large corporations direct access to liquidity. The much-advertised regulation of corporate behavior through the financial marketplace is largely fiction.

Corporations are important buyers of professional services. This means that the leading firms in hometowns and oftentimes in the money center cities as well are "conflicted" out of representing any challengers to the leading corporations. Advertising and public relations expenditures assure the existence of a generally supportive atmosphere about corporate functioning. The glossy business magazines invariably confirm CEOs of the largest advertisers to be "business executives of the year" and the like. When the disastrous mismanagement of a company such as Marks & Spencer was confirmed in 1999, no one thinks back to the recent years in which it had been acclaimed as Europe's best.

The large corporation in today's society is a largely autonomous self-referential energy. This energy can be applied in a variety of ways. It may be applied in the direction of maximization of shareholder values as in the case of Westinghouse (now Viacom) At another extreme, it can be applied to permit the gradual liquidation and decreased relevance of the institution as in the case of General Motors. In the extreme case of Microsoft it can prosper while ignoring and defying political considerations.[31] *The large corporation is intrinsically constructed to exist profitably in society with only minimal consideration of forces outside of the enterprise.* Corporations invoke the metaphor of the self-sealing tire, they are not immune to puncture but they are organized to seal any incursion.

Wisdom from James Hurst

The late James Willard Hurst, the greatest American scholar of the relationship of corporations to society, has described how society stopped legislating the behavior of corporations, and instead began adjusting in response to corporate interests: "We ... ceased to build general social controls into corporate structure because the larger business corporation grew to involve a wider range of interests than the corporation's own internal constitution could mediate; hence, the law moved into an expanding variety of specific subject matter regulations which, though not formally so limited, in fact mainly concerned *adjustment of societal interests* affected by large corporation behavior."

Secondly, Hurst alludes to the problem that government had in dealing with the reality of corporate power. "The trend of policy also implied a judgment on methods of legal regulation in an economy in which large-scale firms were the most influential private decision makers. Experience indicated that nothing short of specialized, continuous executive or administrative attention would supply significant external checks on the responsibility of those who held central power in corporations with large numbers of shareholders."

Hurst pointed out the most effective governmental presence is in the area of finance. "As large corporations increased the range of their impact on society, a wider spread of problems challenged public policy processes – concerning the market as an institution of social control, concerning diffuse public interests in national resource conservation and in public health and safety, and concerning important interests (those of labor, dealers and suppliers, and consumers) outside the formal structure of the corporation but affected in more focussed ways by what the corporation did." He concludes: "Thus, in 1970, as in the 1880s, we had reached an apparent equilibrium of policy in law concerning corporations, but it seemed likely to prove as unstable an equilibrium as that of the 1880s."[32]

In Hurst's view, the impact of large corporations can be accommodated to societal interest either from outside – laws, regulation, the marketplace – or from inside – its charter, its CEO, its shareholders. How one assesses the relative attractiveness of the potential "controls" depends in the first instance on the "language" used to describe the corporation. Lawyers are apt – like Professor Hurst – to seek formal solutions from the courts or the legislature or in the incorporation documents; economists and accountants look to the market; management experts look to the modern "CEO – philosopher king."

These perspectives are too linear to adequately describe the dynamic functioning of a large corporation with its freedom from the market and its power to influence, even to dominate, the rule setters. An historic view with the lens of a particular discipline inevitably will reveal a static series of relationship rather than the ideal expression of human genius that is the modern corporation.

The "genius" of the corporation lies in its unique capacity to respond to change. This is why publicly held companies have triumphed over those managed by the most elite of bureaucrats, why government direction is almost invariably inferior and why co-operatives ultimately have to join the Global environment or perish. The essence of the publicly held company – Microsoft's 180° turn in 1995 and the *hegira* of Westinghouse/CBS/Viacom described earlier in this book – is the pursuit of an identifiable objective with virtually all the resources that management is intelligent enough to identify and charming enough to enlist. This kind of impact is self-evidently beyond the capacity of stationary regulatory mentality and even the finest institutions.

Adapting to change – grudgingly

The corporation is best understood as a "complex adaptive system" with certain imperatives, growth, perpetuation and rejection of containing or challenging forces. What did it take to persuade Dow Chemical not to manufacture napalm in the 1960s; how to stop ITT from bribing foreign officials or Occidental Petroleum from illegal campaign contributions in the United States; how to change Shell's behavior in Nigeria – it took external pressure of various kinds. It took a great amount of pressure. Essentially, the complex system adapts to required change grudgingly – Shell agrees to the "wrong" environment solution with Brent Spar, Microsoft will give minimum satisfaction to the Department of Justice. *Clearly, remediation is simpler if it comes from within.* There is a huge literature on the efficacy of change through "hostile takeover." Whatever the benefits – and they are real – the price is too high. The wrong people make too much money at the expense of the surviving venture. The term owner is cheapened when speculators buy stock (sometimes based on inside information) and then sell to the hostile acquirer.

The level and rate of increase of CEO pay calls the legitimacy of the corporation into question

But when it comes to money, the biggest culprits are the leaders of those corporations themselves, in some cases. The levels of CEO pay exceed any historical precedent, comparison with compensation in other countries, and – most importantly – correlation with increased value for shareholders. Consider the astounding numbers recently appearing in *Business Week*:

> *"In 1999, the average total pay garnered by CEOs at 362 of the largest US companies again shattered the record, rising 17% from 1998's $10.6 million to an average of $12.4 million. That compares with a 19.5% rise in the Standards & Poor's 500-stock index and a 32.8% boost in earnings for 1999. **That $12.4 million is more than six times the average CEO paycheck in 1990.**"[33]* (Emphasis added.)

Forbes magazine, the usually reliable publisher of materials sympathetic with top management, makes it clear that the rise is *not* due to improved corporate performance – the conventional explanation for these large awards: Indeed, a study performed for *Forbes* by Monitor Group Corporate Finance Practice, based in Cambridge, MA, found virtually no correlation between annual changes in pay and shareholder returns. (Monitor Group studied compensation and total return to shareholders for each of the 399 *Forbes* 500s companies included in *Forbes* pay issues from 1995 through 1999. The *Forbes* article about the study concludes:

> *"Compensation committees are hesitant to make pay-for-performance stick. If the stock shoots up, the chief keeps his reward, if it collapses and he manages*

not to get fired, he either gets old options repriced or gets a new slug at the low price."[34]

Through the exercise of their large option grants, now top managers (hereinafter referred to collectively as CEOs) have become substantial corporate owners. Option holdings represent more than 10 percent of the total publicly outstanding stock. Institutional Shareholder Services reported as early as 1992 that the top 15 individuals in each company received 97 percent of the stock options issued to all employees. *Business Week* reported that the 200 largest corporations set aside nearly 10 percent of their stock for top executives, stating that in almost all cases, "it's the superstar CEO who takes the lion's share of these stock rewards."

The lion's share is large indeed. The compensation of top corporate officials in the United States today exceeds by orders of magnitude every comparative measure of pay irrespective of time and place. Today the average CEO makes about 475 times what the full-time factory employee does.[35] The levels and method of compensation of the CEOs of corporations threaten to metastasize into a cancer that will destroy the market-driven free enterprise system now prevailing in the United States and most of the world.

Process of setting pay – gap between appearance and reality

How this has happened is an important story. Law has been followed "to the letter," but to make this possible the entire business community has accepted the use of words directly contrary to their accepted meaning. Process has prevailed over common sense and the result is an emerging hegemony of the CEO, which portends significant change in the role of corporations in this society.

Appearance and reality are utterly different in several critical respects, as shown in Table 3.2.

Through the phenomenon of runaway CEO pay, the corporate system has been significantly perverted. The original ideal of management accountability to boards and shareholders has been stood on its ear. CEOs have used their power and the accommodating skill of their professional advisors to confer wealth on themselves. There is no "free" market in executive pay, it has been rigged. This corruption at the core is a cancer to the legitimacy of the corporation.

Table 3.2 The process of setting pay – the gap between appearance and reality.

Appearance	Reality
1 Shareholders' interests are secured through the *election* of directors who protect their interests.	Shareholder action with respect to the election of directors can best be described as "coerced ratification." No matter how shareholders vote, those individuals listed on the management proxy are elected.
2 The preponderance of directors are "independent" according to the rules of the SEC, the New York Stock Exchange, the Nasdaq Stock Exchange, the Internal Revenue Service, the Council of Institutional Investors, and governance-minded companies such as Campbell Soup and GM, among others.	Boards of directors are *self-perpetuating*. The CEO has at the least the power to veto nominees, but usually actively participates in the selection process. Membership is highly valued and those selected are conscious of benefit conferred on them.
3 Most boards have compensation committees comprised entirely of "independent" directors.	Most directors are nominated and/or approved by the CEO–Chairman. How can anyone be considered "independent" of someone to whom they are personally beholden?
4 Best practice requires the use of "professional" compensation consultants.	The realities of a successful professional practice include not being perceived as insensitive to the needs of those who are retaining you.
5 The "free market" ensures that competitive factors control the levels of CEO pay.	There is no "free market" in top executive compensation. CEOs control the critical stages of the process, including government and professional accounting treatment.

"Why doesn't anybody protest?" you might ask. "Why doesn't anybody do anything?" Graef (Bud) Crystal, a refugee from the compensation consulting business, has cried loud and clear, but his is a voice in the wilderness. Other credible witnesses as to the inappropriateness of the redistribution of corporate wealth earn fine livings, which are controlled by those to whom this wealth is being diverted.

CEO power over government and rule setters changes the accounting for pay

The legitimacy of corporate power must be questioned closely in light of the change in the language and rules for CEO compensation. The Business Roundtable is an organization comprised exclusively of the CEOs of major companies. Their agenda purports to be that of their corporations they lead. In the case of compensation, unfortunately, their agenda is entirely personal. The BRT has led a most successful co-optation both of the United States government and of the previously independent rule-setters for the accounting profession.[36] This was exemplified by the 88–9 vote of the United States Senate in 1994 expressing its "sense" [sic!] that the current cost of issuing options should not be reflected on companies' income statements. The Business Roundtable successfully organized a lobbying effort to pressure the Financial Accounting Standards Board ("FASB") to reverse its proposal that account be taken of the "value" of options at the time they were granted. Thanks to the Roundtable's lobbying skills and power – henceforth, options not only are a one-way street, but they are also "free" – they don't cost anything.

Warren Buffett, whose ability to make money deprived the country of a great literary talent, wrote to Senator Chris Dodd, then Chairman of the Securities Subcommittee of the Senate Committee on Banking:

> "The most egregious example of let's-not-face-up-to-reality behavior by executives and accountants has occurred in the world of stock options. The lack of logic is not accidental: For decades, much of the business world has waged war against accounting rule makers, trying to keep the costs of stock options from being reflected in the profits of the corporations that issue them. Typically, executives have argued that options are hard to value and therefore their costs should be ignored. At other times managers have said that assigning a cost to options would injure small start up businesses. Some of them have even solemnly declared that 'out of the money' options (those with an exercise price equal to or above the current market price) have no value when they are issued. It seems to me that the realities of stock options can be summarized quite simply: If options aren't a form of compensation, what are they? If compensation isn't an expense, what is it? And if expenses shouldn't go into the calculation of earnings, where in the world should they go? ... Managers thinking about accounting issues should never forget one of Abraham Lincoln's favorite riddles, 'How many legs

does a dog have if you call his tail a leg?' The answer: 'Four, because calling a
tail a leg does not make it a leg.' It behooves managers to remember that Abe's
right even if an auditor is willing to certify the tail is a leg."

The CEO community's success in overpowering FASB, the supposedly independent accounting rule-setting organization, flies in the face of public
opinion, which is becoming ever more suspicious of corporations and their
managements.

The American public is profoundly concerned with the extent of corporate power. *Business Week* magazine (September 11, 2000) devoted its cover
and primary article to the question: "Too Much Corporate Power?" *Business Week* together with Harris conducted a poll in the late summer of 2000
which contained the question:

"Which of the following statements do you agree with more strongly?

	2000	1999
US corporations should have only one purpose – to make the most profit for their shareholders – and their pursuit of that goal will be best for America in the long run	*4%*	*5%*
US corporations should have more than one purpose. They also owe something to their workers and the communities in which they operate, and they should sometimes sacrifice some profit for the sake of making things better for their workers and communities	*95%*	*95%*
Not sure/No answer	*1%*	*0%*

Business Week, September 11, 2000,
http://www.businessweek.com/2000

M&A activity increased CEO pay. Furthermore "The American Disease"
threatens to export via merger.

Acquisitions have accelerated the progression (if that is the right word) of
the CEO into an independent entity with entitlements far greater than those
of the corporation's other constituencies. In the recent merger of BP Amoco
(itself the product of a previous merger of British Petroleum and American
Oil) and Atlantic Richfield, BP Amoco paid off the CEO and top officers
for selling a "merger of equals" to those lower in the organization – shortly
to be laid off. Compensation in these deals is out of sight. Not only are all

options vested and all parachutes opened, but CEOs like Frank Newman of Bankers Trust are paid additional king's ransoms simply not to go to work. Donald Marron, the 66-year-old CEO of Paine Webber, has made a piker out of Frank Newman. Not only does he get all the goodies, not only will he not have to retire (like everyone else in the organization), not only will he not have to report to anybody, but he also gets a big customer for his new business – Paine Webber's acquirers – (UBS of Switzerland) – have agreed to put some of their money (reported to be $500 million) to be managed by a new Marron controlled and owned enterprise.[37]

The American experience is inviting imitation from abroad. Following the aforementioned merger of British Petroleum and American Oil, there was a well-choreographed cry that UK salaries should be competitive with those on the world level. As a practical matter, this meant that BP executives received previously unimaginable pay raises. The same pattern was repeated in the Chrysler merger with Daimler Benz with the added fillip that under German law the surviving company discontinued the American practice of disclosing the level of top executive pay.

What has happened to the concept of corporate officers having a fiduciary relationship with other corporate constituencies? Corporations are truly getting to the same place as Church and nation state before them, where the position of the leader rather than the institution becomes paramount. This is the condition that precedes loss of legitimacy and collapse.

A solution

So what is the solution? Is it enough for shareholders simply to rely on market pressures to drive management out of antisocial activities? Society does not speak with a single voice. Gambling and liquor earnings are highly valued; General Electric's persistent refusal to admit responsibility for fouling the Hudson River has not prevented it from being the second most highly valued corporation in the world. Not even GE's occasional lapses into conduct classified as criminal have dimmed its luster. Nor have findings of anticompetitive behavior kept Microsoft periodically from being Number One; UK companies purchase tobacco operations from America without stock market loss or moral encomium. But as we shall see in later chapters of this book, the gains from antisocial behavior are not sustainable. In the long run, shareholders and fund beneficiaries do not benefit from such behavior.

Is it tolerable for the corporate constituencies to acquiesce in the dramatically changed compensation arrangements for the principal executives? Will history record that this was an event comparable to the selling of indulgences by the Church or Marie Antoinette's "Let them eat cake" in signaling the destroyed legitimacy of a previously vigorous institution?

Clearly the tides towards an economically determined world have moved too far, and some solution must emerge. Can government laws alone force good behavior? In most cases, the answer is no. The reason is that the cost of fines for breaking the law in many cases is lower than the potential profits a corporation can make from breaking the law.

What agency, then, if not government, can ensure accountability for today's large modern corporation? The next chapter of this book will identify such an agent – long-term, responsible investors in corporate equities.

Endnotes

1   I reflect at length on Smith's analysis of these in my book, *The Emperor's Nightingale: Restoring Corporate Integrity* (Capstone/Addison Wesley, 1998). (Note that Addison Wesley was the original publisher in the US, but the US operation was subsequently sold to Perseus Books.)

2   In early 2000, Glaxo Welcome PLC paid $76 billion for SmithKline Beecham PLC and Pfizer Inc. paid $85 billion for Warner Lambert.

3   The bill numbers were S 2567 and H.R. 7010.

4   This is the motto proclaimed at jubilee2000.org, which is based in London, England, and part of a larger world movement on the Web called netaid.org. This Jubilee 2000 movement is not identical with the Jubilee 2000 movement of the Roman Catholic Church, which is broader in scope. However, the Roman Catholic Church has endorsed the notion of debt forgiveness for the poorest nations, and has been promoting this cause at Catholic universities and in local parishes. The biblical roots for debt forgiveness in a "jubilee" year can be found throughout the Old Testament book of Leviticus.

5   Robert Lenzner, "Corporate Saboteurs," *Forbes*, November 27, 2000, pp. 157, 158.

6 Jeffrey E. Gartner, "Time for a Shakeup at the Business Roundtable," *Business Week*, October 9, 2000, p. 12.

7 Cover story, *Business Week*, November 13, 2000. See also a previous cover story, "Backlash: Behind the Anxiety Over Globalization," *Business Week*, April 24, 2000.

8 John Plender, Comment & Analysis, *Financial Times*, September 11, 2000.

9 Robert A.G. Monks and Nell Minow, *Corporate Governance* (Oxford: Blackwell, 1995), p. 10, Fig. 1.1.

10 Opinion in *Louis K. Liggett Co. v. Lee*, 53 S. Ct. 487 (1932). (Emphasis and paragraph breaks added.)

11 Caroline Chute, *The Snow Man* (New York: Harcourt Brace, 1999). Revolutionary Abby and other manifestos are sent at different times to friends and members.

12 Jacques Barzun, *From Dawn to Decadence – 1500 to the Present – 500 years of Western Cultural Life* (New York: HarperCollins, 2000), p.784.

13 The full quote was as follows: "It has long been recognized, however, that the special status of corporations has placed them in a position to control vast amounts of economic power which may, if not regulated, dominate not only the economy but also the very heart of our democracy, the electoral process ... The State need not permit its own creation to consume it." Justices Byron White, William Brennan, and Thurgood Marshall.

14 Scott Turow, "The High Court's 20-Year-Old Mistake," *New York Times* op-ed Sunday, October 12, 1997.

15 Jeffrey Goldberg, "Big Tobacco Won't Quit," *New York Times Magazine*, June 21, 1998, pp. 36 (emphasis added).

16 Goldberg, *op. cit.*

17 "Big Tobacco Wins One," *The Economist*. June 20, 1998, p. 32.

18 Jeffrey Taylor & Phil Kuntz, "Despite Polls, GOP Doesn't Fear Voted Heat on Tobacco," *Wall Street Journal*, June 25, 1998, p. A24.

19 Richard Kluger, *Ashes to Ashes: America's Hundred-Year War, the Public Health, and the Unabashed Triumph of Philip Morris* (Knopf, 1996), p. 618.

20 *Ibid.*

21 Common Cause, "Nicotine Fix," in *Return on Investment: The Hidden Story of Soft Money, Corporate Welfare, and the 1997 Budget & Tax Deal*, paper published in Washington , DC, 1997, pp. 30–31.

22 Steve Campbell, "Washington Watch," *Maine Sunday Telegram*, June 21, 1998.

23 Goldberg, *op. cit.*

24 Goldberg, *op. cit.*

25 Clifford J. Levy, "Philip Morris Spends Heavily Behind Scenes to Court Albany Lobbyists," *New York Times*, July 27, 1999, p. A19.

26 *Ibid.*

27 *Congressional Record*, April 17, 1996.

28 Kathy Chen, "In Campaign 2000, Local Stations are Winning Big," *Wall Street Journal*, November 9, 2000, p. B1.

29 Dean Alger, *Megamedia, How Giant Corporations Dominate Mass Media, Distort Competition, and Endanger Democracy*, (Lanham, MD: Rowman & Littlefield, 1998), pp. 13, 14.

30 Jane Meyer, "Bad News – What's Behind the Recent Gaffes at ABC?" *New Yorker*, August 14, 2000, pp. 30, 32.

31 Here, we need just note the widespread criticism of Bill Gates and Microsoft in early 1999 for having failed to make the customary lobbying commitment and campaign contributions in Washington, DC – a prudent business expense to assure even-handed consideration by antitrust authorities. No one ever accused Microsoft of being a slow learner. By the end of the Year 2000 election cycles, at $3.5 million the company was one of the largest donors to political candidates and parties. [Source: Kathy Chen, "In Campaign 2000, Local Stations are Winning Big," *Wall Street Journal*, November 9, 2000, p. B1.]

32 As a rather mediocre student at the Harvard Law School, I am perhaps overly impressed by the rather extraordinary coincidence that each of the three most perceptive students of the relationship of corporate power to a free society – Louis Brandeis, David Engel, and James Willard Hurst – shared the distinction of being the finest students in their respective classes. Adolf A. Berle, whose exquisite early work deteriorated into the commonplace, was also a genuine prodigy at both Harvard College and Law School, although not first in his class. James W. Hurst, *The Legitimacy of the Business Corporation in the Law of the United States, 1780–1970*, (Charlottesville: University of Virginia Press, 1970), pp. 162–3.

33 Special Report – Executive Pay, *Business Week*, April 17, 2000, pp. 100, 102.

34 *Forbes*, May 15, 2000, pp. 213, 214.

35 Depending upon what statistics you use, that ratio amounts to an eight-
    to tenfold expansion in executive pay relative to the rest of the work-
    force in just 25 years. *Business Week, supra*, at 110.

36 I have elsewhere told this story in detail. See *The Emperor's Nightingale*
    (Reading, MA: Addison-Wesley, 1998), pp. 58–63.

37 Charles Gasparino, "Marron's Job at UBS Has Extra Perk," *Wall Street
    Journal*, July 21, 2000.

Chapter 4

The Solution

The New Global Investors

When East India Company ships first set sail in search of spices in 1600, the individuals who had invested in those vessels sailed along in spirit. These first modern owners, although they had limited their liability through the corporate form, were *involved*. If those ships failed to accomplish their stated mission, those owners would have taken decisive action.

Over the course of the next four centuries, however, owners of ever-growing global corporations lost their sense of involvement. They became more passive – starting from the dawn of the twentieth century right through current times. In the previous two chapters, we explained this history – a bright promise tarnished by abuse of power.

At this juncture, we bring good tidings. In the following pages we will show that in the late twentieth century, there emerged a new type of shareholder: the Global Investor – a true owner whose potential will be explored for the remainder of this book.

This new Global Investor means business. Whether based in New York, Boston, or London, Global Investors (often pension funds for state government employees) are buying significant amounts of corporate equity. And in some cases, they are showing signs of responsible ownership as historically significant as investment in early trading companies.

Global Investors: the numbers

The numbers tell the story. Particularly eloquent are numbers telling the size of US outbound investment – both direct investment (in assets and entire companies) and portfolio investments (in stock).

By the end of 1998, the aggregate of foreign direct investment by US investors rose to $993 billion for that year – significantly up from the $251 billion total flowing out in 1985. During this same period, foreign portfolio investments made by US mutual funds went to $1 trillion (up from $39 billion in 1985), and similar investments by US pension funds rose to $606 billion (up from $300 billion in 1985). Adding foreign direct investment and foreign portfolio investments together, the sum outflowing from the US in late 1998 exceeded $2.5 trillion.

Meanwhile, foreign issuers have made more of their equity available in US markets, sparking a dramatic growth in American Depository Receipts (ADRs) traded on US stock exchanges. The number of US exchange listed ADR programs more than doubled between 1992 and 1998 (from 215 to 484) and the volume of listed ADRs nearly quadrupled (from $125 billion to $555 billion).[1]

All this has occurred in a global marketplace for ownership. With few exceptions, all equity markets, large and small, are to some degree foreign-owned today (see Table 4.1).

For additional data, see Fig. 4.1 below and, further below, Table 4.2 on worldwide pension holdings, containing data from Intersec Research Group, a unit (since April 2000) of Deutsche Bank.

Table 4.1 Foreign ownership of equity markets.

	Size of equity markets	Percentage foreign-owned
France	$647 billion	42%
Germany	$825 billion	22%
Japan	$2.2 trillion	n/a
UK	$2.3 trillion	24%
US	$11.7 trillion	27%

Source: Conference Board, *Institutional Investment Report*, International Review, 1999, p.18. We have chosen to record the UK percentage from Phillips & Drew, Pension Fund Indicators (1999), p.18.

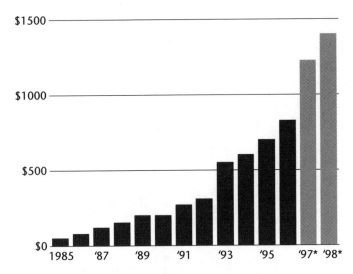

*New estimate based on a Federal Reserve System survey

Fig. 4.1   A flood overseas: US holdings of foreign stocks ($ billions). Source: Securities Industry Association.

The modern investment process

The significance of the global equity movement becomes even greater when we focus on how the modern investment process works. All the institutions described to this point share one common trait: they own shares in publicly traded companies. Because they own shares in many different companies, these investments are called portfolio investments, using the common nomenclature of the Organization for Economic Cooperation and Development (OECD). These portfolio investments, in turn, lead to a type of investment called direct investment or, if the investment is overseas, foreign direct investment.[2]

It works like this: the companies that sell shares to investors use the funds from their sale of equity, along with funds derived from internal cash flow and borrowing, to buy plants and equipment or to invest in research and development – the whole range of assets, tangible and intangible, that help grow their business. This process of corporate investment literally creates the future of society. Here decisions are made that shape the future, determining which regions will prosper, what technologies will be advanced, which jobs will be created, and what educational requirements will be set.

Table 4.2 Worldwide pension holdings (1998 figures obtained in 1999 from Intersec, a unit of Deutsche Bank).

Country	Local equity holdings of domestic pension funds YE 1998 (US$ billion)	Local equity holdings of foreign pension funds YE 1998 (US$ billion)	Total equity holdings by pensions (US$ billion)	% of pension investments held by foreign pensions	Country GDP (World Bank estimates) (US$ billion)	Pension investment as % of GDP	Country market capitalization (US$ billion)	Pension investment as % of market capitalization
Argentina	2.2	3.4	5.6	60.7	298.1	1.88	59.25	9.45
Australia	44.1	22.4	66.5	33.7	364.2	18.26	696.66	9.55
Austria	0.2	2.9	3.1	93.5	212.1	1.46	35.72	8.68
Belgium	2.9	17.0	19.9	85.4	247.1	8.05	136.97	14.53
Brazil	22.1	8.8	30.9	28.5	750.8	4.12	255.48	12.09
Canada	100.7	33.2	133.9	24.8	598.8	22.36	567.64	23.59
Chile	4.9	3.3	8.2	40.2	78.7	10.42	72.05	11.38
Denmark	18.6	7.8	26.4	29.5	174.3	15.15	93.77	28.16
Finland	6.0	13.7	19.7	69.5	125.7	15.67	73.32	26.87
France	8.4	82.9	91.3	90.8	1432.9	6.37	674.37	13.54
Germany	9.4	93.8	103.2	90.9	2142	4.82	825.23	12.51

Hong Kong	4.0	18.2	22.2	82.0	166.6	13.33	413.32	5.37
Ireland	11.9	4.3	16.2	26.5	80.9	20.02	24.14	67.12
Italy	1.9	46.0	47.9	96.0	1171	4.09	344.67	13.90
Japan	304.2	167.0	471.2	35.4	3783.1	12.46	2,216.99	21.25
Malaysia	8.0	8.4	16.4	51.2	72.5	22.62	93.61	17.52
Mexico	0.0	8.4	8.4	100.0	410.3	2.05	156.60	5.36
Netherlands	71.7	54.3	126.0	43.1	382.6	32.93	468.74	26.88
New Zealand	1.0	1.6	2.6	61.5	54.1	4.81	90.48	2.87
Norway	2.3	3.4	5.7	59.6	145.9	3.91	66.50	8.57
Portugal	2.6	5.8	8.4	69.0	106.6	7.88	38.95	21.56
Singapore	6.4	6.6	13.0	50.8	84.4	15.40	106.32	12.23
South Africa	19.9	7.6	27.5	27.6	133.4	20.61	232.07	11.85
Spain	1.8	29.6	31.4	94.3	551.9	5.69	290.38	10.81
Sweden	13.7	23.2	36.9	62.9	225	16.40	272.73	13.53
Switzerland	35.5	70.3	105.8	66.4	264.4	40.02	575.34	18.39
Thailand	0.8	2.1	2.9	72.4	111.3	2.61	23.54	12.32
UK	684.7	158.0	842.7	18.7	1357.4	62.08	1,996.00	42.22
US	3,403.4	358.5	3,761.9	9.5	8210.6	45.82	11,309.00	33.26

Up until the present time, as we write in the year 2001, it has made perfect sense to distinguish sharply between "portfolio investment" and "direct investment." Portfolio investment connoted the absence of power; direct investment, the presence of power. Today, however, these two types of investment – portfolio and direct – are beginning to converge, a trend clearly seen in the behavior of Global Investors. These new Global Investors are traditionally considered to be "portfolio" investors only. But do they not begin to match the OECD definition for direct investment? According to the OECD, direct investors have "the objective of obtaining a lasting interest [which] implies the existence of a long-term relationship between the … investor and the enterprise and a significant degree of influence on the management." The OECD benchmark definition continues:

> *"Investment is the process through which a minimum – say 10 percent – of the shareholders – exercises influence over the constitutional structuring of portfolio companies … An effective voice in the management, as evidenced by an ownership of at least 10 percent, implies that the … investor is able to influence or participate in the management of an enterprise …"[3]*

The 10 percent mark is widely recognized as a threshold of control. For example, US securities laws set this limit as a dividing line between "insiders" and "outsiders" in US corporations. So the momentous question before us is this: are Global Investors still only "portfolio" investors, or have they in fact crossed the line into becoming "direct investors?" We will use the term "Global Investor" to indicate a portfolio investor whose manner of ownership approximates that of the class "direct investor."

Identification challenges, US style

Unfortunately, current compilations of statistics still do not permit precise identification of the characteristics of the Global Investor – despite reams of US governmental and private data purporting to give the most comprehensive analysis of the institutional investor world. I had the very rare personal experience actually of looking at the ballots in a contested election – following my contested candidacy for the board of directors of Sears Roebuck at the 1991 annual meeting. Accompanied by John Wilcox of Georgeson & Company, then and now one of the few genuine experts in the field, I availed myself of the provisions of Delaware law that entitled a losing candidate the opportunity to "inspect the ballots." This privilege was extended from a dungeon-like room in an anonymous government building in the state capital of Dover, Delaware. The ballots themselves were virtually all in nominee name, so it was not readily apparent who had voted how. (As detailed further below, an institution does not typically vote in its own name, but often votes in the name of a "nominee," custodian, or depository trust.) Guessing against estimates derived from our months of direct solicitation, we were able to pull together an approximation of who had voted for and against me.

There were some surprises – notably in the case of two institutions where a personal friend had the power to vote. One friend, who publicly supported me, voted against me. The other friend, who refused to commit himself, had voted for me.

This whole process gave me an indelible feeling that nobody really knows who the stockholders of the modern corporation are, and the stockholders know it. Virtually nobody has the motivation and interest to explore the subject as far as I did, and in my case, I could get only as far as an informed guess.

Let us start with money managers – a category of institutional investor that seems faceless to all, supposedly an individual in a gray suit making investments on behalf of an amalgam of investors, individual and institutional. Let us look further to see if there is not a center of gravity for money manager wealth.

In the US, large money managers (handling more than $100 million) are required quarterly to file with the Securities and Exchange Commission a list of their holdings, called 13F filings for convenient identification.[4] Many commercial enterprises record these filings and generate reports for interested customers. One of the largest and best-established "data" firms in this field is the Toronto-based multinational Thompson Financial, through its Rockville, Maryland, subsidiary CDI. One can arrange all manner of services with CDI right up to a "real time, online" list of the recorded shareholders of every company.

Investigators in search of the elusive Global Investor may encounter their first problems here. One must add to the mix the additional mix of holdings by mutual funds, which are described in filings made pursuant to a different statute (The Investment Company Act of 1940 in contrast to the Securities Exchange Act of 1933). Beyond this, the Investment Company Institute (ICI) publishes data on mutual funds.

With all these filings – both the filings of money managers and the filings of mutual funds – there is a common problem: there is no enforcement of the requirement of filing timely and accurate information. No one has ever been fined or gone to jail because of late or erroneous Form 13F filings. It is thought that the level of compliance is good, but at best the information is three months old and comprises information furnished only by the conscientious.

A few years ago, Michael Clowes, the always-amusing editorial director of Pensions & Investments (which can pass as the industry organ) pointed out the absurdity of the many differing measures of institutional ownership.

"A quick quiz. At the beginning of 1995 private pension plans had (a) $334.8 billion in equities, or (b) $1,091.9 billion in equities. Answer: Almost certainly (b). But both figures come from the government, so nothing is certain. The first figure comes from the US Department of Labor, Pension and Welfare Benefits Administration's Abstract of 1995, Form 5500 Annual Report. It is certainly wrong. The second figure is from the Flow of Funds Accounts of the United States, published by the Board of Governors of the Federal Reserve System. I suspect the Fed's numbers are about right because the Fed has been tracking the numbers for fifty years?"[5]

Clowes goes on to explain that this particular discrepancy arises because of apparently different requirements for accounting for "pooled" versus "individually invested" funds.

One of the reasons that the information is so sloppy is that it is rarely needed in a money-making context. Of course, everyone would appreciate accurate up-to-date information, and the technology exists to produce it. But high-quality records are prohibitively expensive to create and maintain. Typically, such records are generated only where significant money is at stake in the short term. So, no one cares who the shareholders are or how many shares they own except in the context of a proxy contest. Yet even so, how many proxy contests take place in a year where the contesting party considers it economical to identify and reach each and every shareholder? Not many. It is only when stakes are high and elections are close that faulty voting procedures become evident – as seen all too painfully in the US presidential elections of 2000.

To be sure, every public company maintains the ownership registers and, with certain stylized obfuscating, is obligated to make them available to paying and otherwise eligible challengers. But are these ownership registers realistic? In my experience, the answer is no. For example, in examining the ownership records of most public companies, one rarely sees the Public Employees' Retirement System of California – to name just one important institutional investor – yet it is widely known that CalPERS invests significantly in these same companies.

Tracing the tracks of any particular investor (CalPERS in this example) requires an understanding of how CalPERS itself manages its own funds – whether actively or passively.

Actively managed funds are those that CalPERS chooses to invest in particular companies. These investments can be made in the name of a variety of vehicles:

- CalPERS itself
- CalPERS' nominee (it is common to form a "nominee" partnership for the purpose of holding title to stock so as to facilitate transfer)
- CalPERS' custodian (the bank that acts as the depository of the evidence of ownership, as required under the Employee Retirement Income Security Act of 1974, ERISA)
- CalPERS' depository trust company (which is where the certificates actually are held), or in the name of its nominee CEDE & Co.

Passively managed funds are an even more significant factor to take into account when tracing CalPERS holdings. CalPERS, like other public funds, puts most of its equity holdings in index funds.

To figure out how many shares in a particular company are owned by CalPERS (or any other investor), one must know how much money CalPERS is putting into the index fund, as a percentage of the index fund's total incoming money. Then one would need to identify what company shares are purchased by the index fund, and calculate the CalPERS portion.

To give a simplified example, let us assume that CalPERS and two other investors invested $2 each in Index Fund ABC, which has $6 to invest. ABC Index in turn invests $1 each in six companies. And let us further assume that for each of these six companies, the $1 invested represented 1 percent of the company's equity. By this formula, CalPERS, via the Index Fund ABC, would have purchased 0.33 percent of each of the three companies in the fund.

Or, to go about the math in a different way, if we know that CalPERS owns 33 percent of an index, and that Company X's shares in the index represents 1 percent of its equity, then CalPERS owns 0.33 percent of that company.

Using this formula is easy, but finding the factors for it is not, since the investments made by CalPERS (or any other institutional investor) are most likely carried in the name of the index fund, its nominee, custodian, or depository – as explained above. Furthermore, the composition of many index funds, such as the MSCI-EAFE index (which stands for Morgan Stanley Capital International-Europe, Australia, Far East) is proprietary, and thus not fully disclosed. Indexes also change composition on a daily basis as markets change and companies are bought and sold. For more on the subject of indexing, see the end of this chapter.

Identification challenges, UK style

The disclosure system in the UK provides more clarity – although it, too, fails to give us an easy way to "connect the dots" of ownership.

UK companies must not only file names of their shareholders at Companies House, but they must also reveal the "beneficial" owner on the back of the "record" holder on petition under Section 212 of The Companies Act. There is a plethora of information services available in the City of London (the equivalent of Wall Street). Preeminent among them is City Watch which will provide, for a substantial fee, a terminal right on your desk which with flicks of the appropriate buttons will show on the screen the current shareholdings, all of which can be printed out neatly with the press of another button.

Given the differences in US and UK disclosure practices, joint ventures can lead to disclosure anomalies. Consider for example the situation with Hermes Lens Asset Management ("Hermes"), a major UK investment company in which I had a substantial interest.

Hermes has entered into a joint venture with CalPERS. Under the terms of the joint venture, the two investors have agreed to vote each other's shareholdings in its native country. As a result, Hermes regularly receives up-to-date lists of CalPERS holdings of securities in the UK. These lists show substantial investments in a number of major companies – above and beyond any investments made via index funds. I made a bit of a nuisance of myself at a lunch with Judith Hanratty, the formidable corporate secretary of British Petroleum, when I bet her a return meal that she could not accurately identify the shareholders of BP. The derision with which my challenge was greeted abated when it became clear that the corporation's records made no mention of ownership by the California Public Employees Retirement System (CalPERS) – known to be a major BP investor. Could this fact be uncovered by a persistent and knowledgeable user of the Companies Act? Who knows? The fact is that few people can afford the time, money, and sheer struggle required to find out. At some point, we will have to decide whether there is any public interest in knowing precisely who owns these major companies.

Yet no such tracks appear on the record that is available to the general public via the CityWatch print-out. Scrutiny of the records reveals no trace of CalPERS holdings, and only the most rudimentary indications of where to begin to look. Virtually all of the holdings of non-resident owners are held in multiple nominee names, along the lines bullet-pointed earlier, namely nominee, custodian, or depository trust company. This last category is especially vexatious. Many of the depository accounts in the name of large US banks with clients investing abroad include holdings by more than one institution, so no numerical cross-checking is possible.

Getting at the mystery

Given these disclosure difficulties in the US, the UK, and other countries too numerous to describe, it is clear that the real ownership of corporate equities is a great mystery. Companies themselves do not know who their real owners are – and until the ultimate proxy contest takes place between infinitely well-funded, experienced, and committed parties, there may never be any reason to know.

Globally, the problems of data inaccuracy get compounded. In looking through the compendious OECD publications listing Foreign Direct Investment and Portfolio Investment data for all participants, there are time lags of at least two years. Hence, 1998 publications will show 1995 data. The same is true of the World Bank and its UNCTAD publications. Private firms like Phillips & Drew's 1999 study on World-Wide Pension Funds[6] use more up-to-date data. The problem is that none of the figures jibe. Michael Clowes' problem exists in virtually every effort to correlate more than one data source with another.

Overcoming identification challenges

Clearly, the Global Investor is amassing ownership at a rapid rate, and is prepared to use it responsibly. But who exactly are these Global Investors? Identification is difficult, even in the United States, known to be a bastion of good disclosure.

Our first attempts to obtain equity investment information involved trying to locate high quality, summary level information. For this information we contacted the relevant money managers, consulting groups, government organizations, and business reporting organizations. We found this information to be uncommon and of varying quality. Our contacts and sources were the following:

- PIRC – Pensions & Investments Research Consultants Limited
- The Conference Board
- Employee Benefit Research Institute
- Greenwich Associates
- Intersec Research Corp.
- Euromoney Institutional Investor
- US Securities and Exchange Commission
- US Department of Labor
- US Internal Revenue Service
- Wilshire Associates
- Pensions & Investments Online
- Money Market Directories, Inc.
- Princeton Financial Systems
- Datamonitor Financial Services
- Dunn & Bradstreet
- The Carson Group
- Schroders
- Barclay's Global Investors
- Vanguard
- Citywatch

- Watson & Wyatt
- Jefferies & Co
- Morgan Stanley Capital International

We found the money managers unhelpful with this information. If they knew any answers to our ownership questions, we were unable to entice them to provide them. The reporting organizations, such as Pensions and Investments Online, had very general information that they could provide, but no details of foreign ownership.

Fortunately, we found two great allies in the consulting industry: Intersec Research Group (purchased in April 2000 by Deutsche Bank), and Greenwich Associates. We obtained information from Intersec that provided good estimates of total pension investments in 29 countries. These estimates are based on the Morgan Stanley Capital International World Index weightings, and take into account domestic and foreign investments from the US and foreign pension funds. These estimates accounted for $6 trillion. Greenwich was able to provide us with outstanding breakdowns and trends in pension investments over a 10-year period that accounted for $5.6 trillion.

Government sources included the Securities and Exchange Commission, for information on Form 13F. The only foreign companies on this list are those that issue American Depositary Receipts (ADRs), so this list provides little evidence of total foreign ownership. The best government data source that we found was Section 1 Form 5500 Schedule G of the Internal Revenue Service (IRS). Here, US private pension funds can detail their investments, both foreign and domestic. The IRS takes in these forms and sends them to the Department of Labor (DOL) for storage and dissemination through Freedom of Information Act (FOIA) requests.

However, through lengthy discussions with the IRS and the DOL, we determined that there is in all likelihood only one person at the DOL who knows anything about the Form 5500 Schedule G. Even she did not realize that submission of this schedule is entirely voluntary. Apparently the private pensions know more about this form than the DOL, as we were able to find submissions for only two of the 50 largest private pensions in the US Although this information is available through the FOIA, we had to physically go inside the DOL ourselves and search a primitive microfiche filing system for the information. When the Department of Labor announced that it would outsource its Schedule G work to the private sector, I had high hopes for improvement. So did my longtime associate, Barbara Sleasman, who had worked for the Department of Labor during the first 10 years of ERISA. It turns out that our hopes were unfounded. Even today, despite outsourcing, the material is available only in fragmentary, paper record form – an ironic commentary on government in the digital age.

After exhausting the potential sources of summary level ownership information, we went straight to the source: the pension funds themselves. We were able to obtain information on the investments of 30 of the larger pension funds (Table 4.3). Twelve of these 30 gave us complete listings and the other 18 partial listings. From these listings, and knowing the percent foreign ownership of the world's 300 largest pensions, we were able to make good estimates of pension fund ownership of 77 percent of the 1000 largest companies in the world.[7] We show these estimates on our Web site **http://www.ragm.com/library/topics/global_investors.html**.

In addition to the data we came up with from our own sleuthing, we were also able to find a "profile" of global investors based on data from the 1999 Pensions & Investments/Intersec World 300 Pension Funds (published 9/20/1999 by Crain Communications, Inc.) (see Table 4.4).

A major force: retirement funds

All these problems of measurement aside, it seems clear that *the majority of Global Investors are retirement funds.* In the previous discussion, we described the Global Investor generically. Many of our examples, however, involved retirement funds, for this is where the action is.

This "pension fund revolution" is not a new phenomenon. It has been going on for over a decade. In a classic essay published in the *Harvard Business Review* a decade ago, Peter Drucker described the "middle class" revolution that has given a substantial portion of the electorate in the developed world a personal and direct interest in the performance of corporations worldwide. Drucker reasoned that average citizens, whether employed in the private or public sector, have a natural interest in preserving the wealth in their retirement portfolios.[8]

Let us look at the available statistics – as poor as they may be – for confirmation of this assertion. If you believe Phillips and Drew, for example, the 1998 size of US pension fund investment abroad is approximately $800 billion. On the other hand, if you prefer Carolyn Brancato's reports for the

Table 4.3 Ownership estimates of 25 of the largest companies in the world.

Company	Country	Market value ($US billion)*	Estimated pension fund ownership**
Microsoft Corporation	US	407.22	13.41%
General Electric	US	333.05	18.10%
IBM	US	214.81	17.03%
Exxon Corporation	US	193.92	19.41%
Royal Dutch Petroleum Co.	Netherlands/UK	191.32	8.05%
Wal-Mart Stores, Inc.	US	189.55	11.80%
AT&T Corporation	US	186.14	19.44%
Intel Corporation	US	180.24	14.09%
Cisco Systems, Inc.	US	174.09	15.73%
BP Amoco p.l.c.	UK	173.87	9.44%
Coca-Cola Company, The	US	168.99	15.02%
Merck & Co., Inc.	US	159.8	15.96%
MCI WorldCom, Inc.	US	152.24	16.98%
Citigroup Inc.	US	150.94	15.57%
Lucent Technologies Inc.	US	150.34	16.22%
American International Group, Inc.	US	141.62	11.43%
Pfizer, Inc.	US	138.37	10.22%
Bristol-Myers Squibb Co.	US	136.53	17.13%
America Online Inc.	US	129.07	3.28%
Johnson & Johnson	US	124.64	18.59%
Procter & Gamble Co., The	US	124.05	15.70%
Deutsche Telekom AG	Germany	115.02	3.52%
Bank of America Corp.	US	112.87	17.26%
British Telecommunications plc	UK	107.14	45.39%
Roche Holding	Switzerland	103.72	13.71%
	Average ownership		**15.30%**

* Market value estimates come from the 1999 Business Week Global 1000.
** Calculations of ownership estimates are described in Appendix ##.

Conference Board, the totals are a little more than half of that ($432 billion). Beyond this, as mentioned earlier, the Investment Company Institute (ICI) publishes current data (as current as can be, given the high speed of change) on the holdings of the hugely expanding mutual funds – totaling approximately $400 billion outside the US in 1998. We know that much of the funding of pension funds comes from mutual funds, which many companies use as a vehicle for making investments in 401(k) retirement plans.

Table 4.4 Global Investors: a profile.

Rank	Fund	Country	Assets (US$ billion)
1	Stichting Pensioenfonds ABP	Netherlands	159.7
2	California Public Employees' Retirement	US	133.5
3	Assoc. of Local Public Service Personnel	Japan	101.3
4	New York State Common Retirement Fund	US	99.7
5	General Motors Investment Management Corp.	US	87
6	California State Teachers' Retirement	US	82.6
7	Alimanna Pensionsfonden (Board 1,2 & 3)	Sweden	80.1
8	Florida State Board of Administration	US	77.5
9	Nat'l Public Service Personnel	Japan	75.6
10	New York State Teachers' Retirement System	US	71.1
11	Texas Teacher Retirement	US	69.5
12	Public School Personnel	Japan	67.1
13	Federal Retirement Thrift Investment Board	US	64.5
14	New Jersey Division of Investment	US	63.3
15	General Electric	US	58.7

Source: 1999 Pensions & Investments/Intersec World 300 Pension Funds

How much double counting is there? *Brancato + ICI = P & D*? No matter what source we use, the conclusion of rapid increase is unmistakable. The *Economic Report of the President – 1999* records "foreign securities corporate stocks" as of year end 1997 as $1001.3 billion (up from $197.3 billion in 1989).[9]

Retirement plans undoubtedly constitute a major percentage of these totals. This conjecture is supported not only by Brancato/ICI/P&D figures cited above, but also – and perhaps even more persuasively, by the educated guesses of involved participants.

Hon. Felix Rohatyn, US Ambassador to France, the immensely sophisticated former senior partner of Lazard Freres & Co., recently noted that: "American institutions account for between 30 and 40 percent of all equity ownership on the CAC-40."[10] (The CAC-40 is shorthand for the 40 companies listed on the major French stock index – Compagnie des Agents de Change-40.) Rohatyn goes on to tell us that the French government is thinking, "if you can't beat 'em, join 'em ... They're weighing the issue of allowing their *pension funds* ... to take a much more aggressive position in equities." (Emphasis added.)

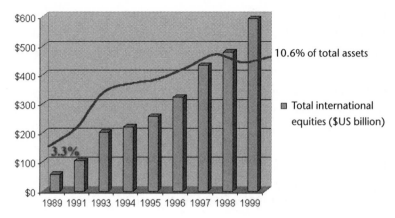

Fig. 4.2 International equities held by US pension funds.

Overfunding: creating a new power base

One symptom of the tremendous potential of these retirement funds is the amount of money they have over and above what they owe – a happy condition called *overfunding*. Over the past 20 years, pension plans have grown to become an enormous economic force. They not only bet on equity, they truly invested in it, and their investment reaped rewards.

During the 1980s, as stock markets recovered from a bear market, pension investment committees began shifting more of their assets away from bonds and into stock. Meanwhile, assets in the plans grew, increasing the plans' ability to make further investments. In the 1990s, during a strong bull market, companies let their overfunded assets keep growing. Many had no choice but to do so. Congress made it more difficult for companies to access the overfunded assets by instituting a 50 percent excise tax on reversions to corporations. The wealth of some overfunded plans was staggering. In fiscal 1998, General Electric realized an income credit of more than $1 billion.[11] Declining markets in 2001 suggest that surpluses may already be a phenomenon of the past.

The April 24, 2000, *Business Week* puts it this way:

> *"Thanks to the longest bull market in history and rising interest rates, which push down corporate contributions, defined-benefit pensions have ceased to be a cost center. For a growing number of old-line industrial companies where many such plans are clustered, they have instead become an important income genera-*

tor ... Across the board, 1999 was certainly a bang-up year for pension-fund investing: The median return for large-company plans was 15.7%, according to pension-fund adviser Wilshire Associates. That contributed to an overall 40% increase in pension assets over the past two years, estimates Eric P. Lofgren, director of benefits consulting for Watson Wyatt Worldwide, a human-resources adviser. At the same time, fund costs are growing much more slowly or, in some cases, falling. A shift to cash-balance plans, which combine attributes of 401(k)s and traditional pensions, has saved some companies millions of dollars a year. And by converting to self-directed 401(k)s, companies can shift much of the cost of retirement to employees. Overall pension liabilities for US companies rose only 5% on average in 1998 and '99, says Lofgren."[12]

This rise in the equity-based wealth of pension plans puts those plans in an important historical position. By exercising their fiduciary duties to increase the wealth of long-term beneficiaries, they can literally change the world, since so much of the world is theirs. Managers, of course, have a short time frame – the vesting date of their options. Many other classes of shareholders are short-termers as well. Only the Global Investor has the perspective and the legal authority to consider the long term.

Defined benefit plans plus defined contribution plans = trillions

Let us take a moment to consider the extraordinary impact of pension fund wealth and power on society. This is the first time in history that society has been devoting such a large portion of its wealth to the elderly. Only a generation ago, members of the oldest generation lived at the home of their children and grandchildren. In some cases, this choice was made out of mutual love. In many cases, however, it was made out of economic necessity. The retired generation simply could not afford to pay for separate living space. Today most senior citizens can choose to live independently – thanks in large part to the US pension system, both public and private.

Pension experts may well point out a precipitous decline in the number of defined benefit plans, and the simultaneous rise of defined contribution plans. They might say that the fiduciaries of defined contribution plans are not the same breed as the fiduciaries of defined benefit plans. But this distinction sets up a false dichotomy. Some plans are classified as defined benefit plans but have features of defined contribution plans, and vice versa, notes Boston-based pensions expert John Dirlam, a partner with Arthur Andersen LLP.[13]

A *defined benefit plan* specifies the level of benefits to be received by the employee upon retirement. It is different from a *defined contribution plan*, which specifies only the level of contribution, not the final amount to be received. The defined benefit plan offers greater security, while the defined contribution plan offers greater upside potential. Defined benefits plans are more common in large companies, and defined contribution plans in smaller companies. (This explains why while the number of defined contribution plans is 10 times greater than the number of defined benefit plans, the number of employees covered is only two times greater.)

In the US, approximately 23 million employees are now paying into defined benefit plans, compared with almost 46 million paying into defined contribution plans – two times as many. And in terms of numbers of plans, defined contribution plans outnumber defined benefit plans ten to one: the US private sector has some 45,000 defined benefit plans versus over 500,000 defined contribution plans. Dirlam notes: "As further evidence of this trend, it is estimated that in a few years there will be more *retirees* in defined benefit plans than *active employees*."[14] Amazingly, however, because of overfunding (see below), these plans will remain solvent.

In any event, the dividing line between defined and contribution plans is very gray, because of the rise in hybrid plans, including cash balance plans, pension equity plans, target benefit plans, and age-or service-weighted profit-sharing plans. Here is a quick overview.

- *Cash balance plans* are popular in big firms. In fact, while there are only about 1000 such plans in existence, they may cover as many as 10 million employees because of their concentration in the *Fortune* 500.[15] A cash balance plan is legally a defined benefit pension plan,[16] but it does not accrue more rapidly as the employee reaches retirement. Each employee is credited with a rate of return tied to a benchmark (usually the 30-year Treasury Bond), but the employee funds are *not* actually invested in the source of this benchmark, but are invested at the discretion of the company – often investments in equity.
- *Pension equity plans* are essentially a variation on the cash balance theme, but they are paid out differently, with an accrual pattern more like the defined benefit plan. There may be no more than 100 to 200 such plans now in place.

- A *target benefit plan* is a defined *contribution* pension plan that bases its annual contributions on some combination of age and service. There are approximately 10,000 target benefit plans in existence. The plan uses a "target benefit formula" that determines each employee's annual contribution, but there is no *guarantee* that the benefit will be there at retirement. The actual investment performance (which is often determined by employee investment choice) determines the actual benefit at retirement or termination, just like a 401(k) plan.
- An *age-or service-weighted profit-sharing plan* is a defined *contribution* plan that tilts the annual contributions to older, longer-service employees. In some cases, the contributions may even be tilted in accordance with the employee's position in the company, although these are somewhat less common because they have more difficulty in passing the applicable IRS discrimination tests. The contributions can also be "integrated" with Social Security. There are probably fewer than 10,000 of these plans in existence today, but the number is growing rapidly.
- *Combination plans* are a kind of defined benefit "floor plan" underlying a profit sharing plan (but not a 401(k) plan). In these arrangements, called *combination plans*, the company sponsors *two plans*. The profit-sharing plan makes contributions each year on the basis of corporate profits. There are probably no more than 5000 combination plans in existence, and the number may be declining with the overall decline in defined benefit plans.

Another variation on the theme is allowing employees to choose their own benchmark – for example either the 30-year Treasury Bond or the Standard & Poors 500 Index. A generation ago, employees would have chosen bonds rather than stocks. Today, in the continuing bull market, stocks remain a strong choice.

The real news behind the switch from defined benefit plans to defined contribution plans is the *huge cost savings* that companies are enjoying from defined contribution plans – savings they are putting right back into the plans, which are getter richer and richer. Here is how a recent *Business Week* article summarizes the situation.

"Some companies have recently reduced their pension costs by switching to cash-balance benefit plans. By spreading pension allocations more evenly over a worker's years and allowing employees to take more money with them when

they leave, these plans benefit newer employees. But they can cut some older workers' payouts. Overall, cash-balance plans have reduced pension costs at 45% of the companies that adopted them, according to a recent study by Watson Wyatt. BellSouth Corp., which made the switch last year, saw 1999 pension obligations fall 4%, to $13 billion, while assets grew 15%, to $21 billion. Electronic Data Systems Corp. also reaped a windfall. According to EDS's 1998 annual report, its transition to a cash-balance model reduced its future benefit obligation by $492 million."[17]

Dark horse fiduciary?

Most of this chapter has emphasized pension funds as the long-term fiduciary of the future. Another Global Investor that might possibly emerge might be the charitable investor market. As scholar Marcy Murninghan reports, based on data compiled by the Foundation Center and factoring in 1999 major gift announcements, the combined market value of assets held by organized philanthropy is roughly $400 billion. With the anticipated intergenerational wealth transfer (producing charitable bequests of up to $25 trillion over the next 55 years, estimate Boston College researchers), these institutional assets could swell to $2 trillion in the next few years.[18]

Community foundations add to the picture. At last count, there were 556 community foundations in the United States. According to figures recently released by the Columbus Foundation, 1998 nationwide assets for community foundations jumped to $25.2 billion, an increase of almost 19 percent over 1997 levels. Boosted by a bull market for equities, and by record-breaking giving levels (1998 gifts to community foundations grew 17 percent over 1997 totals, to $2.8 billion), the family of community foundations has grown by 15 new members each year.

Finally, community foundations preside over a growing number of support organizations. In 1997 and 1998, according to the Columbus Foundation report, 92 support organizations were established under the aegis of community foundations, with combined gifts of $276 million. Taken together, 82 community foundations are now responsible for 290 support organizations. Overall, support organizations comprise assets of $3.2 billion, a nearly fifty percent increase from 1996; most of them hold assets ranging from $1 million to $50 million. In addition to its $400 billion asset size, the charitable investor and community foundation market has value as equity owners, which is waiting to be tapped. In another measure of their growing financial clout, with combined market assets of $25.2 billion, a conservative estimate of community foundation equity holdings ranges from $16 billion (roughly 65 percent of all assets, including domestic and international equities) to $20 billion (roughly 80 percent). Although these institutional owners have not yet embraced their role as active owners, they could do so in the future. If they do, they will be another force to reckon with.

The Boston Foundation established a "Civic Stewardship policy in December 1999:

"As an institutional investor and a public charity, The Boston Foundation knows that it bears greater responsibility for its ownership role, more so than day traders or fund arbitrageurs whose motivations are different.

"As an institutional investor, The Foundation now recognizes that proxy voting is subject to fiduciary standards similar to those affecting private pension plans, that voting rights have economic as well as moral value and therefore should be treated as assets, and that doing so means that proxies are voted in accordance with publicly stated policy and guidelines. It can and should do no less."

Indexing: here to stay

With so much equity-based wealth in retirement plans, charitable trusts, and other long-term Global Investors, we must return to the subject of indexing. The move toward indexation is growing. Chicago consultant Ennis Knupp has recently advised clients to increase the indexed portion of their equity accounts from 50 percent to 80 percent.[19] Earlier we mentioned that CalPERS makes some 'passive' type investments via index funds. CalPERS is not alone in this respect. Many institutions have invested through the medium of "index funds." This fact is well known, but poorly documented. The reason is that money managers, investing on behalf of pension funds and others, want to avoid having their style of investing classified as "indexing," because they receive such low fees for this type of passive investing.

Consider the case of Wells Fargo, the original money manager for the Federal Employees' Retirement System (FERS), which I helped select and oversee when I served as one of FERS' original trustees. The bid from Wells

Fargo for managing the indexed equity portfolio was *minus* 15 basis points: they would pay us for the privilege of allowing this type of investing.

The use of indexing, because of its passive nature, may seem to contradict our notion of the active Global Investor.[20] The fact is that pension funds like CalPERS will continue to make both "active" and "passive" investments. The financial community worldwide agrees that active government involvement in private sector companies should be minimized or avoided entirely. The only way to permit public sector employees to participate through their pension funds in the economics of private companies is through indexes where government has literally no choice of sector or security. As investing has become worldwide, the relative ignorance of managers about specific companies in remote locations has increased the desirability of investing through an index.

The question arises as to how the indices are compiled, what considerations the compilers take into account, what accountability the compilers have. In other words, even if the investors in index funds are passive, the funds themselves are not. They, too, are Global Investors in the full sense of this word.

Significantly, a World Bank subcommittee is analyzing the issue of index funds as part of the Bank's Global Governance Forum initiative

Mrs Firestone

How important are Global Investors? The following quote from a recent Wall Street Journal article, speaks volumes:

> "*Klaus Pohle, chief financial officer for German drug maker Schering AG raised eyebrows a few years ago when he described to a Berlin audience how he made decisions. 'I go to Boston and visit Mrs Firestone,' he said 'She tells me what to do.' Karen Firestone, a portfolio manager at Fidelity Investments, is no longer Schering's main contact, but Mr Pohle says the investment company is even more influential these days.*"[21]

This statement may exaggerate the importance of institutional investors over the fate of their portfolio companies, but there is an important kernel of truth here. Global Investors have the capacity to influence how their equity dollars are spent:

- *Will equity dollars be spent for short-term profits for the gain of hangers on – be they short-term investors or corporate managers?* That result will surely obtain if Global Investors remain within the classical boundaries of portfolio investment.
- *Or will equity dollars be spent for the long-term maximization of shareholder wealth through proper attention to the rights of all constituencies?* This result is preferable for true "investors" in the full sense of the term, and for society in general.

Our rhetorical question yields a working definition of investment made by Global Investors. At the outset of this book, we defined investment as the process of foregoing immediate expenditures in order to build a more prosperous future. When it comes to Global Investors, we can be even more precise. In their case, investment may be defined the commitment to become involved sufficiently in the functioning of portfolio companies to assure certain minimum practices. A company having true "investors" is more valuable than one without such investors.

A worldwide movement

The Global Investors are well positioned to impose baseline rules in conjunction with the investment of their funds. They may be able to foment change in countries that lag behind the governance curve. The movement is not just in the US, but worldwide, often with a glance back at America.

Europe has become a theatre of increasing shareholder activism. US Treasury Secretary Lawrence Summers has noted (on July 7, 1999, on CNBC television) that "The priority in Europe, as many people in Europe have recognized, has to be on developing an appropriate domestic growth strategy. That means restructuring companies, allowing *empowered shareholders* to do the work of restructuring. It was these kinds of changes from the bottom up that I think contributed, along with deficit reduction, to the prosperity that we're enjoying in the United States." (Emphasis added.)

ABP, the largest pension fund in the Netherlands and one of the largest in the world, has recognized the need to change its policies and to become oriented to the activist requirements of ownership.

"ABP will proceed to exercise its voting right as the occasion arises, but more actively than in the past. When appropriate, ABP will attune with other institutional investors and vote by means of a proxy procedure to be further agreed upon. In the case of clear differences of opinion with the company's management, ABP will not hesitate to vote against proposals. When possible, the company's management will be informed of this prior to the general meeting of shareholders."[22]

Asia will follow in Europe's wake. Already Japan, a common recipient of Global Investor capital, has recognized the importance of pleasing outside investors. JETRO, the Japanese trade organization, has recognized as much. In a recent press release it stated that:

"[T]he trend toward economic globalization has increased the mobility of capital, which now flows to the asset classes and locations that provide the highest return on investment. This is a very tough fact for Japanese companies, as they have proven less attractive to investors than many competitors in other OECD countries in recent years."[23]

Indeed, one of the astonishing aspects of Japanese post war economic development is the rapidity of real change under the guise of paralyzing inactivity. The shape of the change is very clear from a 1998 report of the Corporate Governance Committee of the Corporate Governance Forum of Japan, Corporate Governance Principles – A Japanese View (Final Report), May 26, 1998:

"[1–1] The Globalization of the marketplace has ushered in an era in which the quality of corporate governance has become a crucial component of corporate survival. The compatibility of corporate governance practices in an international context has also become an important element of corporate success. The practice of good corporate governance has become a necessary prerequisite for any corporation to manage effectively in the globalized market.

"[1–2] The publicly-owned corporation, the basic constituent of corporate society throughout the world, is actually a system of cooperative relationships between various stakeholders, including shareholder, management, employees, consumers, clients and creditors. But shareholders in particular, the providers of equity capital are given a special position. As they constitute the final risk-takers of the company who are entitled to claim the residual profits of the company,

they are often considered the owners of the company. In this sense and under the system of private ownership, shareholders are granted the right of governance over the company for the benefit of their own interest in the form of maximized returns on their investment."[24]

It seems likely that shareholder power may well be more influential than the government in Russia–US affairs. As the *New York Times* recently reported, "Investors representing about 15 percent of [United Energy System] stock met with Aleksandr Voloshin, the Kremlin chief of staff. Mr. Voloshin, an important figure in President Vladimir V. Putin's administration, is also chairman of United Energy's board ... [Mr. Voloshin] was surprised by how strongly the investors felt about the restructuring, a person close to the situation said."[25]

And the sweep of change is not limited to the US, Europe, and Japan. Even in developing economies outside of these known regions, we see a rise of interest in better governance through shareholder activism. Scholar Enrique Rueda-Sabater notes:

"There are even stronger reasons to believe that corporate governance/business practices can significantly affect the bargaining power of host countries to attract foreign investment. For developing countries corporate governance issues, therefore, are not only a factor influencing the distribution of income and wealth but also a key factor affecting their competitiveness and ability to grow rapidly."[26]

Following the investment collapse in East Asia in the fall of 1998, the World Bank, working jointly with the Organization of Economic Cooperation and Development, created a task force of active investors. The task force is led by the redoubtable Ira M. Millstein of Weil Gotshal and Manges, who chaired the OECD group that created and achieved consensus on a set of corporate governance principles in May 1999. One goal of the World Bank task force, of which I am a member, is to encourage meaningful application of these principles around the world. Our mandate is to facilitate investment in the Third World by acquainting leaders with the governance concerns of potential lenders and investors. We have already held learning sessions in Brazil and Russia, and plan many more.

Global standards for action

Clearly, the rise in power of the Global Investor is occurring on a scale and at a pace not reported, and hardly imagined, in contemporary scholarship. This new concentration of power will eventually be expressed in action.

Many Global Investors would prefer to ignore the signs of their power. They are not anxious to be identified; they are not anxious to be required to expend the resources necessary to function as owners; they do not want to stick their necks out and affront present or potential customers. Nor do these institutions have either the culture or the personnel necessary to perform the necessary monitoring function.

But the reluctance of these uninvolved owners should not determine the world's economic fate. Society cannot afford to permit property to be held without genuine accountability for the power of management. Thus our collective future must take its cue from the few owners that have asserted their interests on the global scene – albeit without leaving many traceable tracks.

True Global Investors collectively share a common objective: they want to preserve and enhance the wealth they safeguard. As such, they have a natural interest in improving the quality of global equity markets. *Fortunately, they are in a position to impose globally consistent standards for the behavior of corporations. In every country, they can assert these standards as criteria for making their investments in those corporations' shares.* The notion of global standards is quite new and exciting. I sensed this excitement when I spoke at the fourth meeting of the International Corporate Governance Network in Frankfurt in July 1999. This was the first time that a significant portion of the world's owners had gathered to plan collective ways to advance their interests as owners.

The Global Investor is likely to make good decisions for the long-term of society, because it can afford in most cases to take a long-term view, and a diversified view. An ordinary domestic investor may need to reap profits in the short term. As such, that domestic investor may choose to invest in a corporation that externalizes the brunt of the harm it is doing. But importantly, *nothing is external to a global shareowner.* Institutions having investments in all countries have virtually no incentive to permit environmental and hiring practices in the poorest countries that can only have the impact of competing with their own investments elsewhere. Why lower third-world production costs through pollution only to compete with your own products manufactured elsewhere when you own all of the comparable enterprises?

Leading firms, exemplified by Royal Dutch Shell, are turning their significant resources in this direction, as outlined further in Chapter 6.

Convergence

What should be clear from the barrage of statistics is Global Investors, especially retirement funds, are making inroads all over the world. To be sure, the way they cluster differs from country to country. In the US and the UK, the dominant institutional investors can be found in pension funds, public and private, and in investment companies, also known as mutual funds. Many of these institutions engage in the active defense of the value of their shareholdings. By contrast in Europe (for example France and Germany), as well as in Asia (for example Japan), corporations invest in one another in a practice called cross-shareholdings. These institutions follow a relationship style for their more "closely held" equity.

Despite these different practices, however, there is a convergence of behavior. As The Conference Board (New York) predicted in a press release dated May 1999, soon " 'closely-held' equity will be replaced by *global equity*,' which is certain to be accompanied by increased corporate governance pressures."[27] This is the subject of our next chapter.

McKinsey & Company published in June 2000 the results of a series of surveys conducted to discover how shareholders perceive and, importantly, value corporate governance in both developed and emerging markets. Undertaken in co-operation with the World Bank and the *Institutional Investor's* regional institutes, the surveys gathered responses about investment intentions from over 200 institutional investors, who together manage approximately US $3.25 trillion in assets. The overwhelming majority of investors say they would pay more for a well-governed company. The survey defined a well-governed company as having a majority of outside directors on the board with no management ties; holding formal evaluations of directors; and being responsive to investor requests for information on governance issues. In addition, the survey said, in the well-governed company directors hold significant stockholdings in the company and a large proportion of directors' pay is in the form of stock options. The actual premium investors say they would be willing to pay for good governance differs by country, but it ranges between 18 percent in the UK to 27 percent in Indonesia or Venezuela. While these results confirm the performance of activist investors in recent years, their uniformity and size are startling. What changes in strategy, sales, manufacturing, management, financing could one imagine adding a *fifth* to the value of an enterprise? Governance is clearly an important factor in corporate value.

Global corporations and the problem of independence

The modern corporation has no geographical home – it buys, sells, manufactures, hires, pays taxes, and complies with laws in virtually every country on earth. Corporations can be understood in the terminology of complexity theory as "Complex Adaptive Systems." With their underlying dynamic for survival and growth, corporations will organize themselves to circumvent efforts at restraint, no matter whether such originates from business competitors or from sovereign governments. Corporations by their nature focus on seeking profit. They do not make social policy, which is the exclusive preserve of elected officials. Their social conscience comes from monitoring by owners acting in their own self-interest. This is the key to "governance revolution" which is based on the necessity for a process by which the managers are accountable for their performance to some independent class or group not under their control.

True independence, however, remains elusive. The ubiquity of corporate power has made it difficult to identify any genuine independence. In theory, owners are independent, almost as a matter of definition. In practice, however, the institutional owners are not independent, because the appointment of the trustees of these institutions is usually "in the gift" of corporate management. In a pluralist society, it is to be expected that large institutions would have commercially significant relationships with the corporations in which they invest. Yet these relationships frustrate the essential purpose of investment trusts. The law, particularly with reference to pension funds in the United States, is very clear; the trustee must consider investments "solely" in the interest of beneficiaries. The pension trust must be administered for the "exclusive benefit" of plan participants. On March 6, 2001 the Myners Commission recommended that the same standard be made in the law of the UK.

In the next chapter, we shall begin to explore new incentives and means for doing this.

Endnotes

1 Conference Board Press Release #4484, May 6, 1999.

2 *OECD Benchmark Definition of Foreign Direct Investment* (3rd Edition, 1996), section 8, p. 1.

3 *OECD Benchmark Definition of Foreign Direct Investment* (3rd Edition, 1996), section 8, p. 8.

4 The origin of 13F is Form 13F under Rule 13f-1 of the Securities Exchange Act of 1933. Rule 13f-1 covers "Reporting to Institutional Investment Managers of Information with Respect to Accounts Over Which They Exercise Investment Discretion."

5 Michael J. Clowes, "DOL Pension Figures Useless," *Pensions & Investments*, July 26, 1999, p. 10. (NB: Clowes merely *suspects* that the numbers are *about right* – for what compelling reason? Oh – that they have been compiling them for a long time.)

6 Phillips & Drew, "Pension Fund Indicates a Long-Term Perspective on Pension Fund Investment," 1999, p. 18.

7 We calculated ownership estimates of the 1999 *Business Week* Global 1000 (*BW* 1000) companies by the world pension funds. Our methods were as follows: *Pensions & Investment's* Top 300 (*P&I* Top 300), published by Crain Communications, Inc., plus TIAA-CREF. (TIAA-CREF is not included in the *P&I* 300 because they have recently been reclassified as a mutual fund. However, we believe that TIAA-CREF is largely representative of pension fund investments and have added only their pension fund assets to our totals in the list of world pension funds.) The *P&I* Top 300 is an annual survey and ranking of the 300 largest pension funds in the world with total assets of $5.2 trillion in 1999. The total assets of the 1999 *BW* 1,000 companies were $19.7 trillion.

We endeavored to collect lists of equity investments (actual numbers of shares held) from the world pension funds. We were successful in accounting for complete equity investments of 12 of the larger pension funds and partial lists from 15 additional pensions. In this way, we were able to account for pensions totaling $1.1 trillion assets, or 21 percent of the total value of the world pensions. Using the total shares of each of the *BW* 1000 companies held by the pension funds, we calculated an "average percent composition" for the world pension funds. This "average percent composition" represents the fraction of a pension's total assets represented by ownership of a given BW 1000 company. We then took the average percent composition, multiplied this number by the total assets of the pensions we were unable to account for, and summed these fractional ownership estimates to arrive at an estimate of world pension fund ownership estimates for the *BW* 1000.

After eliminating estimates that were obviously unreasonable (over 100 percent ownership) and companies which had merged into other *BW* 1000 companies, we were left with ownership estimates for 77 percent of the *BW* 1000. Because equity investment lists were generated between mid-1998 and mid-1999, we calculated share prices and, thus, ownership estimates for 12/31/1998 values of the *BW* 1000 companies. Although the BW 1000 was generated in mid-1999, we calculated the valuation of the 1999 *BW* 1000 companies for 12/31/98 so as to provide estimates that would be more time-congruent with the equity investment estimates of the pensions.

8 Peter F. Drucker, "Reckoning With the Pension Fund Revolution," *Harvard Business Review,* March–April 1991, pp. 316–318.

9 *Economic Report of the President, transmitted to the Congress February 1999,* Table B-107 p. 449.

10 Riva Atlas, "In Paris, Rohatyn Remains the Man Who Saved New York," *Institutional Investor,* July 1999, p. 22.

11 Ellen E. Schultz, "Joy of Overfunding: Companies Reap a Gain Off Fat Pension Plans: Fattened Earnings," *Wall Street Journal,* June 15, 1999, p. A1.

12 "The Perils of Fat Pension Plans Investors Beware: Corporate Income is Being Puffed Up," *Business Week,* April 24, 2000, online edition.

13 John K. Dirlam, "Hybrid Retirement Plans: The Best of Both Worlds?" *HR Director: The Arthur Andersen Guide to Human Capital* (New York: Profile Pursuit, 2000).

14 *Ibid.*

15 "Consultants now believe that between 500 and 1000 plans have been converted to cash balance programs, most in the past five years." Source: Fred Williams, "Seagram Mixes Three Plans to Create Cash Balance," *Pensions & Investments,* March 6, 2000, p. 6.

16 Most cash balance plans are amendments to a pre-existing defined benefit pension plan; very few such plans have ever been started from scratch. For example, as reported in the March 6, 2000, issue of *Pensions and Investments,* when the Seagram Co. established a cash balance plan

for its 8900 US employees, it combined three existing pension plans to do so.

17 *Business Week*, April 24, 2000, online edition, *op. cit. supra.*

18 This section is excerpted and adapted from Marcy Murninghan, "Institutional Investors & Civic Stewardship: Prime Time for Good Players," a January 8, 2000, memorandum to Amy Domini, Jamie Heard, Peter Kinder, Steve Lydenberg, Bob Monks, and Nell Minow.

19 Joel Chernoff, "Ennis Knupp Strategy Could Lead to Reallocation of Billions," *Pensions and Investments*, November 27, 2000, p.1.

20 "… [T]he only resort for an indexed fund manager to improve returns is to become engaged. Presumably he is not doing his job under trust law if he does not try to increase the absolute return on his indexed portfolio in this way." Private communication from Alastair Ross Goobey, February 1, 2001.

21 Greg Steinmetz and Michael R. Sesit, "Rising US Investment in European Equities Galvanizes Old World," *Wall Street Journal*, August 4, 1999, p. 1.

22 ABP, *Corporate Governance*, second revised edition, November 1998, pp. 12–13.

23 "Japanese Cabinet Approves Industrial Revitalization Plan," JETRO, press release, July 21, 1998.

24 Corporate Governance Committee, Corporate Governance Forum of Japan, *Corporate Governance Principles – A Japanese View (Final Report)*, May 26, 1998.

25 Sabrina Tavernise, "Battle over Russian Energy Concern Moves to the Kremlin," *New York Times*, June 29, 2000, p. C4.

26 Enrique Rueda-Sabater, "Corporate Governance and the Bargaining Power of Developing Countries to Attract Foreign Investment," paper delivered May 1999 at Nottingham Business School, p. 2.

27 Conference Board Press Release, *op. cit. supra.*

Chapter 5

The Fiduciary Framework

A Setting for Investments

For much of the twentieth century the separation between ownership and control of corporations has been the subject of exhaustive analysis. One of the most important consequences of this phenomenon has hardly been noticed: the death of corporate social responsibility.

When corporations had shareholder "owners," it was plain who was responsible for the impact of corporations on society. This was a matter of law (within the constraints of "limited liability" protection), a matter of practicality, and a matter of culture.

When shareholders ceased being in control of ventures it was plainly futile to place responsibility for corporate functioning at their door. The loss of shareholder power resulted in the loss of a specific corporate constituency that would be responsible for how the corporation would accommodate the interests of society as a whole.

Responsibility has costs, so it is hardly surprising that no one has come forward to assume it. So long as shareholdings devoid of responsibility have the same value in the marketplace as those encumbered with it, traditional owners will be reluctant to take action.

The need for such action seems clear, given the record of the past century.

Twenty years before Adolphe Berle and Gardiner Means wrote their book on *The Modern Corporation*, the Pujo Committee reported in 1913: "None of the witnesses (the leading American bankers testified) was able to name an instance in the history of the country in which the stockholders had succeeded in overthrowing an existing management in any large corporation. Nor does it appear that stockholders have ever even succeeded in so far as to secure the investigation of an existing management of a corporation to ascertain whether it has been well or honestly managed."[1]

Ownership without power

The tendency during this period has been the dilution of the controlling blocks of shares to the present situation of institutional and widely dispersed ownership – ownership without power. "In fact, it is a process which seems to be culminating in our time with Cheshire cat disappearance of 'ownership' of large publicly held companies in any meaningful sense of the term."[2]

Dean Bayless Manning has suggested, "An arbitrary model of a corporate structure may prove helpful in attacking the problem. Assume a large modern corporation similar to its typical commercial counterpart in all respects but two. First, the model abandons the *a priori* legal conclusion that the shareholders 'own the corporation' and substitutes the more restricted conception that the only thing they 'own' is their shares of stock. Second, the shareholder in this model corporation has no voting rights. His position would be quite similar to that of a voting trust certificate holder with all economic rights in the deposited stock but no power to elect or replace the trustees by vote. Given this corporate model, there can be no talk of 'corporate democracy' or rejoining 'control' and 'ownership.' In such a corporate world how would one go about ensuring the desired degree of management responsibility while permitting corporate officers the necessary discretion to run the business?"[3]

Manning concludes that there would be need of new government mechanisms to ensure that management did not abuse its position of trust and resolve conflicts of interest egregiously in its own interest. He did not consider that there was any element of public interest that was damaged by the absence of participating ownership.

The philosopher king

This conclusion coincided with that period of time in post-World War II euphoria that America briefly flirted with the CEO as philosopher king.

Those same persons whose productive genius had brought victory in war and hegemony in peace would look after society's interest. As historian James Willard Hurst recounts, "There were those – both within the corporations and outside of them – who argued at mid-century that top management was developing a working character which in itself legitimated the power resident in large corporations. The argument rested largely on the significance of expertise, institutional procedures, and continuity in the existence of the big firms ... Statesmanship in corporation decision making meant fidelity to the productive function coupled with readiness to seek fair adjustment among all major elements closely affected by what the big company did – not only its shareholders but its workers, suppliers, dealers, and customers – and to be a good citizen in its relation to the general community."[4]

With surprisingly little scrutiny, this benevolent dictatorship has continued in American business, more or less diluted, through the balance of the twentieth century. While the law provides that the shareholders elect the directors, it is plainly recognized that no one accedes to a board except at the direction or concurrence of the CEO; while directors generally are thought to be responsible for succession planning, the preponderant pattern is for CEOs to pick their successors; emerging notions of good practice recite that CEO pay is fixed by "independent" directors, serving as an "independent" compensation committee, using the service of independent pay consultants. The reality is that all serve at the CEO's pleasure. Nothing proves more clearly the reality of CEO rule as the expansion of top pay from every previously normative ratio to limits unimagined in other times or places. Today's CEO can receive, for a few months of mediocre work, sums larger than the entire annual budget for the government of a country.

Worldwide attention to the annual pay of their CEOs provides unusually clear insight into the ethical and economic dynamics of American corporations. CEOs do what they are paid to do. Boards of Directors are responsible for creating compensation arrangements for key officers that align their interests with those of the owners of the corporation. Nell Minow in **http://www.thecorporatelibrary.com** has compiled all of the available current contracts for CEOs of the S&P 500 companies. Among several other financial publications, the *Wall Street Journal* annually provides a statistical and analytic review of CEO pay, a series edited by Joann Lublin. This torrent of information consistently shows that much of the energies of the modern corporate system are committed to increasing the wealth of corporate leaders.[5]

While the "CEO/philosopher-king" has been a convenient theory in accommodating many needs at low apparent cost, it has been unstable, having no support in law or in fact. The law continues to base corporate legitimacy on shareholders. In fact, corporate leaders – no matter how great their vision – enjoyed no mandate from the citizenry and could not credibly substitute their judgement for that of elected officials. It is this absence of "legitimacy" that was called forcefully to the world's attention with the failure of the World Trade Organization talks in Seattle in November 1999, and the disruption of International Finance Corporation/World Bank talks in April 2000, as described in Chapter 3.

Until the sundering of control from "ownership," corporate legitimacy fitted comfortably within the concepts of property developed in the West since John Locke. As Adolphe Berle explained, "Most fundamental of all, the position of ownership has changed from that of an active to that of a passive agent. In place of actual physical properties over which the owner could exercise direction and for which he was responsible, the owner now holds a piece of paper representing a set of rights and expectation with respect to an enterprise. But over the enterprise and over the physical properties – the instruments of production – in which he has an interest – the owner has little control. At the same time *he bears no responsibility with respect to the enterprise or its physical property*".[6] (Emphasis added.)

Birth of the passive shareholder

No one passed a law, no agency recognized a change of status, and shareholders became passive pursuant to the inevitable dispersion of their interests over a long period of time.

The passive shareholder has been subject to universal scholastic scorn. The argument runs that investors in equities should not be entitled to the full protection accorded by society to property because shareholders have failed to exercise the responsibilities that legitimated their ownership. "Must we not, therefore, recognize that we are no longer dealing with property in the old sense? Does the traditional logic of property still apply? *Because an owner who also exercises control over his wealth is protected in the full receipt of the advantages derived from it, must it necessarily follow that an owner who has surrendered control of his wealth should likewise be protected to the full?* May not this surrender have so essentially changed the logic applicable to his interest in that wealth?"[7] The shareholder is perceived as victim – no one points out that the shareholder has apparently escaped a burden.

George Cabot Lodge excoriates the Business Roundtable's 1978 recitation of the conventional wisdom of corporate legitimacy. "The statement implies that the board derives its authority and legitimacy from the shareholders, but it ignores the problem that *shareholders neither have nor want to have anything to do with the naming of directors. Furthermore it is quite clear that Roundtable managers do not want them to have any more to do with it.*"[8] (Emphasis added.)

It is clearly in the interests of management to work in a system where the appearance of accountability can be advertised while the reality is otherwise. This has taken place against the backdrop of the neutering of the ownership authority/responsibility implicit in a share of stock. This is surprising, if for no other reason than because trading records on various exchanges around the world consistently demonstrate that the vote has value.

The ever-imaginative Dean LeBaron suggested in the early 1980s that the theoretical questions about the value or efficacy of voting rights could be settled by allowing their separation from shares and creating a trading market in them. The issue is complicated by the practical incapacity of small holders to correlate any ownership effort on their part with any impact, to say nothing of any increase in value, on the corporation as a whole. Why should owners spend their time and money to no effect? So long as the question is posed as one of ownership rights, there appears nothing amiss in having such small shareholders decline to act.

Creative tension

Ownership involvement can provide a valuable "creative tension" disciplining corporate energy to be compatible with the needs of society. Over the last half-century vast energy, imagination, technology, and investments have been committed to ensuring the easy transferability of the maximum number of shares of stock each day. The ethics of the exchange preponderate. Anything making transfers easier is good, anything inhibiting them is bad. Thus we have gone to a system of universal ownership in nominee name with physical possession of all certificates by a single depositary trust company (Cede & Co.). Any friction delaying or reducing the volume of transactions will encounter ferocious resistance.

The notion that shares of stock be encumbered with some enforceable obligations goes counter to the dominant energy of the times. The exchanges have been uniquely effective in creating meaningful governance standards – the requirement of independent directors composing a majority of an audit committee is a conspicuous example – but have not been able to deny trading privileges to non-voting and diminished voting shares of stock.

Exit shareholders, enter government

This general agreement in the appropriateness of shareholder inactivity leaves out one essential aspect – the public interest. Governments flirt with the notion of explicitly requiring fiduciaries to vote, a process described recently by an astute observer as "government's yearning not so much for a return to a world that has passed, but for a return to a world which, if Adam Smith is to be believed, had probably never existed: a world of committed corporate shareholders, assiduously working to ensure that managers run enterprises efficiently with a view to the long-term development of corporate assets." [9]

With the elimination of meaningful accountability to ownership, corporate energies can only be molded to the public interest through explicit laws and regulation. The relative ineffectiveness of law in shaping corporate policy leaves society in a tenuous position. The questions must be asked directly: Can corporations be permitted in the absence of informed and involved shareholders? Is the social cost of neutered owners too high?

Over the last dozen years many Western European countries have "privatized" all manner of enterprise previously owned by the state. The unstated informing logic behind this process is that ownership matters. It matters on several levels: it matters whether a corporation has owners; it matters who the owners are; and – if the first two concerns are appropriate – it must matter how the owners conduct themselves with reference to the corporation. If ownership were utterly irrelevant, we could return to the model sketched by Bayless Manning and simply trust in the integrity and scope of the unelected corporate managers.

Denationalization is understood by the electorate as meaning that anybody other than the government is a preferable owner. This can take the form of the lottery distribution system in the Czech Republic or the more conventional underwritten public offering in the UK, Italy, and France. What does it mean to have owners? It certainly does not mean that all owners will inform themselves and become involved in corporate affairs. At the very least, it means that some group of owners will coalesce and form a ruling bloc.

Thus, it is not so much important that all shareholders be involved as it is that there be a viable segment of the shareholders that will undertake the responsibilities of, and, as is most often the case, assume authority over the venture. Oftentimes, these control groups maintain their prerogatives through methods that are unfair to the balance of the shareholders. The Ford Motor Company has displayed conspicuous leadership in May 2000 by volunteering to "improve" the environmental and conservation characteristics of its most profitable line of motor vehicles. In a time of general price decline for the automobile industry General Motors' stock went down a great deal more than Ford's, so it was no surprise that they decided in August to compete on a social as well as economic level. The 40 percent voting position of the Ford family was confirmed in a summer recapitalization, notwithstanding the family's withdrawal of increasing portions of its collective investment. Some may criticize the arrangement as violating the "one share one vote" ethos, but let us remember that the point of that ethos is to enable effective ownership. This said, however, we must return to the wisdom of Bayless Manning: there will always need to be an independent adjudicator for situations involving conflicting interest between shareholder groups.

The need for an independent adjudicator can be seen as an American, as opposed to European or Asian, perspective. The basic principle of American constitutional government is suspicion of power – hence our balance of power among the branches of government. Inefficient it certainly is, but it has inclined to prevent the violent twists characteristic of other places. The corporate system can co-exist within a constitutional political system only to the extent that it has a compatible system for the accountability of power. A corporate system with no effective constraints would represent an unacceptable threat to the constitutional system.

This has been best summarized in the context of denationalization in the UK by then–executive director of the Bank of England, David A. Walker (now Sir David Walker and the Chairman of Morgan Stanley UK):

> *"One of the major arguments for privatisation has been the difficulty of establishing satisfactory working relationships between successive governments and the boards of the nationalised industries of which, until recently, they have been sole shareholders. The counterpart to this observation is that institutional shareholders of newly privatised businesses are expected to be able to establish better relationships with their boards. But there is plainly a question how confident we can be about this.*
>
> *"One difficulty is cultural. Whereas boards are accountable to shareholders, this accountability has until recently and in many cases tended to be a formality, with not much disposition on either side to give it substance. Yet the reciprocal of the accountability of the board to the shareholders is the duty of the shareholder to satisfy himself as to the quality and composition of the board. This becomes a more than ever important responsibility with the growing concentration of equity holdings, especially given the growing influence of major discretionary managers. The proposition is not of course that fund managers should interfere in the running of the business. They have no competence to do so. But they should stand ready to exert their influence. It is their **right and their responsibility** to promote better boards.*
>
> *"Let us consider the alternatives. For an individual fund manager with a small holding in a company where the board seems deficient, disposal of the shares may be the best course. Although a large holder can reduce the weight of his holdings, he is unlikely to be able to go far without moving the price against himself. All that remains for him is thus either to sit tight for the time being, taking no action but hoping that bidders will come along, or to take some initiative designed to strengthen the board. Such initiative is of course much easier to prescribe than to achieve, and I do not belittle the effort needed and difficulties involved in bringing effective influence to bear on a chairman who is not keen to respond to what he may regard as unwelcome outside interference. But how can it be regarded as 'outside' interference? – for, after all, **you are the members of the company and the board is accountable to you**.*
>
> *"In any event, whatever the difficulties, let us reflect for a moment on the potential cost of shareholder inertia, which means either no signal to the board,*

or, in effect, an implicit signal that the shareholder is content with what is going on. This is relevant to the question whether institutional shareholders should exercise their voting rights save in special situations, such as on a share option resolution where they may have a strong view. It seems that, in general, even the larger fund managers do not exercise their votes as a matter of course. While it plainly takes time and effort to exercise voting rights, foregoing their use on a regular basis does involve the loss of a potentially useful influence on boards. I do not want to exaggerate the significance of voting, and it will be of little value as against abstaining if votes are always cast in favour of management. But not to vote risks being interpreted as a signal either of disinterest or of approbation, neither of which may be the intended or most appropriate message."[10] (Emphases added.)

Peter Drucker, not for the first or the last time, was the harbinger of new circumstances in his *Pension Fund Socialism*, published in 1976, which announced the arrival of the new institutional investor and reconfigured ownership. Because of tax encouragement, savings in the Anglophone world were directed toward pension plans, which in the language of an influential NBC documentary in the summer of 1985, quickly became "The biggest lump of money in the world."[11] I was astonished when Reuven Frank, then president of NBC News, came to call on me at the Department of Labor's Frances Perkins building in the spring of 1985. He asked me to participate in a televised study of the US pension system. I readily complied, offering my views on the worldwide importance of pension policy and shareholder involvement. The results appeared on prime time television the following year – but it was like a shot in the dark. The program failed to change the world as I (and I believe Reuven Frank) had hoped. It is fortunate that I am not of a despairing nature, for I certainly could despair over the subsequent decade and a half of public and media indifference to this important topic. The OECD began keeping track of the increasing investment by transnational corporations outside of their home domicile (called foreign direct investment or FDI). As we have discussed in Chapter 4, the confluence of FDI and portfolio investments from the mutual and pension funds has created a situation in which a relatively few owners have influential positions in virtually every publicly traded corporation in the world. The crippling impracticality of action has largely disappeared.

The obligation of ownership

The English scholars Anne Simpson, long the conscience of UK corporate governance, and Jonathan Charkham, with a distinguished career in the Bank of England and as a member of the Cadbury Commission, have recently suggested that corporate ownership of a certain size – either as a percentage of the total or as a total value of investment – imparts ownership responsibilities.

Their suggested "obligation of significant ownership" is based on broad justification. "It is because the good working of the market-based system demands it for economic, social and political reasons. The economic reason is that there needs to be a mechanism for controlling boards that do not work well so as to prevent unnecessary waste of resources; the social reason is that listed companies are a crucial and integral part of the fabric of a modern society and their success reduces alienation; the political reason is that the limited liability company has achieved its far-sighted originators' aims beyond their wildest dreams, of producing concentrations of power and resources, and that those who exercise these powers must be effectively accountable for the way they do. The power and influence of the leaders of companies in domestic politics – and indeed internationally – are considerable."[12]

Charkham and Simpson ultimately conclude the necessity for shareholder involvement because all of the alternatives are demonstrably inferior. In their view, the virtues of the corporate system are so plain that an effective and credible system of accountability is an absolute necessity. The need for shareholder involvement bumps up inconveniently against the inveterate legal limitation of liability to the amount of investment. One of the critical advantages of the corporate form of organization is that the investors can have confidence in the limits of their own exposure. How can this be squared with an "obligation of significant ownership?" Who are these owners?

The interests of an arbitrageur are different from those of a participant in an index fund; an option holder has different considerations than someone borrowing stock; a tax-exempt institution has a different calculus of value than individual investors. All are different, and all are shareholders. Plainly, there cannot be an "obligation" that will be equally appropriate for all elements in the ownership spectrum.

The law makes no distinction between the different kinds of shareholder, apparently unconcerned by the anomaly of mandating broad accountability

to a class without common interests. All fiduciary institutions are characterized by a division between legal and beneficial ownership; a trustee holds
and administers shares for a variety of beneficiaries – the plan participants in
pension schemes, the beneficiaries of various mutual funds, participants in
insurance plans – but all share a fundamental interest that the corporation in
which they hold shares generates long-term value.

The largest component of "institutional investment" – both from the
perspective of size of assets and number of participants – is the pension system. There is fairness, therefore, in posing the hypothesis that managements
should consider the beneficiaries of pension schemes to be those shareholders for whose benefit they manage the enterprise. This hypothesis does not
appear contrary to the interests of other classes of shareholders.

By formally identifying a coherent object for management duty, we
begin to make some of the fiduciary relationships – the obligation of fiduciary owners to beneficiaries, for example – susceptible to articulation and
meaningful enforcement.[13] The fiduciaries plainly are obligated to manage
the trust assets – portfolio securities – in a manner that enhances long-term
value. There is substantial evidence that informed and involved shareholders increase the value of an enterprise.

Drawing from the experiences of Warren Buffett in a dozen major American companies to the investment record of special purpose partnerships like
Lens and Relational Investors in the US and Hermes in the UK, it is plain
that activism adds value. The obligation to act arises out of the legal status of
the trust relationship and does not impinge on the limited liability character
of the trust.

Martin Ebner, the self-made Swiss billionaire, is probably the leading
shareholder activist in the world. "Mr. Ebner's tried and tested strategy for
improving the management of Swiss companies is to become a big (ideally,
the biggest) shareholder and use this position to press for change … Mr.
Ebner set up his BZ group from scratch, and made his name through financial innovation before starting his crusade for better Swiss corporate governance."[14]

An unenviable position

We need pause to consider the situation of the trustees. It is not an enviable
one. In common law, trustees were not allowed to offset any losses they

might have occasioned with gains; they were not allowed incentive compensation; they were subject to criticism and possible liability if they behaved in a manner different from other trustees. While statutes – conspicuously, ERISA in the US – have further accommodated traditional trustee
functioning with the realities of the twenty-first century economy, cost-
benefit analysis does not justify activity other than as specifically required
and universally practiced. Thus, no single trustee is going to be comfortably
activist unless the law is perceived as requiring the same level of commitment from all comparable trustees. As a commercial matter, no trustee will
take the risk of alienating its customers until and unless there is unequivo-
cal requirement that their competitors follow the same standards. (See letter
from Frank Cahouet below.) [15]

Where are the charities?

We mentioned earlier (in Chapter 2), Marcy Murninghan's idea of the "covenant" between society and for-profit business. Certainly nonprofit foundations should feel such a bond. And certainly they have the financial clout
to become powerful, active owners. But as Murninghan points out, they
have not stepped into the ring. What is their excuse? While commercial obstacles can predictably inhibit commercial trustees, why have not the great
universities and private foundations provided leadership in this area?

Stephen Viederman stands alone in his decade-long reformist efforts as
president of the Jessie Smith Noyes Foundation. He has made great strides
in trying to reduce the dissonance between investments and philanthropic
activities. He put it in the Foundation's 1999 review of its seven-year effort:
"During the 1980s, board and staff believed strongly that the Foundation
should move to make things as seamless as possible between our giving and
our investing." [16]

Perhaps the most striking example of dissonance was the investment
by foundations and universities in companies doing business in apartheid
South Africa or the manufacture by Dow Chemical of napalm used to de-
spoil Vietnam. What is disappointing is the failure of the most prominent
fiduciary organizations to follow the lead of Noyes. Epitomized by Harvard
University, with its ever-balanced "case studies" of corporate problems and
the exhaustive yet ever-neutral analyses of the Investor Responsibility Research Center of Washington, DC, the "top people" simply will not put

Mellon Bank Corporation
Frank V. Cahouet
Chairman, President and
Chief Executive Officer

August 17, 1998

Mr. Robert A.G. Monks
Principal
LENS
Suite 800
1200 G Street, NW
Washington, DC 20005

Dear Bob:

Thank you for your letter and I will pull up the article on Mellon. I also appreciate your taking our position with *The Financial Times*. For whatever reason they were in the Bank of New York's camp. I suspect to them it is all a matter of numbers. I hate to think of where we would have been if we had done the Bank of New York transaction, what with the need of taking $800 million of costs out, handling the year 2000 issues, and building the company in a very compressed period of time. In our view, our shareholders would have been punished.

We are very reticent to position ourselves as an activist shareholder in domestic or international securities. The problem for us is how we are perceived by our customer base. The risks are such that it probably does not make sense for us to take an aggressive position. I can imagine many of your partners do have a lot more freedom since they apparently have no other business interests with portfolio companies. [Emphasis added.]

It is always great to hear from you and I want to stay close as my own career changes at the end of the year.

Best personal regards,

Frank

themselves into a position of seeming to criticize their peers, even if to do so is the right thing and is legally required. There has developed a sophisticated language in the effort to justify this reality, or, rather, to avoid having to confront it.

In the late 1950s and early 1960s, largely due to the efforts of the late Dr. Paul N. Vlvisaker, a highly renowned philanthropy and urban policy expert, Ford pioneered the concept of "program-related investing" – that is, the use of assets as loan capital to support projects in keeping with the Foundation's charitable goals and mission. As an investor, however, Ford (along with most other foundations) has been far more reluctant than public or union funds to assert its ownership power on corporations, either in the boardroom or through the proxy process. Ford rarely initiates social proxies, even though it has a proxy review committee, votes each proxy, and "take[s] the proxy responsibility very, very seriously."[17]

As is the case with most funds, Ford has a board-level investment committee responsible for charting investment policy and overseeing its performance. There are no explicit social responsibility guidelines, other than support for the Sullivan Principles regarding corporate activity in South Africa (this was before the late-September call of Nelson Mandela before the United Nations General Assembly to suspend economic sanctions).

"Our fund is monitored by a high-powered board of trustees of movers and shakers, business and academic types, from all over the world, and there is an investment committee on the board which prepares investment guidelines that I am required to operate under," says Ford's John English. "But I think the generic guideline that I follow is that I do not hold any security that I would not be willing to have published on the front page of *The New York Times*."[18]

> *"I like to think that we are socially responsible in what we're doing with our investments here. But the net of everything I do is that the proceeds of our investments are used to do good works around the world. We have one office here and over fifteen offices in developing countries. My job is to generate the income required to keep these places going. I might feel differently about my job if what I was trying to do is to make rich people richer. What I am trying to do is to create money which will change human lives. When we get to the question of, what is the definition of something being socially responsible – that's where it gets a little*

bit fuzzy because somebody has to make a value judgment that such and such an activity is desirable or undesirable, and I have some difficulty with that."[19]

Under the rubric of "fiduciary duty," much is justified. The unexceptionable fiduciary requirement that trustees may consider "solely" the interests of beneficiaries is adduced to justify non-involvement in "social" or "political" investments. Activism is dismissed as being unrelated to adding long-term value to the trust portfolio. Jay Vivian of IBM,[20] known to have an overfunded pension with a surplus over $10 billion, stated that the company had cut back sharply on the scope of pension department activity, and would have no ability to investigate this area. IBM's disinterest in continuing its institutional leadership is doubly ironic. First, the company had been active in this field. IBM's Joe Grilles served as president of the Committee on Investment of Employee Benefit Assets (CIEBA). Second, the company's own earnings had benefited from large plan surpluses. Indeed, financially speaking, IBM's pension fund assets may be its most important business.

Some of the large fiduciaries actually claim that they are inhibited by budgetary constraints. Yet the activities of LENS in the US, and Hermes in the UK – to name only two examples close to this author – demonstrate year after year that activism in fact does add value.

ERISA permits a complicated system of delegation of fiduciary responsibilities (in this regard, it departs from the common law). The finance committee of General Motors, which is the named fiduciary under its employee benefit plans, is permitted to delegate responsibility for managing trust assets to qualified investment managers. This option of delegating permits some funds to stay inactive.

While there is no requirement that the trustees delegate both investment and ownership responsibilities to the same institution, there is no prohibition against it. The imaginative Gordon Binns, for a long time the principal spokesperson for the private pension system as well as manager of GM's funds, took the position that he expected his managers to exercise their discretion as to appropriate levels of activism for the various securities in the portfolio.

The fact that none of these managers (themselves involved in competition for corporate business) have ever seen fit to recommend activism did not bother Gordon. Delegating to someone you know will agree with your own views of inactivity has been one of the principal explanations for the practical disappearance of "ownership" as an effective component of share-ownership. In the foundation and university world, there is organizational separation between mission and money.

The people on the mission side are generally sensitive to the thought of harmonized activity. There is a bright line that few dare to cross. Nobody questions the integrity of the money managers, particularly after several decades of spectacular performance.

On the endowment side, John English knows how to invest big money. As the former vice president of the Ford Foundation, he was responsible for overseeing the investment of its $6 billion in assets, the nation's largest foundation fund. English, who is now retired, came to Ford in 1981 after serving 26 years at AT&T where he was responsible for the investment of its pension fund; AT&T is the nation's largest corporate pension fund, currently valued at over $46 billion. He is also affiliated with the General Board of the United Methodist Church, which has an endowment of over $4 billion. In his opinion, the legitimate co-mingling of financial and moral concerns is best achieved through his institution's grantmaking practices rather than through corporate governance reforms.

In early July 2000, the International Corporate Governance Network (ICGN) – 330 delegates from 26 countries – met at the headquarters of TIAA/CREF on Lexington Avenue in midtown New York City. Notwithstanding the number and diversity of attendees, there was no one from the Ford Foundation three blocks away on Forty Second Street, no one from General Motors Pension fund over on Fifth Avenue, and no one from the endowments of Harvard, Yale, and Princeton, each of which maintain a club within ten blocks of the conference. The ICGN, together with initiatives by the World Bank and the OECD, represents a pioneering effort by Global Investors to inform themselves on matters of common interest. This is the necessary precursor to their effective action as owners. It is telling that the private pension plans, foundation and university endowments would absent themselves from such a meeting. Their absence accurately casts shareholder activism today as a rump movement. The inability to attract involvement by all fiduciaries limits the credibility and effectiveness of those who do act.

A clear responsibility

Some formal action will be necessary before widespread trustee involvement is possible.

In the meantime, those trustees who are active are able to define the ownership agenda without the competitive involvement of the private company plans and universities and foundations. The public pension plans have enjoyed unfettered dominion, but the meeting of several dozen countries' labor organizations having funded pension plans in Stockholm on November 3, 1999, suggested that a new energy will be present. This was confirmed in early December 1999, when the US AFL-CIO announced its opposition to the Vodafone takeover of Mannesmann in Germany. Possibly, the effective involvement of the public and labor plans will cause "the great and the good" to reconsider their passivity. An expanded group of funds met in Brussels in October 2000 to coordinate an activist shareholder agenda.

Assuming that the various fiduciaries (bank trusts, foundations, universities, and mutual funds in the US, in addition to pension trusts) take on an activist mode, does this "restoration of ownership" reinstate corporations within the traditions of property in a free society? If owners are responsible in a meaningful way for corporate functioning, the scope of necessary or justifiable government involvement should be reduced.

It is plain that relatively few institutions comprise numerical control of the preponderance of multi-national corporations. Frequently, it is recited that each of these owners faces the classic conundrum of collective action – that what is plainly in the interest of the class as a whole is nonetheless not attractive to each individual component of the class. There is less talk about the conflict of interest problems arising out of the dual functioning of financial conglomerate organizations – both as fiduciaries for pension participants as well as providers of services to the plan sponsor companies.[21] The conflict between the sponsor corporation and beneficiaries of its sponsored pension funds is an admitted contradiction that is accepted in order to induce employers to set up defined benefit retirement plans.[22]

In the US, one looks in vain over the last 20 years for a single shareholder initiative emanating from those who manage money in the private company pension system beyond the conspicuous leadership of TIAA/CREF.[23] In both the UK and the US, the plain fiduciary duty of trustees to act solely in the interest of their beneficiaries has been watered down in the case of pension funds and their delegate managers to the point that the inaction of this large portion of company ownership is condoned.[24] If value adding through activism is so clearly established, why cannot one simply rely on the market place to create an appropriate level of shareholder involvement? Will not self-interested parties take such steps as conducive to higher values?

In the most compelling analysis currently available of this situation, Allen Sykes, the distinguished English commentator, reluctantly concludes the necessity of – at least a temporary – formal government involvement.[25] A generation, which has prospered mightily under the informing principle that the least government must be the best, will not take readily to Sykes' recommendation, notwithstanding his Okhamlike analysis. Wishful thinking, however, cannot be allowed to distort reality. There is simply no evidence that the needed reforms will occur in the absence of effective government involvement.

The marketplace of shareholder rights does not work because the largest single component of the market is allowed to decide not to participate out of regard for its own interests and without regard to those of the ultimate owners.[26] As A.A. Berle wrote a quarter century after his initial work,

> *"The ten billions or so which are devoted to common stock equities by these funds represent an appreciable potential. They do not represent a control position in a number of important industries only because pension trust managers as a rule have endeavored to avoid the power position. Continued avoidance of that position, however, seems impractical as a permanent policy. Pension trusts grow as a matter of necessity. The investment is not a matter of choice with them: they must invest as part of the law of their being ... **honest managers of funds cannot honorably refuse interest in or decline concern with management of those enterprises in which they have large investments**. For another, it is too much to expect of human nature that power position will not eventually excite the interest or the ambition of men who hold it. Thus, we must forecast a time when these funds now valuating to comparable size with the other great pool of private investment – insurance companies – will emerge as a major and perhaps decisive element in choosing the managers and influencing the policy of the more decisive sectors of American production."[27] (Emphasis added.)*

Pension funds: beyond excuses

The private pension system continually develops language and argument to excuse itself from the need to be activist. The trustees either delegate their duty to vote to independent money managers or to specialist firms and do not concern themselves with the appropriateness of other kinds of involvement – such as changing the board or the executive management. Within corporations, responsibilities for pension management are so defined that literally no one is in charge of ownership obligations.

By creating a system in which "ownership" is nobody's concern, the private companies have effectively neutered the vote of their system. This is in contrast with the public pension plans, some of which are conspicuously activist, and the labor plans that are beginning to think in global terms. The result has been to keep in place in America an amorphous system of corporate power incest. With smoke and mirrors and good lawyers, the great and the good have preserved their own continuing position of power.

> *"In every interview we conducted, fund executives talked at length about assuming, assigning, or avoiding responsibility. As we listened to them, it often seemed as if the funds had been designed for the purpose of shifting responsibility for decision-making away from identifiable individuals. They described four specific mechanisms for displacing responsibility and avoiding blame: burying decisions in the bureaucracy, blaming someone else, blaming the market, or claiming that their hands were tied by the law."[28]*

The private pension system is the American metaphor for the *keiretsu* in Japan and the banks in Germany – the largest shareholder who can be counted on to support management. In America there have been other elements in the corporate constellation, so the result has not yet been so stagnating as in Europe and Asia, but we should remember with humility the respect with which the German and Japanese close relationships were viewed barely a decade ago.

If the language of ERISA is so plain and the evidence of value added through activism so indisputable, why have not disgruntled activists found relief in court? And why has the Department of Labor, the bedrock of fiduciary concern, not enforced the law? There are several reasons, most of them of the kind that appeal only to lawyers. There is the problem of proof. How can it be proven that the vote, or failure to vote, of a single shareholder *caused* a specific amount of damage?

Even in those exceptional cases where a particular shareholder's vote was *the* difference between whether a motion carried or failed, how can it be proven that the fate of this one resolution was *the reason* that loss was incurred. And votes are the most tangible of shareholder prerogatives; the problems of proof and causality become more attenuated when talking of questions like replacing board members or changing strategy. If the courts are to be the institutional instrument for articulating and enforcing a *national law of ownership*, the legal issues will have to be framed differently. An affirmative duty of owners under certain circumstances need be articulated either by court or legislature. Here is a sample statement:

> *"If a corporation has underperformed[29] drastically[30] for a substantial period of time, it can be presumed that the fiduciary shareholders[31] have failed to take appropriate action to safeguard the interests of their beneficiaries."[32]*

This formulation would effectively place on ERISA fiduciaries[33] the burden of proving that failure was not attributed to their inaction. Many questions of "process" would need be addressed – should it be enforceable by courts or by executive branch agencies, should it be a governmental or a private right? However answered, this may be the *only way to cure the present dysfunction.*

Even when loss is plainly attributable to trustee action, the conflicts and intricacies of the legal process can prohibit effective retribution. Such problems are virtually insurmountable for even the most victimized of plaintiffs. This is particularly true in the case of the beneficiaries of employee benefit plans, who are in the least enviable position of all potential plaintiffs. First, they must be willing to sue the people for whom they work. Second, they must overcome the many barriers to collective action (always more difficult to take than individual action).

I ran into such doubly frustrating barriers in my early work as the federal official at the Department of Labor responsible for the enforcement of ERISA. (I was the Administrator – now an Assistant Secretary position – for the Pension & Welfare Benefits Program.) In 1985, I launched a lawsuit against Bank of America and Carter Hawley Hale. The letter and spirit of the law were on my side, but the government was not. During the Reagan Administration any suit brought by any part of the federal government had to be approved by the Department of Justice (DOJ).

Why did the DOJ deny our request? Some saw political motivations here – namely, protection of the Southern California establishment[34] – but ideology explains it best. The Administration truly believed in small government, and was willing to circumscribe government powers in the short term whatever the cost.[35] Whatever the White House's reasoning, employee-shareholders experienced a devastating reduction in the value of their plan accounts.

Several years later, I led a shareholder effort to stop the destruction of values at Stone & Webster, an engineering company with a worldwide business in nuclear power plants.[36] With my colleagues at the investment fund Lens, Inc., I zeroed in on a key problem – alleged value destruction occurring because of misconduct by the trustee of the pension fund, Chase Manhattan Bank (this was prior to the Chase-Chemical merger). We went to court in 1995 to engage Chase in a dialogue. It was a matter of record that Chase declined even to meet or talk with other shareholders.

As plaintiffs in this case, we made a number of points. First, we contended that the Chase Manhattan Bank was in fact a "controlling shareholder" of Stone & Webster because, as trustee, Chase held 35 percent of Stone & Webster stock. Furthermore, we contended that Chase was violating a fiduciary duty to plaintiffs as minority shareholders, by "not exercising independent judgment in the management and voting of its controlling shares, by failing to maintain confidential voting (for the employee/beneficial owners), by refusing to make materials tendered by plaintiffs available to the employee plan participants, and by voting its controlling shares in favor of management of the Company without consideration of the interests of plaintiffs and other fellow shareholders."[37]

Judge Keeton firmly dismissed the claims we made on our own behalf, and made light of the claims we were making on behalf of beneficiaries of the firm's pension plan. He wrote: "To the extent that the allegations relative to the alleged failure to ensure confidential voting, plaintiffs have not shown that this in any way has caused an injury to them, even if it is assumed that it has caused an injury to the beneficial owners of the stock held in trust." And, further: "Plaintiffs point to no authority for the contention that Chase owes plaintiffs a duty to distribute plaintiffs' materials to the beneficial owners. Nor have they shown that Chase owes plaintiffs a duty to vote the beneficial stock in a manner that plaintiffs would prefer. This claim must fail."[38]

At the time of that lawsuit, Chase was the long-time trustee for all the Stone & Webster plans. In 1998, however, the Stone & Webster board appointed Putnam Fiduciary Trust (Putnam) to that position. Putnam came into a troubled situation.[39] The affairs of Stone & Webster had long been in decline. Our activism, along with complaints from other shareholders, had forced a number of changes – including significant restructuring, the resignation of several long (too long!) serving officers and directors, and the recruitment of new talent. Hardly was revival underway when the East Asian financial crisis in late 1998 hit, decreasing demand for the company's services – and halted several major projects in mid-stream.

Despite – or perhaps because of – the company's desperate straits, the company's employee retirement plan purchased one million shares of treasury stock from the company on December 16, 1999, at a price of $15 13/16th per share. Was the price too high? Not according to the "fairness opinion" accorded to Putnam by Houlihan, Lokey, Howard & Zukin, financial advisors for the transaction. But at least one man may have had his doubts: In January 2000 perhaps the most valued "new" director, John P. Merrill, resigned in mid-term, without public notice. Yet business went on as usual. The company auditors certified financial statements for the year ending December 31, 1999.

In the course of "due diligence" investigation in April and May 2000, a would-be acquirer, Jacobs Engineering, uncovered some financial performance problems only thinly masked by the company's financial statements. The problems proved insurmountable: Stone &Webster, one of the great engineering companies of the last century, went into bankruptcy in June of 2000. Later in the year Shaw Engineering acquired its operating assets.

Who suffered as a result of these events? Employees did. In fact, the largest owners of Stone & Webster are employee plans – four in total:

- an employee retirement plan – 1,079,800 shares
- an employee investment plan – 1,279,262 shares
- an employee stock ownership plan (ESOP) – 2,408,417 shares
- an employee-funded stock ownership plan (PAYSOP) – 51,778 shares
- *Total:* 4,819,257 shares or 33.9 percent of the total shares outstanding.

These shares now have a market value of approximately $3 per share. Stone & Webster employees have suffered an aggregate loss approximating $75 million – $13 million of which is attributable to the December 1999 purchase.

Without pausing to consider other relationships between Putnam and the company and the employee plans, we must ask – did the trustee, owning a full third of the voting stock, manage these assets (meaning the Stone

& Webster shares) as ERISA requires? That is, did it manage those shares "with the care, skill, prudence, and diligence under the circumstances then prevailing that a prudent man acting in a like capacity and familiar with such matters would use in the conduct of an enterprise of a like character and with like aims."[40] It is supreme irony that Putnam's behavior must be measured by this "prudent expert" rule, since the rule was originally articulated by Justice Samuel Putnam in the case of *Harvard College v. Amory* [1830].

It is obvious that something is seriously wrong – either within the company or with the external auditors – when financial statements presented in March are proved by the due diligence of a prospective purchaser in May utterly to misrepresent the company's financial position. We will not pause long here to speculate on the possibilities, including the responsibility of a dominant shareholder with respect to the integrity of financial statements. They will be exhaustively considered in the course of the several litigations now being pursued by shareholders.

Accountability to outside shareholders through voting is little more than theoretical in a situation like this one where employee benefit plans are the largest single shareholder in the company.[41] The employee benefit plans' trustee, typically selected by company management, has such a large holding that the other shareholders are effectively disempowered. Without the support or, at least, the acquiescence of a trustee such as Putnam, no outside shareholder could hope to challenge existing directors or to muster regulatory and shareholder approval for remedial action. Yet Putnam insulated itself from other shareholders by refusing to respond to shareholder concerns.

Furthermore, Stone & Webster employees have lost an enormous amount of money in accounts that were theoretically "protected" by federal fiduciary law. And yet there may be no practical way in which an individual beneficiary can economically and successfully bring a claim. Cruelly exacerbating the plight of employee beneficiaries is the working of ERISA's provisions disallowing contingent fee arrangements (intended to protect them) so as to discourage class action lawyers from aggressively pursuing their rights. Short of declaring pension and securities laws a massive fraud perpetrated on American workers and shareholders, only one solution seems feasible: the government must act to enforce those laws for the good of all.[42]

Government inaction in enforcing the trust laws has created this obstacle to market functioning. It is incumbent on government to remove the obstacle. The choice is clear: either enforce relationships within established trust traditions or stop misleading the public and participants and find a more appropriate legal vocabulary to define the existing situation.

In the meantime, CalPERS' board has decided to apply sweeping social criteria to investment decisions, particularly in emerging markets.[43] Carefully articulating their reasoning along the lines appropriate for fiduciary compliance, the CalPERS trustees argued that "equity in corporations with poor social and ethical records could represent an excessive fiduciary risk because such firms court boycotts, lawsuits, or labor activity." Some might call this policy a blue-collar agenda, but even the white-collared can recognize its financial merit, given the clear long-term cost of investment inactivity.

Hermes Investment Management Ltd, under the leadership of Alastair Ross Goobey, Peter Butler and Michelle Edkins, has become the most professional practitioner of responsible institutional ownership. On January 23, 2001, Hermes published the following outline to guide portfolio companies on the importance of social environmental and ethical matters.

Guidelines for reporting on social, environmental and ethical matters

The board

The company should disclose in its Annual Report whether:

1.1 The formal schedule of matters reserved to the Board takes account of social, environmental and ethical (SEE) matters.

1.2 The Board has identified and assessed the significant risks to the company's short and long term value arising from SEE matters.

1.3 Account is taken of SEE in the training of directors.

1.4 The Board has received adequate information about SEE matters that may affect the company's short and long term value.

1.5 The remuneration committee, in designing and implementing performance related remuneration schemes, has considered the effect on the company's performance of SEE.

Policies, procedures and verification

The Annual Report should:

2.1 Include information on SEE matters that significantly affect the company's short and long term value.

2.2 Describe the company's policies and procedures for managing risks to the company's short and long term value arising from SEE matters. If the annual report and accounts states that the company has no such policies and procedures, the board should provide reasons for their absence.

2.3 Include information about the extent to which the company has complied with its policies and procedures for managing risks arising from SEE matters.

2.4 Describe the procedure for verification of SEE disclosures. The verification procedure should be such as to achieve a reasonable level of credibility.

Global standards for investment

Clearly Global Investors are in a unique position to bring positive change. They will be helped in this regard by the OECD's June 1999 Principles of Corporate Governance. These were crafted one by one with care by a committee representing all of the organization's 29 members, namely the following:

- Australia
- Austria
- Belgium
- Canada
- Czech Republic
- Denmark
- Finland
- France
- Germany
- Greece
- Hungary
- Iceland

- Ireland
- Italy
- Japan
- Korea
- Luxembourg
- Mexico
- Netherlands
- New Zealand
- Norway
- Portugal
- Poland
- Spain
- Sweden
- Switzerland
- Turkey
- UK
- US

The principles adopted by these 29 countries were in essence a distillation of the governance codes promulgated by many countries and companies over the past decade. It makes eminent sense for Global Investors and corporations alike to take them to heart.

These global standards cover five main areas:

1 The rights of shareholders.
2 The equitable treatment of shareholders.
3 The role of stakeholders in governance.
4 Disclosure and transparency.
5 Responsibilities of the board.

Global standards for corporate governance: a closer look

We will look at these quickly one by one, as they might apply to Global Investors.

Global principle one: the corporate governance framework should protect shareholders rights. Shareholders have a right to receive relevant information about the company in a timely manner, to have the opportunity to participate in decisions concerning fundamental corporate changes, and to share in the profits of the corporation, among others. Markets for corporate control should be efficient and transparent, and shareholders should consider the costs and benefits of exercising their voting rights.

Question. As an investor, do you question management about fundamental corporate changes? (These include amendments to statutes or articles of incorporation, authorization to issue additional shares, and sales of the company or substantially all of its assets.)

Global principle two: the corporate governance framework should ensure the equitable treatment of all shareholders, including minority and foreign shareholders. There should be full disclosure of material information and prohibition of abusive self-dealing and insider trading; all shareholders of the same class should be treated equally. Members of the board and managers should be required to disclose any material interests in transactions.

Question. When you buy stocks in a company, do you ensure that directors are free from conflicts of interest? Do the boards of your portfolio companies have a policy in this regard? US state law imposes a "duty of loyalty." (Similar concepts exist in jurisdictions outside the US.)

Global principle three: the corporate governance framework should recognize the rights of stakeholders in corporate governance as established by law, and encourage active cooperation between corporations and stakeholders in creating wealth, jobs, and the sustainability of financially sound enterprises.

Question. Do the boards of your portfolio companies have any committees devoted to nonshareholder constituencies, such as customers, employees, lenders/suppliers, communities, suppliers, and the general public? Do you ask for information from management pertaining to these constituencies? How would you rate the companies' relations and information flow with these groups?

Global principle four: the corporate governance framework should ensure that timely and accurate disclosure is made on all material matters regarding the corporation, including the financial situation, performance, ownership, and governance of the company. Material should be prepared, audited, and disclosed in accordance with high quality standards.

Question. How do the boards of your portfolio companies rate in quality and timeliness of disclosing material information on the following: the financial and operating results of the company, company objectives, major share ownership and voting rights, membership and pay for board and key management, material foreseeable risk factors, material issues regarding employees and other stakeholders, governance structures and policies?

Global principle five: the corporate governance framework should ensure the strategic guidance of the company, the effective monitoring of management by the board, and the board's accountability to the company and the shareholders. Board members should act on a fully informed basis, in good faith, with due diligence and care, and in the best interests of the company and the shareholders.

Question. Do you as a fiduciary pay attention to the quality of the directors on the boards of companies in your portfolio?
Where board decisions may affect different shareholder groups differently, the board should treat all shareholders fairly.

Question. Do the boards of your portfolio companies respect the rights of minority shareholders?
The board should ensure compliance with applicable law and take into account the interests of shareholders.

Question. Do the boards of your portfolio companies have a process to ensure legal compliance?
The board should fulfill certain key functions, including the following:

• Reviewing and guiding corporate strategy, major plans of action, risk policy, annual budgets and business plans; setting performance objectives; monitoring implementation and corporate performance; and overseeing major capital expenditures, acquisitions, and divestitures.
• Selecting, compensating, monitoring, and, when necessary, replacing key executives and overseeing strategic planning.

- Reviewing key executive and board remuneration, and ensuring a formal and transparent board nomination process.
- Monitoring and managing potential conflicts of interest of management, board members, and shareholders, including misuse of corporate assets and abuse in related party transactions. *Author's note: Boards need conflict of interest policies. The independence of board members can help reduce the incidence of conflicts of interest. There are many definitions of director independence; the most authoritative US definition was recently adopted by the stock exchanges for audit committee members.*
- Monitoring the effectiveness of the governance practices under which it operates and making changes as needed. *Author's note: The current mechanism for this is a board committee. It may be a nominating committee, sometimes renamed as (or supplemented by) a corporate governance committee.*
- Overseeing the process of disclosure and communications. *Author's note: Disclosure is important not just for shareholders, but for other constituencies.*

Question. Are the boards of your portfolio companies independent? How can you make them so?

Boards should consider assigning a sufficient number of non-executive board members capable of exercising independent judgment to tasks where there is a potential for conflict of interest. Examples of such key responsibilities are financial reporting, nomination, and executive and board remuneration.

Board members should devote sufficient time to their responsibilities.

Question. Are the directors of your portfolio companies spending the necessary time to oversee them?

In order to fulfill their responsibilities, board members should have access to accurate, relevant, and timely information.

Question. How good is the information received by directors of your portfolio companies?[44]

These principles are a good beginning – and promise to become a benchmark for the rest of the globe. They are mentioned prominently in a newer document, *Corporate Governance: A Framework for Implementation*, published in August 1999 by the World Bank. The World Bank document explores how countries outside the OECD can work toward adopting similar principles.

In September 1999, the World Bank formed a Global Governance Forum to adapt these principles to a broader world market, naming a number of governance activists, including this author, to its various task forces. When we task masters complete our work, the era of the Global Investor will arrive in full force. For the present moment, however, the era is only beginning. We must all contribute to it through thought and action – as detailed in the following chapters.

Endnotes

1   Quoted in Louis D. Brandeis, *Other People's Money and How the Bankers Use It* (National Home Library Foundation, 1933), p. 41.
2   Abram J. Chayes, "Introduction" to John P. Davis, *Corporations: A Study of the Origin and Development of Great Business Combinations and of their Relation to the Authority of the State* (Capricorn, 1961), p. xviii.
3   Bayless Manning, *J. A. Livingston, The American Shareholder* (review), 67 Yale L.J. 1477, 1490 (1958).
4   Hurst, *op.cit. supra*, p. 105.
5   One might say that it is shareholders, not only CEOs, who are enriched by the system, since CEOs pay tends to rise with stock price. However, as previously noted, CEO pay may rise with stock price, but it does not fall with stock price. The relationship is not linear; the correlation is weak.
6   Adolph A. Berle and Gardiner C. Means, *The Modern Corporation and Private Property*, (Transaction Publishers, 1991 [originally published 1932]), p. 64.
7   *Ibid.*, pp. 297–298.
8   George C. Lodge, *The American Dream* (Knopf, 1984), p. 286.
9   Paddy Ireland, "Enlightening the value of Shareholders: to Whom should Directors Owe Duties?" In *Directors' Conflicts of Interest: Legal, Socio-legal and Economic Analysis*, eds Mads Andenes and David Sugarman (Kluwer, in press), p. 119.
10 David A. Walker, "Some Perspectives for Pension Fund Managers," NAPF Investment Conference, Eastbourne, 27 February 1987.
11 NBC White paper: "The Biggest Lump of Money in the World," 1985, National Broadcasting Company, Inc.

12 Jonathan Charkham and Anne Simpson, *Fair Shares – The Future of Shareholder Power and Responsibility* (Oxford: Oxford University Press, 1999), p. 224.

13 By expressing the rights of corporate constituencies – in particular, those of employees – in the mode of ownership, two objectives are achieved: (1) ownership accountability as the core energy of governance is enhanced and legitimated; and (2) expanding the pool of "owners" will add new elements to the definition of long-term value optimization.

14 "Swiss Corporate Governance – Crusading Again," *The Economist*, November 4, 2000, p. 81.

15 Frank Cahouet is my lifelong friend since age 8, as well as a classmate and supporter. His personal integrity is luminous and his ethics are impeccable, so I empathize with the position in which he is placed.

16 Jessie Smith Noyes Foundation, Annual Report, 1999.

17 *Ibid.*

18 *Ibid.*

19 Marcy Murninghan, *Corporate Civic Responsibility and the Ownership Agenda – Investing in the Public Good*, John W. McCormack Institute of Public Affairs, University of Massachusetts at Boston, October 1993, p. 77–78.

20 Phone conversation with author on December 20, 1999.

21 The only reference that we could find in the various codes and commission studies to the "different" interests of corporate fiduciaries who also have fiduciary relationship with the pension fund is in Financial Reporting Standard 8 (FRS8): "The fact that certain pension funds are related parties of the reporting entity is not intended to call into question the independence of the trustees with regard to their fiduciary obligations to the members of the pension scheme. Transactions between the reporting entity and the pension fund may be in the interest of its members but nevertheless need to be reported in the accounts of the reporting entity." The accounting profession, apparently, is not put off by split personalities.

22 In the US, control by the settlor corporation of the appointment and removal of trustees is referred to as the "fundamental contradiction of ERISA."

23 This echoes Louis Brandeis' conclusions at the beginning of the century cited at the opening of this chapter.

24 *Condoned* or *acquiesced* seems to describe the present situation, in which pension scheme participants, plainly having a right to require "loyalty" from their trustees, have virtually no practical capacity to enforce this right. The language of trust is being used in full knowledge that the traditional rights of the beneficiaries are not susceptible of enforcement.

25 *Capitalism for Tomorrow: Reuniting Ownership and Control* (Oxford: Capstone, 2000), p. 145 ff.

26 "The significance of institutional activity should not be exaggerated, however. Institutions typically hold a small proportion of the shares in a large number of companies. ...External fund managers may be reluctant to incur the costs of intervention, *since the benefits will often be deferred and will accrue to their clients rather than themselves.*" (Emphasis added.) John Parkinson's words describing current institutional behavior in a January Letter to Working Group E of the DTI Study of Corporation Law could well be used by a Judge as his definitive finding of fault in an action by a beneficiary against a conflicted trustee.

27 A.A. Berle, *Power without Property* (Harcourt Brace, 1959), p. 50. (The italics in this quotation are added to raise the readers' question as to whether Berle's 1958 notion of "honor" is obsolete!)

28 William M. O'Barr and John M. Conley, *Fortune and Folly, the Wealth and Power of Institutional Investing* (Irwin: Business One, 1992), p. 85.

29 Performance can be quantified with reference to the industrial average as a whole or particular industry subsegments.

30 How bad is bad? This will be impossible to answer to everyone's satisfaction, but it might be useful to think of total return to shareholders over several periods of time – the *Wall Street Journal* does an annual edition showing returns over 1, 3, 5 and 10 years – and say that drastic underperformance is assumed to be the bottom decile or even quintile.

31 Institutional investors in the US (top 100 companies) and UK own collectively over 60 percent of the total outstanding stock. There are public records as to who these owners are; there are competitive proxy advisory services that allow for cost-effective decisions on ownership alternatives. The new task now is to oblige each institution to work with fellow shareholders in drastic situations. This happens often, naturally, in both the US and the UK.

32 In demonstrating how conduct was in aid of beneficiaries' interests, it will be essential – when appropriate – to explain the other business relationships with the focus companies and how those commercial interests were effectively subordinated.

33 Before concluding that this is unfair and places too great a burden, one should understand that money managers and consultants are among the most highly paid classes of worker in the world, including movie stars, football players, and talk show hosts. Ned Johnson, the inheritor and builder of Fidelity, is thought to be worth in excess of $5 billion. If you wonder why institutional investors have failed so utterly in their indispensable role as monitors of corporate conduct where managers have conflicting interests – quintessentially in the area of setting their own pay – it is good to remember that they do not relish bringing up compensation as a topic.

34 Benjamin J. Stein, "A Sage of Shareholder Neglect," *Barron's*, May 4, 1987, pp. 8–75.

35 In a statement to Stein (*ibid.*) Michael Horowitz, General Counsel of the Office of Management and Budget, said the matter was purely one of government intervention: "We were concerned that a part of the government seemed to be expanding its role through litigation and we did not want any part of the government making policy through litigation. Our feel was in no way related to the personalities or even the dollars involved."

36 Our case, filed in the United States District Court, District of Massachusetts, was Civil Action No. 94–10787-REK

37 Memorandum and Order, June 29, 1995 p.50.

38 *Ibid.*, p. 51.

39 As of the date of publication, it is impossible to verify whether Putnam Fiduciary Trust became trustee of the Employee Retirement Plan at the same time as it became trustee of the other three employee benefit plans. In the event that Chase Manhattan Bank remained as trustee the fiduciary problems would be even more serious.

40 ERISA Section 404(a)(1)(B)

41 Many companies, following the decisions of the Delaware Chancery and Supreme Courts in 1989 in *Polaroid*, have used the device of employee benefit plan ownership of large percentages of stock as an effective antitakeover device.

42 See Appendix II.

43 Stephen Davis, "CalPERS becomes biggest fund pushing social invest-ment criteria," *Global Proxy Watch*, Vol. IV, No. 42, November 17, 2000.

44 The author acknowledges the contributions of Ira M. Millstein and his colleague Holly Gregory to the articulation of these principles. I also thank the research department at the National Association of Corpo-rate Directors for providing background material for this section on the OECD principles.

Chapter 6

The Language of Accountability

How to Depict True Corporate Value

Understanding corporate investment requires understanding corporate value. Value lies at the very heart of any corporation. Indeed, a corporate system is one in which substantial resources – of property and personnel – are organized within a society in order to "optimize" economic gain, traditionally defined as profit. The currently fashionable conservative economists, such as Frederick Hayek and Milton Friedman, argue strongly that only the pursuit of economic gain legitimates the existence and functioning of collective resources outside of government.

This formulation has some merit, and may be better than any other. The discipline of profit pursuit prevents corporate management from straying into the areas of social policy – a good thing, since they are not elected political officials.

But defining corporate purpose as the pursuit of economic gain raises substantial problems when the gain sought is merely profit maximization. Virtually any activity can be bundled under the rubric of long-term profit, including activities that are not beneficial to society or in fact conducive to profit. After all, to pursue profit does not necessarily mean to make it. There is no formula for surefire profits; no definitive lexicon of profit-enhancing activities and their converse. Can we be confident that a particular activity is or is not associated with the achievement of profit?

Optimized long-term value

The challenge is to articulate an inclusive concept of optimized long-term value. There is no inherent quality either in corporations or in managers necessitating a value system incompatible with human welfare. The informing dynamic is competition. If all companies need to adhere to the same standards, there will be little resistance within the organization to complying with them. The emergence of Global Investors makes the acceptance of a uniform and universal standard more than a pipe dream.

The Organization for Economic Cooperation and Development (OECD) has for many years been trying to secure acceptance of a minimum code of investment standards. This so-called Multilateral Agreement on Investments (MAI) became the target of an intense lobbying effort in Paris during the spring of 1998, and the proposition has been withdrawn. In the meantime, the OECD has secured ratification of codes prohibiting bribery and creating minimum standards of corporate governance. The World Bank has virtually adopted the OECD governance conclusions and has created task forces to advise of their adoption throughout the world. One of these task forces has recently challenged the compilers of investment indexes to use governance screens when including particular companies and countries.

In the meantime, commerce has moved faster than the rule makers, as Thomas Kamm has reported in the *New York Times*.

> "*Of course, many say Europe has a right to define its own model of capitalism and try to soften what Mr Peyrelevade calls the 'dictatorship of the market.' But in a global contest to attract capital, signs of wariness toward the market could be costly. 'We have to bow to Anglo-Saxon cultural norms,' says Gérard Mestrallet, chief executive of French utilities giant Suez de Lyonnaise des Eaux.* **Capital is in the hands of the Anglo-Saxon pension funds that can choose where to invest.** *Those that don't play the game risk sending capital and activities elsewhere.*"[1] (Emphasis added.)

The "green" or "social" funds have begun the normative process by declining to invest in companies engaged in a variety of activities of which they disapprove. (The defining event for this category was the disposition of South Africa stocks during the apartheid years.) Social investors refuse to purchase shares in companies with characteristics that they oppose – liquor, tobacco, armaments, nuclear energy and environment insensitivity are some of the most common. They go further and file shareholder resolutions in appropriate companies and support the resolutions of others along publicly disclosed lines. The cumulative impact of this effort is to call attention to different kinds of corporate functioning and to mobilize concerned constituencies.

The Department of Labor, in deciding that "social" investing is inappropriate for ERISA funds, makes clear that a trustee's duty is to invest "solely" and "for the exclusive benefit of" plan participants. The department, however, makes clear that the accomplishment of social objectives – for example, financing "union only" construction projects – does not invalidate an investment that can be justified on its merits. This encapsulates the problem of definition – what one reasonable person calls "social investment" another might view as involving a long-term view of optimized value.

Fifteen of the most prominent socially responsible and environmentally friendly funds – including Calvert Group, Domini Social Investment, Evergreen, Global, Parnassus, and Walden – have decided not to buy any stock in the Mitsubishi Corporation because of its plans to build the world's largest salt factory at Laguna San Ignacio, California, on the shores of gray whale breeding grounds.[2] The lagoon is one of only four in the world where gray whales come to mate and calve each year. This announcement was coupled with running advertisements in the *New York Times* and the *Wall Street Journal* by prominent environmental activist groups.

While a United Nations task force has prepared a report that is generally favorable to the project, the principal scientific investigation has yet to be performed. From the company records, there is no evidence that the "green" funds are shareholders of Mitsubishi. This project illumines the strengths and weaknesses of "social" investors – their greatest strength is in asking questions. Their weakness is endemic. Having no sustaining interest in the company, they cannot afford more than passing scrutiny, which reflects more the conventional wisdom than the results of professional evaluation. It should be noted that the Mexican government and Mitsubishi "postponed" the project early in 2000. The superior investment performance of many of these funds usefully provides support to the proposition that informed involvement (even to this limited extent) can help increase corporate value.

Next stage

Our experience is that this is a consciousness-raising effort, but that it is not enough to truly change corporate conduct. For that level of corporate commitment, we must move to the "next stage" in the words of John Hancock: the intelligent and effective involvement of a cadre of permanent shareholders with substantial holdings.

> *"The next stage in socially responsible investment is one where funds buy stocks in businesses of whose practices the fund managers disapprove. This, of course, is quite incompatible with the avoidance type of fund and cannot really be said to be in line with the support type of fund. However, this type of investment strategy is practiced by churches and charities who would bring the force of their money and their argument right to the heart of a business, using their position as major shareholders to engage in a constructive dialogue."[3]*

The core requirement for all kinds of investment is that *returns must exceed the cost of capital*. These calculations are both simple and complex. Simply, one tries to take more cash on leaving a company than one originally invested, taking into account whatever time cost of money is thought appropriate. Traditionally, accounting conventions have been helpful in determining values and their change over time. Classical cost-based accounting has proven to be inadequate for the demands of an economy where value is increasingly knowledge-based.

The problem with GAAP

There is widespread dissatisfaction with Generally Accepted Accounting Principles ("GAAP") as a useful indicator of corporate values. It is felt that GAAP is not only inadequate to explain value, but is actually miscorrelated with market values in the modern world. With the advent of companies whose value is based almost entirely on the ingenuity and enterprise of the participants, the absence of a convention for valuing "intellectual property" has doomed GAAP to obsolescence.

Before turning to several imaginative suggestions about how to value corporate assets, we need face up to the equally challenging problem of the lack of an adequate language to explain corporate liabilities. Corporations inevitably have an impact on society beyond that reported on the conventional financial statement. Some of that impact is negative and creates expenses for society. Indeed, one of the ongoing principal questions in political life is an appropriate allocation of costs between society and business. While the fact of "negative externalities" is plain to all, assigning costs is little better than a guessing game. However, it is important to guess, because the numbers are very large and need to be reflected. Only then can we see a corporation's true sustainability in relation to society. As accounting scholar Ralph Estes observes "A recent and admittedly rough attempt to estimate the social costs that corporations shift to others puts this figure at $2,622 billion per year (1994 dollars) a figure almost double the entire federal budget and equal to almost half of the nation's 1990s gross domestic product."[4] We need to close the ignorance gap so as to have a better idea of the true impact of decisions that we are making and condoning.

We can learn from commentator Cy Mintz who notes in *CFO* magazine, "Despite increasing awareness that the value of knowledge assets now approaches or even exceeds the value of reported book assets, rule makers in the US have largely dodged the issue ... Skeptics predict unintended and unwelcome results if knowledge assets find their way onto financial reports. Far from clarifying performance, in their view, knowledge assets will instead mislead investors, distract managers, and foster uncertainty. These fears are overblown. There are more serious deficiencies in an accounting system anchored to physical assets. The value of a single knowledge asset may indeed rise or fall unexpectedly, but successful long-term corporate performance demands optimal control over the levers of value creation."[5]

Baruch Lev, possibly the most imaginative analyst in this field in the world today, has developed a technology for valuing knowledge on a company's balance sheet. "As a systematic model for evaluating knowledge assets, the Knowledge Capital Scoreboard attempts to capture a critical dimension of value that conventional accounting has failed to grasp. Reliance on public information and broad assumptions make it available to everyone... With access to a credible performance-based estimate of knowledge capital and a three-year average investment in R&D, the ROI of R&D comes into view. According to our estimates, every dollar Dupont spends on R&D creates $16.89 of knowledge assets, while each dollar Merck spends creates $32, a gap consistent with the observation that pharmaceuticals constitute a more valuable business franchise than commodity chemicals do."[6]

Let us consider some of the specific elements that would need be changed so as to enable a meaningful accounting language.

Accountant Rob Gray makes a relevant observation:

> *"So, most if not all of the limitations of conventional economics apply with equal force to conventional accounting. Both are only interested in property rights exchanged for money; both are informed by a narrow and limited conception of morality and both are motivated by an exceptionally narrow view of efficiency; both ignore the social and environmental consequences of actions to the extent that they are not priced, and both are immensely powerful in modern society … Sustainability has provided a new theoretical challenge within which to reconfigure social and environmental account… This in turn has led to an emerging line of research which tries to assess the extent to which accounting-driven organizations are incapable of delivering sustainability and to use the conventional accounting concept of **capital maintenance** to calculate the extent of a corporation's **unsustainabilty** via estimation of its 'sustainable cost' – a notion which echoes similar work in 'new economics.'"[7] (Emphasis added.)*

There is no agreement as to whether training costs and research and development are proper costs to be charged against operating earnings or whether they are assets to be amortized like bricks and mortar; while it is clear that brands, technology and patents are important sources of future revenue, it is not clear on what basis they should be valued on the company balance sheet. On neither the asset nor the liability side is a firm suggestion of the modern financial statement even discernable. What is increasingly evident is the importance of pursuing the work. Even in its elemental form, full asset and cost compilations are essential if the corporation is to avoid functioning contrary to society's interests.

The only way to understand current accounting practice is to assume that for some reason it was decided that the results of corporate functioning would be reported in Latin and Roman numerals would be used for the accounts. Everyone knows that Latin is a traditional language lacking a business vocabulary. Roman numerals are clumsy. The transcending consideration is that the previous year's results were stated in Latin permitting consistency in approach. Everyone knows that the language and mode of presentation is inadequate and yet no one has a better language, so it continues. The legally required audit numbers are a beguiling place of beginning for analysts. Rather than simply replacing the system, everyone tries to make adjustments so that the publicly used numbers can be a credible basis for valuation multiples and for compensation purposes.

The theoretical needs for an holistic reporting system were particularly well summarized in an article by Paul Hawken and W. McDonough, entitled "Seven Steps to Doing Good Business."[8] These should be understood as a statement of ideal objectives, not an enumeration of priorities for action.

1   *Eliminate the concept of waste.* This involves transforming the making of things. There can be only three types of products. The first are consumables. This includes the designing of products suitable for the compost heap. The second are products or services which would always belong to the original manufacturer who retains responsibility for their disassembly after they have been used by the "customer." The third category is the unsalables – toxic material, which always belong to the original makers who retain indefinite responsibility for their storage.

2   *Restore accountability.* When any corporation continually affronts and damages the public trust, citizens should have the right to revoke the corporation's charter.

3   *Make prices reflect costs.* "For example, the World Resources Institute in Washington, DC has estimated that the cost of a gallon of gas, when pollution, waste disposal, health effects, and defense expenditures like the Persian Gulf War are factored in, is approximately $4.50, four times what we pay at the pump. A study by the University of California in San Francisco showed that a pack of cigarettes costs citizens in the state another $3.63 in health care and related costs." Replace the entire tax system. The objective would be a green-fee system – taxes that are added on to products, energy, services and raw materials so that prices more nearly approximate true costs. The cheapest things should be the best thing for the customer, the worker, the environment and the company.

4   *Promote diversity.* We need to find out what's here, who has it, and what we can and can't do with it.

5   *Make conservation profitable.* "Imagine a system in which the resource utility benefits from conservation, makes money from efficiency, thrives through restoration and profits from helping sustain the environment."

6   *Insist on the accountability of nations.* Replace the current concept of most favored nation with most sustainable nation. This would involve a system of tariffs that encourages sustainable practices.

7   *Restore the guardian.* Business and unions have to get out of government.

Perhaps the most ambitious effort to codify important components of intellectual capital is the Skandia *Navigator.*[9] This management tool was developed early in the 1990s by Leif Edvinsson, former director of intellectual capital at Skandia Group, an $8 billion Swedish financial company. The Navigator is applied differently, by each company but it follows a unique five-part format:

*   financial focus;
*   customer focus;
*   human focus;
*   process focus; and
*   renewal and development focus.

Skandia hopes to publish audited figures for the Navigator in its 2001 annual report – placing non-financial measures for the first time fully on par with financial ones.

Many consulting firms have developed new technologies for determining the cost of capital and evaluating returns. What particularly concerns us here is that traditional accounting has been found wanting. It will have to be very drastically changed if it is to continue to have other than anecdotal value.

In the meantime, however, most progressive companies are satisfying themselves with a dual approach. They maintain the traditional accounting but add on a supplementary process, duly certified, giving evidence of sensitivity to their externalizations. The Institute of Social and Ethical AccountAbility (ISEA) **http://www.AccountAbility.org.uk** was founded in 1996 in the United Kingdom in order to develop consistent professional practices in social and ethical accounting, auditing and reporting. AccountAbility 1000, exposure draft November 1999, was designed as a "foundation standard" to offer a common currency of principles and process to underpin and therefore provide reassurance about specialized standards of what constitutes good practice in accountability and performance management.

In the US, Ernst & Young has joined with *Forbes ASAP* and the University of Pennsylvania Wharton School to measure nonfinancial performance of S&P companies in what they call a Value Creation Index. The Index weights the relative importance of nine separate factors – innovation, quality, customer relations, management capabilities, alliances, technology, brand value, employee relations and environmental and community issues – in "explaining market values beyond what could be attributed by traditional accounting of assets and liabilities."[10]

The massive oil spills by Exxon Corporation in Valdez Sound gave birth to the CERES principles to which many major transnational corporations subscribe. The principles are:

1   protection of the biosphere;
2   sustainable use of natural resources;
3   reduction and disposal of wastes;
4   energy conservation;
5   risk reduction;
6   safe products and services;
7   environmental restoration;
8   informing the public;
9   management commitment; and
10 annual audit and report.

The Coalition for Environmentally Responsible Economies (CERES) created the Global Reporting Initiative (GRI) in late 1997 with the mission of designing globally applicable guidelines for preparing enterprise-level sustainability reports. Sustainability at the enterprise level includes three principal components – environmental, social, and economic. This is often referred to as the "triple bottom line." Table 6.1 illustrates the scope and intention of the report designers. The core consideration is the full disclosure of the impact of the organization on various aspects of society – be they governmental, social or environmental. This might be styled an "Externalities Report." There is no effort to assign values to particular responses or even to the reports as a whole.

One area where some real progress is being made is in company attitudes towards the environment. Innovest, a Toronto and New York City based financial advisory firm specializing in environmental finance and investment, **www.innovestgroup.com**, has studied the environmental impact

Table 6.1 Global reporting initiative: March 1999 exposure draft for comment and pilot testing. Illustrative application of themes to major dimensions of sustainability.

Sample themes	Sample economic dimensions	Sample social dimensions	Sample environmental dimensions
Diversity *An enterprise's mix and balance of activities and human, ecological and economic resources*	• Business diversification	• Employee diversity, including employment of minorities and disabled people and empowerment of women	• Resource use diversity • Consumption of non-renewable natural resources • Consumption of renewable resources
Added Value *Increasing of relative worth, utility or importance as a result of enterprise activities*	• Return on capital employed • Shareholder value • Economic value added • Investor satisfaction	• Intangible value (e.g. good will) • Information or knowledge held by employees • Employee satisfaction • Customers satisfaction	• Conversion of waste to usable or salable product • Activities to offset negative effects of other activities [e.g. carbon sinks for CO_2 emissions] • Local impacts such as landscaping
Productivity *Effectiveness in creating results, benefits, profits or other forms of value*	• Profit margins • Stability of economic imports on communities	• Rate of employee turnover • Customer retention rate • Involvement in civic activities	• Resource efficiency • Material efficiency

Integrity *Adherence to principles and ideals*	• Bribery • Political contributions • Lawsuits • Qualified accounts; exceptions to auditors/verifiers' statements • Information disclosure policies and practices	• Complaints • Lawsuits • Public opinion • Membership in social responsibility fora • Information disclosure policies and practices	• Lawsuits • Environmental management systems • Membership in environmental responsibility fora • Information disclosure policies and practices
Health *Soundness and resilience*	• Profitability • Demand of products or services • Solvency/liquidity • Rating by investment agencies	• Health of workforce (e.g. employee injury rate, lost time days) • Healthcare entitlements/benefits • Health of community • Local health risk of manufacture or service	• Health risk of product or service • Consumption of critical natural capital • Remediation • Contribution to ecological problems or changes (such as climate change contribution)
Development *Evolution, growth, progression*	• Innovation programs • Investments or capital expenditures	• Employee training and development • Contribution to or impact on local infrastructure or services • Socially or ethically targeted investments	• Investment in environmental technologies • Product line substitution • Environmentally targeted investments

Reprinted by permission of the Coalition for Environmentally Responsible Economies (CERES) of some 800 international equities and has classified industries into a top and bottom half. Over more than a two year period concluding in March 2000, the top half has outperformed the bottom by 21.8 percent in Global forest products, 15.9 percent in US chemicals, 17.2% in US Petroleum and 12.4 percent in US electric utilities. Over this same period of time, an "Eco-enhanced" S&P 500 has outperformed the actual index by 11 percent.[11] It is already clear that the market assigns a significant positive value to companies having an environmentally sensitive policy.

Similarly promising results were achieved in a more recent analysis conducted in late 2000 by the independent quantitative analysis specialist firm QED. This study used an even more sophisticated "time-series" approach and, as in the Morgan Stanley test, all of the other known investment factors which could have explained the out-performance were normalized out. What remains is "pure" environmentally driven out-performance.

As the chart in Fig. 6.1 illustrates, depending on how much emphasis was given to the EcoValue '21 factors, the out-performance margin ranged from 180 to 440 basis points (1.8–4.4%). None of this out-performance can be explained by traditional securities analysis.

Innovest has concluded that the highest environmental grades coincide with the highest value accorded in the marketplace. We will use Innovest's

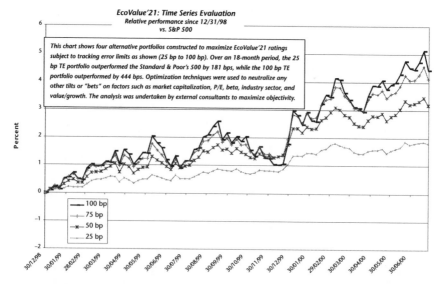

Fig. 6.1 EcoValue'21: preliminary FTSE analysis. (Source: QED International/ Innovest Strategic Value Advisors.)

work on the International oil industry as the basis for our own value projections in Brightline (see Appendix I).

Nonfinancial criteria for investment make sense, as Matthew Kiernan and James Martin recently noted in *Investment & Pensions Europe*:

> *"In the UK, Europe, and the US, pension fund sponsors and their advisors have perpetuated the misconception that they are precluded from considering 'non-financial' investment criteria by their fiduciary responsibilities. They have no choice, it is argued, but to strive to maximise investment returns; to consider 'extraneous' factors, such as environmental or social performance, would constitute a dereliction of duty.*
>
> *"But overwhelming recent evidence suggests that Fund managers, plan sponsors and the consulting industry have all had it backwards. We now have the financial technologies to demonstrate convincingly that environmental considerations do have financial ramifications for investors, and that they can be quantified and forecast with some precision.*
>
> *"Given the recent availability of these technologies, it is now fair to say that to fail to consider available information about companies' environmental risk, performance and strategic positioning is to fail to discharge one's fiduciary responsibilities, not to honour them. Traditional notions of fiduciary responsibility will need to be turned on their heads, and the forthcoming UK pension reform regulations should provide some much-needed impetus in that direction. Can the pension regulators – and institutional investors – in the rest of Europe be far behind?"[12]*

Innovest is the most advanced firm and environmental impact is the most tangible – apparently the easiest to value – of the many aspects of corporate functioning not accounted for by traditional methods. Over time, the work of pioneers like Innovest and Baruch Lev may generate quantifiable values for important corporate characteristics and a new accounting system could be devised.

The Centre for Tomorrow's Company was created in London to follow up on work initiated by the Royal Society of Arts. The Centre is business led and its focus is to enable sustainable success through an inclusive approach. Directed with energy and grace by Mark Goyder, the Centre has provided leadership in the discussions of corporate functioning through meetings, pamphlets, books and tapes.

Prototype PLC Core Company Report 31 December 2000 explicitly accounts for a company's functioning in a new way. It speaks of "success models" for the various corporate constituencies and provides feed back dialogue. There are quantitative targets for success and accounting for achievement of those goals. Beyond this, the traditional financial statement is captioned "providers of capital" and values are assigned to such categories as banks, knowledge bank, technology and patents. Research and development and training are listed in a way that permits them to be considered as expenses or as investments. This brave beginning does not consider the appropriate treatment of external costs attributable to corporate functioning. One should not blame Columbus for not being Magellan! Mark Moody Stuart, the CEO of Shell, is personally committed to creating disciplined indicators that can provide guidance for the management and evaluation of a socially responsible venture. Together with accounting firms such as KPMG, the company is devoting thousands of hours in the effort to understand and to articulate those specific criteria which management will be held to accomplish across the whole spectrum of Shell's impact on society. Once the matrix has been devised, it will be appropriate for executive compensation systems to reflect those standards. (See letter from Mark Moody Stuart.)

Impact of new accounting

At the commencement of the twenty-first century, many of the building blocks for a measurement system reflecting human concerns are in the process of creation. It is important to have identified a "fiduciary" duty of involvement by Global Investors and to have expressed with some precision the class of people to whom they are accountable. This gives content and therefore enforceability to the beneficiaries of the institutional trustees. That these owners are, in fact, Global Investors eliminates the principal theoretical objections to an accounting system based on internalizing all costs so that the market place in corporate goods and services can function according to human-scaled values.

"Best practice" has decreed an elaborate "ritual" through which the board of directors creates a Compensation Committee consisting entirely of "independent" directors. The independence of the directors on the compensation committee is adduced in explanation of the reasonability of executive pay. Likewise, when the independent members of the compensation

Sir Mark Moody-Stuart KCMG
Shell Centre
London
SE1 7NA

Mr Robert A.G. Monks
Suite 800
1200 G Street, NW
Washington, DC
United States of America

30th October 2000

Dear Bob,

Thank you for your letter. It was indeed a pleasure to meet you. And thank you for clarifying for me the complex issue of funding for the US political system.

I agree that just as we as a corporation recognize the benefits of sustainability to business it is logical that our pension funds also take such issues into account, having as they do an impact on the long-term health of businesses. The question is how exactly to apply this in practice, and to how to express it publicly as a strategy.

Best wishes,

Yours sincerely,

Mark Moody-Stuart

committee appoint an independent executive compensation consultant to assist them, one need suspend disbelief as to the appetite of personal service organizations to bring unwelcome advice to their clients. The reality is that very intelligent people have deliberately misused language and structure in describing the process by which the pay for principal executives of American corporations is decided.

The National Bureau of Economic Research (US) has recently made clear that the abuse of power by CEOs that has led to the grotesque compensation profile of today is attributable to poor governance, specifically, to an absence of any effective involvement of ownership. "In practice, executive compensation seems to be better characterized by either the skimming or the contracting model depending on the extent to which there is an active 'principal' (or principals) present to actually design pay contracts. Better governance means that there is more of an active principal and optimal contracting fits better. Worse governance means that there is less of an active principal and the CEO is more likely to set his own pay."[13]

Maybe this is what Stephen Byers had in mind: "It may be appropriate for the board to discuss aspects of directors' remuneration with investors…"[14] This responsibility must be laid at the door of the trustees, themselves; it is utterly unrealistic to expect money managers, hardly ill compensated and dependent on the good will of corporate management, to discharge the function of "principal." It is time to "Get Real."

Real corporate directors

CEOs do what they are paid to do. Boards of Directors are responsible for creating compensation arrangements for key officers that align their interests with those of the owners of the corporation.

Many corporations have made efforts to create a public image that is more sympathetic than that of the mechanical profit seeker. We will consider at some length a variety of performance codes over the last three decades and their relationship to corporate functioning. Elsewhere I have suggested that it would be inappropriate, and possibly illegal, for a corporate management to pursue objectives beyond long-term value maximization.[15] What we will first try to understand is how the adoption of values that cannot be numerically related to profit maximization and their inculcation throughout the corporate system can be expected to influence results.

As Peter Drucker wrote me several years ago, the "market" is not a magical indicator.

> "… And one of the basic problems is that management has no way to judge by what criteria outside shareholders value and appraise performance – the stock market is surely the least reliable judge or, at best, only one judge and one that is subject to so many other influences that it is practically impossible to disentangle what, of the stock market appraisal, reflects the company's performance and what reflects caprice, affects the whims of securities analysts, short-term fashions

and the general level of the economy and of the market rather than the perfor-
mance of a company itself."[16]

Choosing the right performance measures is a difficult process – one subject to frequent error and requiring constant supervision, measurement and change. As the *Financial Times* has noted, "The choice of measures must be linked to factors such as corporate strategy, value drivers, organizational objectives, and the competitive environment. In addition, companies should remember that performance measurement choice is a dynamic process – measures may be appropriate today, but the system needs to be continually reassessed as strategies and competitive environments evolve."[17]

Certain companies have taken up the challenge of demonstrating consciousness of their need to co-exist with others in the universe. Sir John Browne, CEO of BP Amoco, broke ranks with the rest of the oil industry in a speech at Stanford in May 1997 by conceding that global warming may be real. Browne pledged that BP would achieve real reductions in the level of carbon dioxide emissions. He has been the industry leader in adopting pro environmental policies towards developing cleaner fuels and disposal of wastewater. In response to the question – What is the ultimate goal of your environmental policies? Browne answered: "In the end, it's just good business. We know that people are concerned about the environment, that they want to buy products that don't pollute, that governments want to deal with companies that are sensitive to environmental issues, and that people are motivated to work for companies that respect the environment. The big thing is to get the timing right. Our ambition is always to be ahead of the curve, although of course you can get too far ahead of it."[18]

*"**Reward Philosophy** – the remuneration of executive directors in BP Amoco will be based on the following guiding principles: ... total potential rewards will be earned by the achievement of demanding performance targets based on measures which represent the best interests of the shareholder in the short, medium and long term ... Levels of reward for meeting business targets will be fully competitive within the appropriate market while outstanding rewards will be given for delivering world class results ...*
*"**Long-Term Performance Plan (LTPP)** – LTPP focuses on performance within the oil sector and looks at performance against demanding three year shareholder return, profitability and growth targets [in relation to other oil companies] ... ;*

*"**Share Options** – option grants will be related to performance comparisons with a wide selection of global companies. The Remuneration Committee will take into account the ranking of the company's total shareholder return (TSR) against the TSR of the FTSE Global 100 ..."[19]*

BP has gone to great lengths to be sure that executive incentive is virtually congruent with shareholder enrichment. There is protection in the program against the more usual opportunities for manipulation by corporate executives. For example the use of share repurchase programs being choreographed with option grants so as to lock in profits would not be availing to BP Amoco executives. The quest for incentive compensation can be counted on to elicit ingenuity and persistence.

Remaining questions

The question remains as to the effective impact of the company's commitments in the environmental area. Is anyone's pay materially dependent on achieving these objectives? Even if there is no linear connection, will company culture justify a higher market price? Will the market accord higher value to BP Amoco than to a company with less ambitious announced environment ambitions? The auditors of BP Amoco's 1998 Environmental and Social Report consider that management processes could be strengthened through "objectives relating to the implementation of the ethics and relationship policies within performance contracts for business units and key managers."[20] It would certainly give more public confidence in the company commitment to long-term environmental goals if a substantial portion of the ultimate compensation of Sir John Browne and his principal officers were tied to attainment of those goals.

Pearl Meyer is one of the foremost authorities in the US on executive compensation. She advises that many of the largest corporations use nonfinancial-based measures of compensation for executives (not for the top one, however!). These range from the "Customer Value Added" and "People Value Added" tests used by AT&T to the "4-Es" of General Electric Company. Merck focuses on fostering a productive work environment so as to attract and retain employees with the skills, abilities, and attitude to meet present and future business requirements. These companies' leaders have the personal energy to welcome and deal with the speed of change, the ability to create an atmosphere that energizes others, the edge to make difficult decisions, and the ability to consistently execute.

There is considerable interest in tying managerial compensation to employee and customer satisfaction. Even in such companies (for example Eastman Kodak), the CEO's pay is based almost exclusively on traditional performance measurements.[21] Timothy D. Schellhardt of the *Wall Street Journal* reports:

> *"Employee satisfaction, though, remains difficult to measure, and that has been a big impediment to the survey's use in setting executive pay ... What's surprising about Nortel's reluctance to link employee satisfaction with executive pay is that the company has found that satisfied employees add significantly to the bottom line. By analyzing the employee surveys the company has taken for some time, Nortel found that on its scale of 1 to 5, an 0.2 increase in the mean score for specific questions related to productivity conditions can increase profitability by 6.8%. And an 0.2 increase in the mean score of items relating to 'employee engagement' – how satisfied the employee is and whether he or she feels valued – can translate to an increase of 4.5% in profitability. Still Mr. Kozyn concludes, unless shareholders 'start getting vocal about how companies deliver results in respect to how they relate to their people, you won't see a huge movement' toward tying executive pay to employee satisfaction."*[22]

The question lingers – does the market place higher value on a company with earnings of "x" and a good record with respect to employee satisfaction than another also with earnings of "x" with mediocre employee relationships?

The compensation and option committee of Ford Motor Company – composed of Michael D. Dingman, Chairman, Carl E. Reichardt, and Robert E. Rubin – explicitly included normative values in determining the 1999 compensation of top executives: "The grant of Restricted Stock Units depends on the achievement of several major Ford goals based on progress in becoming the world's leading consumer company for automotive products and services with superior shareholder returns: strong global brands, superior customer satisfaction and loyalty, best total value to the consumer, nimble organization with leaders at all levels, and corporate citizenship."

David Murphy, Vice President of Human Resources, describes how Ford has tied the annual bonus to "customer satisfaction" in the effort to delight both customers and shareholders. For 6000 of the top executives worldwide, 50 percent of their bonus is at stake in terms of their contribution to customer satisfaction. A very substantial effort has been made to "harden" the metrics that define customer satisfaction. The company divides the total scoring into three equal parts – one third allocable to the initial sales/service experience at the time of acquisition of the vehicle; one third to the attitude after three months, and the last third in light of customer feelings after three years. One can poke holes in the "formula," but that would miss the point: having this system in place will sensitize the Ford organization as nothing else could do to "customer satisfaction."

Unfortunately the company has found it difficult to apply the same relevant values to its longer-term, higher-level compensation programs. The relevant values in this case express themselves entirely in share price. In principle, the congruency of shareholder and manager incentives is the core on which governance is built. The "numeraire" of executive compensation should, therefore, always be shares in the company. The question, though is how to determine the number of shares. Should this be tied to customer satisfaction or some other measure? Murphy was very open that the company had discontinued this practice because it is difficult to develop credible metrics.

Notably, Ford Motor Company has a "principal" in the ownership of the Ford family and the presence of a family member as chairman of the board of directors. The stature and experience of the committee members are without peer in the commercial world.

The Ford Motor Company is providing leadership in directing CEO energy along lines that are congenial to the interests of society as a whole. This is the right road. We hope that industry as a whole will follow. It is not an easy commitment. The Conference Board has noted the challenge of change: "Given the history of other companies that took a lead in 'doing the right thing,' though, Ford shouldn't expect an unhindered path toward an enlightened future. There are real risks with tampering with the [traditional] business model: risks to the company's profits, its share price, and its reputation."[23]

Paul O'Neill, Secretary of the Treasury, in the Administration of George W. Bush, showed keen sensitivity to the need for "defining values" while Chief Executive Officer of Alcoa. "But, O'Neill didn't hold his troops to criteria that CEOs commonly use, such as profit margins, sales growth rates, or share appreciation. His singular standard: time lost to employee injuries … His safety commitment won over labor unions. By requiring managers to measure up, the program also got employees used to meeting benchmarks; O'Neill later expanded 'stretch goals' to financial results."[24]

Multiples and Coke vs. RJR

Performance criteria have the appearance of exactitude that is often at variance with reality. Most management attention is devoted to creating earnings and cash flows. Market values over many decades have come to be understood as a multiple of earnings or cash flows, or sales for that matter. While it is felt that companies having essentially similar characteristics should be valued with comparable multiples, there is little understanding why those multiples will vary greatly from year to year.

Contrast Coca Cola and R.J. Reynolds – both involve global businesses with global trade names, essentially addictive retail products. Over the years, Coke is valued at thirty to forty times earnings while Reynolds is stuck below ten. This admittedly dramatic example illustrates how the market can value earnings from one company at four or more times as it does those from another. Plainly, the market suspects that tobacco companies will be involved in litigation, will be required to pay damages, and will therefore not be able to support their current profit margins into the indefinite future. These concerns have not been as strong in viewing Coca Cola. If the "multiple" is by a factor of four times the key element in explaining the market value of a company, should not more attention be focused on how those multiples are derived than on the traditional earnings and cash flow elements?

Towards activism – Shell vs. Mobil-Exxon

The Royal Dutch Shell Group was rudely jolted in the summer of 1995 by public protest and customer boycotts over its political involvement in Nigeria and its proposed disposition of the Brent Spar drilling platform. A great deal of corporate soul searching has produced perhaps the most comprehensive Statement of General Business Principles available to date in *How do we stand? People, Planet & Profits. The Shell Report 2000*. Shell has provided an enormous corporate focus on identifying the categories relevant to performance measurement. These are not only related to business and governance mechanics, but are also environmental, social, and ethical values. For each category, working with their stakeholders and other professional groups, including the GRI, they have strived to identify so called Key Performance Indicators ("KPI"). The effort to quantify KPI components will be continued over a five-year period. Shell is working towards producing "integrated reporting." The ultimate objective is a single "bottom line" that will serve as an accurate indicator for the market place to use in making decisions. Shell has committed the resources of money and personnel necessary to assure that this effort is the best in the world. The ultimate questions still cannot be answered: How does one classify the intangible, how does one create a meaningful quantification of the subjective? Is it possible to combine different languages so as to end up with a single result? Shell's leadership is a source for optimism.

Shell adopted the so-called Brundtland Commission definition of sustainable development – "A way that meets the needs of the present without compromising the ability of future generations to meet their own needs" and the obligation to be accountable in financial, social and environmental terms. The company adopted a timetable and a mechanism for disclosure and enforcement. There is always the need to question whether companies genuinely are facing up to a serious challenge or whether they are using the pocket and professional capacity of the world's largest company to create an elaborate appearance. It is most disturbing that Royal Dutch Shell acknowledges that financial statements reflecting quantified costs for externalities so as to permit socially compatible pricing in the market price is the real objective, but that "a truly integrated Annual Report is beyond our remit and poses huge challenges to the traditional verification and accounting profession."

We have discussed two of the great international oil companies, so it is only right to record that the colossus of the industry, the recently merged Exxon/Mobil take an entirely different approach. In their view, success in the conventional mode of measurement is satisfactory and they proudly assert: "Our model has become the benchmark for others to try and emulate … But an increasingly vocal minority is asking not only whether being the world's premier petroleum and petrochemical company entails, other, special responsibilities, but also whether Exxon Mobil needs to look more to such companies as BP and Shell if it is to thrive in the future."[25] In comparing market valuation of Exxon as against BP and Shell, we can understand on a real time basis the extent to which the market places importance on factors not covered in the conventional financial statements.

Shareholder activism – informed and constructive – is essential to "critical tension" necessary for the optimum management of a business venture. There is now available substantial evidence that special purpose – activist funds add value. In the US, the LENS fund has operated for more than seven years with more than 25 companies and has succeeded in outperforming the S&P index during this period. The portfolio for the three-year period culminating March 31, 2000, is some 1800 basis points better than the S&P. Our analysis of LENS' focus companies over this time period suggests that our investments succeeded because we "lost small" rather than "won big." Our activism was more effective in stopping companies from continuing to lose value than it was in helping them generate new profits.

The Hermes fund in the UK over eighteen months has consistently outperformed the FTSE averages. Andre Baladi's ABF Euro V.A. fund, which is the only pan-European corporate governance focused and shareholder value driven fund outperformed the FTSE – Europe by 3.25 percent during its first year and as of December 8, 2000, the figure has reached 7.8 percent.[26] These are funds with publicly disclosed portfolios that are managed for the purpose of demonstrating that informed activism adds value to portfolio companies. In each case, the plan sponsors never themselves owned large enough shares in the "focus companies" to compel change without the support of the preponderant institutional owners. Investment coupled with active involvement is rational in an economic sense.

The externalizers

Corporations that externalized too many costs to the public, such as Occidental Petroleum, Gulf Oil and ITT, generated a sub industry for corporate reform. Ralph Nader recommended federal incorporation requirements so as to permit consistency and tighter control by the domicile; General Motors produced a Public Interest Report in 1977–78; definitive volumes on corporate ethics abounded and corporations such as Cummins Engine appointed chief ethics officers. The Foreign Corrupt Practices Act was passed, and with help from the OECD and the German based Transparency, bribery has officially been condemned virtually around the world. Michael Hopkins writes:

"The 1980s also saw business and profits in a different light. The fall of the Berlin wall and the subsequent collapse of the Soviet Union and Communism was a landmark. At first the West thought that the score was unbridled market capitalism – 1 socialism – 0. But the rules of the game were quickly revised as it became clear that the winners could not ignore social questions such as un-employment in the First World and poverty in the Third ... Consumer activist groups successfully attacked products which were dangerous or of poor quality and groups such as Friends of the Earth and Greenpeace challenged conven-tional wisdom which had allowed the trashing of the seas and the atmosphere for so many generations. Society's growing awareness of the fault of some businesses combined with business' own errors became the motivation behind the further development of the field of corporate social responsibility and the notion of ethics in business."[27]

Business has a continuing need to demonstrate its legitimacy in a world with many continuing social needs. The attractiveness of equity markets around the world will be diminished if business is perceived as unwilling or unable to respond with sensitivity and effect. Michael Jensen, who has provided some of the most insightful analysis of the creation of corporate value, says that we need to provide management with a framework within which to understand value maximization. "We must not confuse optimization with value creation or value seeking. To create value we need not know exactly where and what maximum value is, but only how to seek it, that is how to institute changes and strategies that cause value to rise. To navigate in such a world in anything close to a purposeful way, we have to have a notion of 'better,' and value seeking is such a notion. I know of no other scorecard that will score the game as well as this one. it is not perfect, but that is the nature of the world. We can tell (even if not perfectly) when we are getting better, and when we are getting worse."[28]

We must recognize that it may be very difficult to prove (and we must prove it to the satisfaction of senior officers) that good Corporate Citizen-ship on balance creates market value. Time frames may well be asymmetri-cal. Long-term value for shareholders will not be the same thing as the pe-riod for vesting option rights in management. If we are to join traditional and social values so as to generate a single language of quantitative criteria we need to begin with a new accounting system. In constructing the system, we need to keep in mind some theoretical guiding concepts. Some of these – in particular the need for full costing – are the practical bases for a new way of keeping scores; others reflect possible different kinds of approaches towards the objective of accountability.

The protests were a warning that people will not allow the ascendancy of US-style capitalism and the "corporate values" of profit-at-any-cost to continue unchecked. The perception – valid or not – that large multinational corporations function with flagrant disregard for the environment, for workers' rights, and for the growing disparity between rich and poor, is gaining ground.

If history is any guide, protesters, politicians and trade treaties are more likely to arrive at band-aid compromises rather than permanent solutions. The best way to assure the immortality of capitalism is to use existing mechanisms to fix it from within. From within the constellation of corporate constituencies – owners, workers, suppliers, customers, managers – the leadership, imagination and tenacity to create a financial language encouraging corporate conduct congenial to human society must emerge.

First step

How, then, can the Global Investors begin to claim their rightful position as owners?

The first step that the Global Investors could agree would be the adoption of a very simple Global Corporate Constitution containing three elements:

- Full disclosure of all (excluding confidential information) impact on society. This standard is not as visionary as it may first appear. If the requirement is unequivocally on the company to make public the consequences of its functioning, the level of disclosures will be regulated by the courts in determining liability and damages. Corporations will want to disclose in order to reduce insurance costs and diminish tort liability. Information about external costs is essential if the market place is to function consistent with society's interests. No one should imagine that this information will, in fact, be read by individuals; it is like the information in SEC prospectuses – it is available to professionals who develop businesses in making the essential information available to the various consuming publics. This is the process that occurred with proxy information.
- Restraint in dealings with government is admittedly a very imprecise standard. Perhaps, it should be stated otherwise as the requirement to

disclose fully all expenditures and resource commitment to the elective, administrative and regulatory public processes. If there is full disclosure, entrepreneurs will create businesses to simplify, summarize and communicate that information to the constituencies interested in paying for it. It is felt that no meaningful restriction can be placed on the involvement of corporations with various stages of the governmental processes, but that disclosure will permit those adversely affected to take effective counter moves. The object is not to cripple corporations, but to make clear the extent of their involvement in the governmental processes.

• Obey the law. Oftentimes, in the US compliance with law is considered as one of a number of cost/benefit decisions. One calculates the probability of detection, the amount of potential fines, the costs of litigation against the burden of compliance. This attitude needs to change. The Global Investor can require an annual report of "compliance" and a compensation structure that rewards and penalizes behavior.

These three elements form an interrelated and self-reinforcing conceptual basis for corporate accountability. Corporations are required (1) to obey the law, which is based on (2) informed action by a legitimate government that has (3) not been improperly influenced by corporate power. Laws so developed can be taken as the expression of the popular will.

These elements require shareholder sponsorship because they involve a corporate commitment beyond, indeed outside of, the realm of profit maximization. If corporations are going to "give away" property, it must be solemnized through the informed consent of the owners. These elements are the foundation for harmonious corporate existence within society. There is need for further action.

Under the rubric of "internalizing sustainable development," distinguished professionals known as the Advisory Committee on Business in the Environment, under the chairmanship of Gerry Acher of KPMG, have made gains in this struggle to develop a vocabulary in words and in numbers that will permit discussion and agreement on those elements which need be included in a meaningful financial statement. Clearly, a great deal of effort is being committed to the effort to create a language of accountability. Even the great companies like Shell encounter the obstacle that they cannot do it all themselves, they cannot get out ahead of the professional groups or the regulators. There is a limit to their capacity to lead.

Leadership

The Global Investors are in a unique position to lead – but only they have interests in all major companies for an indefinite time period. Their perspective is the creation and maintenance of an environment congenial to equity investment.

Global Investors are likely to discover the true costs of externalities, and take action accordingly. As explained in Chapter 4, Global Investors own some of all publicly traded stocks in the world. As universal owners, they bring a new perspective to the troublesome and time-honored question as to whom between the corporation and society should pay for the externalized costs of corporate functioning. For example, there is no long-term profit for a Global Investor to transfer polluting operations from a strict to a lax domicile.

Brightline®: a basis for activism

The world of investment needs an accounting language that recognizes, and, if possible, rewards investment in categories such as job creation, pollution reduction, sustainability technologies. Who will urge such a language? The Global Investor. Why?

Because Global Investors are in a position of requiring consistent concepts of value from the management of companies in all parts of the world. If their leverage proves enduring, this could result in the inclusion of the full costs of corporate functioning in financial statements, and the beginning, therefore, of a marketplace that will be able to compare market prices that include appropriate consideration of sustainability values.

Global Investors are trustees. They need some substantial basis for concluding that activism in aid of decreasing corporate externalizing will create value for their beneficiaries.

Now they have a tool for that purpose. Using the interactive agent software ("Swarm") developed at the Santa Fe Institute, we at LENS have created a program called Brightline® to stimulate the competitive performance of corporations under different conditions. The assumptions are simple – in the era of the Global Corporation costs have become standardized. Even top management is no longer a variable as Executive Search firms have become worldwide.[29] Cost of capital, cost of raw materials, cost of plant, availability of work force and executives, transportation costs are converging. The significant "competitive advantage" that a firm enjoys is in the appetite of its domicile for externalized costs. The greater the tolerance for externalized costs, the more profitable the venture appears – at least in the short term. In many ways, this is a pattern of today's world with the differing needs of different regions dictating a range of permissiveness about different externalities.

The relevant time frame for different corporate constituencies is widely misunderstood. Managements are prone to complain about the short termism of institutional investors. There are many money managers who live on the tick of the tape, but there are also many long-term holders including an increasing volume of "indexers" or permanent shareholders. One needs to decide who is the "shareholder" for whose benefit management is to run the company. We will suggest that the Global Investor has the appropriate characteristics to personify the object of management energy. Managements are typically most concerned about matters happening "on my watch." Recent commercial history is replete with examples of high profile managers dominating the occurrence and reporting of significant events so as to coincide with their own tenure. The Global Investor is a trustee with long-term beneficiaries; their influence on corporate managements will be in the direction of spacious and long-term consequences.

The Brightline® program has permitted tens of thousands of simulations, testing with many variables, the hypothesis that over a reasonable period of time (six to ten years), a corporation that has a spacious view about complying with law will be more successful than one without such scruples. The purpose of this program is to give the trustees, legally acting for the new class of Global Investors, a prudent basis on which to direct their portfolio to adopt a spacious attitude about compliance with rules in the countries where they operate.

Endnotes

1   Thomas Kamm, "Continental Drift – Europe Marks a Year of Serious Flirtation with the Free Market," *New York Times*, December 30, 1999, p. 1.

2   Vineeta Anand, "Salt plant poses whale of a problem," *Pensions & Investments*, November 1, 1999, p 8.

3 John Hancock, *The Ethical Investor – Making gains with Values* (Pearson Education Ltd, 1999), p. 105.

4 Ralph Estes, "The Public Cost of Private Corporations," *Advances in Public Interest Accounting* Vol. 6 (1995), p. 372, as cited in Stan Lugar, *Corporate Power, American Democracy, and the Automobile Industry*, (Cambridge: Cambridge University Press, 2000), p. 192.

5 Steven L. Mintz, "A Better Approach to Estimating Knowledge Capital," *CFO*, February 1999.

6 *Ibid.*

7 Rob Gray, *Briefing: Social and Environmental Accounting Research*, ESRC Global Environmental Change Programme, http://www.dundee.ac.uk/accountancy/csear/briefing/.htm

8 Paul Hawken & W. McDonough, "Seven Steps to Doing a Good Business," *Inc Magazine*, November 1993, p. 79.

9 The work of Baruch Lev, a professor in NYC and London, has been particularly helpful in attempting to develop a new technology that permits valuation of "intellectual capital."

10 Bill Mahoney, "Appraising Value Beyond the Numbers," *Shareholder Value Magazine*, October/November 2000, pp. 28, 32.

11 Letter from Dr Matthew Kiernan to R.A.G. Monks, March 21, 2000. Matthew Kiernan is the Chief Executive of Innovest, a consultancy based in Toronto, New York and London.

12 Matthew Kiernan & James Martin, "Eco-efficiency warriors," *Investment & Pensions Europe,* December 1999.

13 Marianne Bertrand & Sendhil Mullainathan, "Do CEOs Set Their Own Pay? The Ones without Principals Do," Working Paper 7604 (March 2000), National Bureau of Economic Research, p. 6.

14 Consultative Document, Chapter 7.

15 Robert A.G. Monks, *The Emperor's Nightingale* (New York: Perseus, 1998).

16 Letter to Robert A.G. Monks from Peter F. Drucker, July 17, 1993.

17 Christopher Ittner & David Larcker, "Non-financial Performance Measures: What Works and What Doesn't?" *Financial Times*, Mastering Management Series, October 16, 2000.

18 *Fortune*, p. F-89, March 6, 2000.

19 BP Amoco, *Annual Report and Accounts, 1999* – Remuneration Committee Report, February 2000.

20 BP Amoco, *Environmental and Social Report 1998* – Ernst & Young Attestation Statement March 31, 1999.

21 Timothy D. Schellhardt, "Bottom Up Pay – Companies regularly survey how employees feel about their bosses, But they rarely use the ratings to set," *Wall Street Journal*, April 6, 2000, p. R5.

22 *Ibid.*

23 Andrew, W. Singer, "The Perils of Doing the Right Thing," *Across the Board*, October 2000, pp. 14, 19.

24 Michael Arndt, "How O'Neill Got Alcoa Shining," *Business Week*, February 5, 2001, p. 39.

25 Hillary Durgin, "Giant that Sees No Evil," *Financial Times*, August 11, 2000, p. 10.

26 *Global Proxy Watch*, Vol. IV, No. 44, December 8, 2000.

27 Michael Hopkins, *A Planetary Bargain and the Bottom Line: Corporate Citizenship, Financial Performance and Staying Power* (Geneva: ILO Enterprise Forum, November 1999), p. 7.

28 Michael Jensen, excerpted from the Harvard Business School working paper "Value Maximization, Stakeholder Theory, and the Corporate Objective Function," April 2000.

29 "Rise in Number of Foreigners Running Companies" – survey by Spencer Stuart's Dennis Lyons, *The Economist*, July 24, 1999.

Where We Are and Where We Are Heading

How to Restore Authentic Corporate Ownership

This book began with a success story – the transformation of Westinghouse into CBS/Viacom – and then explored the origins of that success in the famed English East India Trading Company. These stories show how corporations – even more than religion or politics – can serve as the ideal way for human beings to translate their genius into prosperity for many.

But these successes have been hard-won. For every corporate success in liberating human genius, there is at least one that stifles it, both from within and without. Why? Because from the beginning, corporations have had to contend with internal contradictions – side-effects of their most beneficial traits.

Modern corporations derive much of their beneficial powers from their ability to seek unlimited life, power, size, and license. Yet as Adam Smith noted in *Wealth of Nations*, these can make corporate entities dangerous to society.

The problems inherent in the corporate structure have lain dormant for centuries, but they are now manifesting themselves in ways that average citizens can see.

Through a variety of means, as described in Chapter 3, modern corporations have taken full advantage of their unlimited life, size, power, and license. A brief recap may be appropriate here.

- As for life, fines and bankruptcy no longer have the ability to put inept firms out of business; through creative accounting and reorganization under tax code bankruptcy chapters, such firms can go on indefinitely despite poor management.

- As for size, large corporations are larger than any entity ever imagined – provoking suspicions that they may exceed their capacity to manage their own resources.
- As for power, the proliferation of political action committees (PACs), combined with PACs' utter immunity to reform, prove undeniably that corporations wield power in the domestic political realm. Internationally, corporations are filling the power vacuum left after the worldwide collapse of Communism. The "military-industrial complex" (dubbed so by US President Dwight D. Eisenhower a generation earlier) has now shifted into becoming a purely industrial complex with tremendous power over the lives of people everywhere.

All this adds up to license for corporations to do what they will. They may choose to be good corporate citizens or, conversely, they may take actions that cause various social problems, which the public protests in waves. Pollution, the ill effects of tobacco, the problem of Third World debt ... these are all mere symptoms of the problem of unlimited license.

The problem of corporate legitimacy

Corporations exercise a gigantic influence over the lives of the citizenry. How can this vast power exercised by unelected officials be legitimate in a free society? Readers are invited to revisit Chapter 3 to witness some of the atrocities inflicted on society by corporations that lack the due process imposed by informed, active investors.

These problems will not go away of their own accord. Someone must take action – now. In the beginning of the book, we commented on the behavior of the three servants who received funds in the Parable of the Talents. Two chose to be active investors, and were rewarded for this choice, while one chose to be inactive, and received punishment for his error. Is this not the situation that confronts us today?

Crossroads

Modern investment is at a crossroads. Investors in equity will either continue to reap strong returns in years to come, like the two servants who turned to an active marketplace, or they will find themselves struggling just to maintain the value of their investments, like the servant who buried his talent in the ground. Activism will make the difference. Will investors bury their talents in the ground through passive investment, or will they participate in the marketplace as involved owners?

In this book, we propose a solution: responsible ownership in the form of active long-term global owners, notably pension fund fiduciaries, acting through a clear fiduciary framework. We also describe a new language of accountability that corporations can use to communicate with these active owners and with the public in general.

Not all shareholders need to be activist. Some owners may participate meaningfully in equity risk/reward through indexes or other non-voting arrangements – so long as there exists somewhere in the corporate constellation an *informed and effective nucleus* of participating owners. The significant percentage that pension funds own in corporations worldwide suggests that they will be able to rise to this challenge – but will they? The time to do so is now, when success is all around us, rather than tomorrow, when it may be too late.

Lessons from the Founding Fathers

The present situation bears a profound resemblance to the situation confronting the Founding Fathers at the birth of the US, which has become an unrivaled bastion of capitalism.

In 1776, when drafting the Declaration of Independence, the founders had struggled with the word property. Some wanted to say that among the rights of mankind were "life, liberty, and the pursuit of property," so highly was ownership esteemed. Famously, the words changed to the "pursuit of happiness," but the theme of property continued.

In the summer of 1787, during the Constitutional Convention, a great deal of discussion took place concerning property qualifications for the vote. Many of the states would not allow an individual to vote unless he owned property. Convention notes leave this significant record:

"Mr. Hamilton observed that individuals forming political societies modify their rights differently, with regard to suffrage. Examples of it are found in all the States. In all of them some individuals are deprived of the right altogether, not having the requisite qualification of property. In some of the States, the right of suffrage is allowed in some cases and refused in others. To vote for a member in one branch, a certain quantum of property is required, to vote for a member in another branch of the Legislature, a higher quantum of property is required."[1]

The framers of the Constitution opted against a property requirement for the vote, leaving the question up to the states. But it is interesting to note that many states continued to tie votes to property, and the last property requirements were not dropped until the middle of the nineteenth century.

Why did the founders of the US believe so strongly in the connection between having a stake and having a vote? What was it about property that connoted such high value?

Elbridge Gerry of Massachusetts, speaking on June 7, 1789, shed light on the matter when he noted that "the people have two great interests: the landed interest, and the commercial interest, including the stockholders." He was particularly concerned about the composition of the branches of government, but his insight has a more general application. Gerry worried about "security to the latter interest; the people being chiefly composed of the landed interest, and erroneously supposing that the other interests are adverse to it." In saying this, Gerry was suggesting that ownership of tangible property is not the only kind of ownership worthy of protection. In any case, he, too, saw a connection between ownership and democracy – even when the ownership involved intangible property.

Now we have come full circle in America. As a people devoted to free enterprise from its infancy, we recognized early on the connection between citizenship and property ownership – or, more generally, between having a voice and having a stake. The old formula was this: to be a voter, you must be an owner. This idea passed away, but the valid connection it makes between property and responsibility is still true. To be a voter, one might not need to be an owner, but surely *to be an owner, one must be a voter* in the fullest sense of suffrage.

In short, throughout modern history, active ownership has consistently been recognized as the essential base for the exercise of legitimate power, whether this power is in the political sphere or in the increasingly important corporate sphere. The ownership phenomenon literally has sprung into significance during the last 25 years and the emergence of the global investor has only definitively materialized within the last two or three years.

Corporations have become the most useful legal structure for the conduct of business world wide, so we might as well refer to the "corporate mode" rather than the economic or business mode. To be sure, the nation states created modern business with very different characteristics – including the *dirigisme* of France; the several forms of Communism in the former Soviet Union and Yugoslavia, Eastern Europe, and China; the various manifestations of socialism in Western Europe; bank capitalism in Germany and Switzerland; and *zaibatsu/kereitsu/chaebol* business in the East. But as we discussed in Chapter 2, there appears to be convergence towards the model of the globally owned corporation.

The value of direct participation

The key element in many of humankind's most ingenious institutional creations is the participation of the members. The democratic myth survives most vividly in the memory of Greek city-states built in human proportions – these democratic units were limited to the number of people able to fit into an amphitheater and hear a man's voice. In modern garb, the New England town meeting is a living reminder of the value of direct participation by all those involved.

Globally there is nearly universal agreement that participatory democracy provides the best governing alternative. Modern nation states provide opportunity for the involvement of all adults. The low level of voting in most countries is taken as evidence of lack of vitality in the democratic process. Why, then, is true democracy still an elusive dream for large publicly held corporations, which now elude control by their owners?

Corporations have been delegated the authority to organize for the pursuit of profit. As mentioned in Chapter 3, Adam Smith described such enterprise (and thus corporations) as the pursuit of private interest, which through an "invisible hand" works for the public good. It is important to recognize that this is a limited delegation and does not extend to areas of public interest, which are in the political domain.

Difference between political and corporate modes

This is the point at which we need consider the difference between the political and the corporate mode. In the exercise of its primary obligation to ensure the safety of citizens from internal and external aggression, government is the only entity authorized to use physical force. In the corporate mode, a different kind of power is at issue. Corporate owners provide a *discipline on the exercise of power by managements.*

This monitoring function can be performed by any group, which is independent of management, informed, motivated, and competent. The best group today for this purpose would be the trustees of pension plans. There is significant accountability already inherent in the interaction between trustees and beneficiaries in the administration of employee benefit plans.[2] For example, trustees are now required to inform and follow the voting instructions of plan participants in situations where a tender offer is involved.

In the situation of pension plans, the trustees are fully accountable for making the electoral machinery work. There are provisions for the voting of shares as to which no valid instructions have been received. They can be "mirror votes," which means that they will be deemed to have been voted in the same percentage as those as to which valid exercise has been received. Alternatively, the trustees can be required to exercise their own discretion as to voting them. The pension plan will normally retain up-to-date addresses for participants. Participants will usually open mail from the trustee – it might contain a check! There is clear responsibility on the trustee for making the voting process work.

The corporate mode can exercise legitimate power because of the informed participation of the ultimate beneficial owners. In the political mode, we can only hope. As Henry Jacoby opined in his classic treatise on bureaucracy, "That is why the future of democracy is so dependent on the restoration of a politically reliable, aware public."[3] Participation is enabled through the practical ability to hold trustees responsible for making the electoral system work.

The Global Investor: an ideal arbiter of corporate action

Why substitute a new institution – pension funds – for an existing one – large corporations? The answer is simple: pension funds have more of a stake in the good of society and the world. The emerging Global Investors comprise the first institution that is *genuinely global.*

Global values are in the process of being developed in word and deed – through the OECD, through the World Bank, and even through those with different perspectives on the streets of Seattle and Washington, DC, to name only a few anti-corporate hotspots.

The need and desire for investment capital is the force that ultimately will cause values to converge. Investment makes possible certain societal gains, with certain costs. Over time different societies will arbitrage this cost/benefit calculation so as to attract the optimum external investment.

It was the US government's successful effort to stimulate individual savings that transferred corporate control into the hands of pension funds. And it is up to the government now to force the funds to fulfill their legal duties. If pension funds can be liberated from the dead hand of tolerated trust abuse, this significant ownership element can function as the independent force that can call management to account. In the global world, there can be no more effective controlling mechanism for corporations. We cannot afford to dismiss the potential benefits from activist pension funds. There is no other choice.

What happened to democracy?

Nobody decided one day to remove the element of democracy from corporations. In 1932, Adolf Berle pointed out simply that it had already occurred in the US. Much has been written about this phenomenon over the past seven decades but there has been virtually no change in law or practice to reflect its significance. A state of suspended disbelief exists. While virtually every practitioner in the English-speaking world knows the contrary to be true, the corporation laws of every state, providence, and nation continue solemnly to recite that the shareholders (or members) elect the directors.[4]

When intelligent, honest professionals repeatedly use a legal term in a manner contrary to its commonly accepted usage, we are entitled to ask why. When the corporation laws of 50 states recite that the stockholders "elect" directors; that shareholders "vote" for their choice of "nominees"; that proxies are solicited for the "election" of directors, we are given an impression contrary to the actual practice. Excellent arguments can be made why boards of directors should be self-perpetuating. The benefit of – indeed the need for – collegiality in a managing board is one compelling reason. Why, then, the nearly universal reluctance to call a spade a spade? In addition to their responsibilities to assure that corporations are competitive, directors are responsible that they function legitimately.[5]

The "independent" board of directors is supposed (and assumed) to hold power granted to it by the owner shareholders. Its actual power in fact derives from the CEO – which tends to dilute its legitimacy not only generally, but quite specifically in determining the CEO's pay. The fact that the board's power is self-perpetuating and not derived in any meaningful way from the shareholders may explain the persistent language of "election," "voting," "nomination," and "independence."

It is true that in many countries – for example in the UK and the US – shareholders have the power to remove directors, but they rarely exercise it. In no country do the principals, in fact, truly elect or select their agents.

The ominous significance of indexing

This erosion of democracy in the corporate form is particularly alarming in light of the rise of indexing, the automatic selection of stocks based on a predetermined formula. This robotic process is a very profitable activity for many funds, compared to the costs of more active investment based on choice. Fees for indexing are a very small fraction of those charged for active management. Indeed, they can be a minus number.[6]

Many public funds use indexing, including such well-known funds as the California Public Employees Retirement System (CalPERS) and the British Telephone and Postal System (BTPS).

Indexation also appeals to the trustees of private pension funds governed by ERISA. It constitutes an absolute defense against any possible perception of meddling with competitors, suppliers, or customers. The "Golden Rule" for private fund fiduciaries has been rudely coined. "My pension fund will do unto your management, as your pension fund does to mine." The single normative provision in ERISA relative to investment urges maximum "diversification," which is virtually a mandate for indexing. As investment becomes increasingly global, it is almost unimaginable that pension trustees would expose themselves to the liability of faulty stock selection in foreign lands, so the index mode seems likely to expand in that direction as well.

Finally, index performance – particularly when the lower management fees are taken into account – has been, over many years, fully competitive with active fund management.[7] This brings us to the realization that the entire pension system – holding approximately 15 percent of the total public equity in the world – does so (permit a touch of hyperbole) without a single human judgment about any particular company.

This is, indeed, a new mode of ownership – and indeed a new creature akin to Dr Frankenstein's monster. We have created a power and have left out the means of controlling it. At this same time, the global nature of investments makes the likelihood of effective government involvement in corporate governance even more remote than at present. As the flyleaf of this book states, "things" – mechanical processes such as indexing – "are in the saddle." We have to stop them "riding mankind," or at least get human hands on the reins.[8]

The retirement connection

How did this happen? The origins of the Global Investor phenomenon can be traced to the creation over the last thirty years by several governments of tax policy encouraging the accumulation of savings in trust form. This policy created problems from the very beginning, because of the many levels of remove between the ultimate beneficiary of a defined benefit pension plan and the holdings of a particular company held in a fund. As discussed in Chapter 4, these defy enumeration.

We need governments to undo the harm they have done by creating retirement systems that have unintentionally interfered with the proper functioning of ownership in the governance of corporations. The pension systems are uniquely a creation of government. Their primary purpose must continue to be providing retirement security for plan participants, but this should not deter their acting as the responsible owners of portfolio assets. As we have suggested earlier, it is not essential that all owners be activist. It is only important that each corporation have some informed owners who are effective. Earlier chapters have pointed out that the cumulative holdings of the pension system provide an adequate basis for the responsibility of governance.

Some may say that it is unfair to put the primary burden on the pension system. They believe this will give a "free ride" to other shareholders, including infamously those who consider themselves leaders (like universities and foundations).[9]

Are we placing a financial burden on pensioners by requiring them to expend resources without a reasonable prospect of increased returns? No. The investment records of Warren Buffett and Carl Icahn and the special purpose funds – LENS, Focus, and Relational – over more than ten years show activism outperforming the indexes. LENS has developed Bright-line® to permit those interested to experiment with normative activism under many hypotheses. Indeed, it might be argued that pension funds are receiving the full benefits of a healthy equity sector of the market with only nominal contributions. The difference between the fees for indexation and for actively managed equities could be considered by the most scrupulous fiduciary as a justifiable expenditure – even an intelligent investment.

Initiating change

How to begin? In my most recent book, *The Emperor's Nightingale* (1998), I called for the creation of a new type of trust company, formed under existing trust laws and acting according to them with new vision. I still believe that this is a valuable step in the reform process but in the past three years, with the dramatic growth of the Global Investor, I have come to see that more is possible.

Ultimately the political process must answer the question of the appropriate relationship between private business and the public interest. Government must make a determination that the governance of corporations through the involvement of their owners is a solution in the public interest. No new laws need be passed, no new regulations promulgated, no new agencies formed.

National leaders – for example the President of the United States and the Prime Minister of Great Britain – can simply state that as a matter of policy the public good and the law of the land require effective and informed shareholder involvement in the governance of public corporations. In order to provide guidance both to regulators and the public, this policy statement should be supplemented through public hearings and formal reports. A good model for this would be the report on "The Department of Labor's Enforcement of the Employee Retirement Income Security Act (ERISA)" prepared in April 1986 by the US Senate Governmental Affairs subcommittee on oversight of government management, chaired by Sen. William S. Cohen.

Distinguished law professor Alfred F. Conard has suggested that this might be accomplished in the US through an explicit amendment to the various laws regulating institutional shareowners:

> *"The control of business enterprises by their shareholders, including their institutional shareholders, should be declared a purpose of each of the laws that govern securities, employee pension and benefit funds, mutual funds, foundations, and other institutional investors that are the subject of federal legislation. The purpose clauses of these laws should be expanded to articulate this objective."*[10]

The work currently (Spring 2001) in progress at the UK Department of Trade and Industry and the findings of the Myners' Commission "Review of Institutional Investment" (UK) will go far to create a public understanding of the role of owners in corporate governance.

The essential question in all jurisdictions is the same – it is the definition of "fiduciary duty" of pension trustee in the context of portfolio holdings.

We have spelled out why institutional and individual investors would profit from being informed and activist shareholders. We must also acknowledge that they are not. What is needed? The current laws are adequate in theory. In practice, they have not been enforced. Institutions do not dare risk being seen as insensitive to management's wishes. Individuals – especially the beneficiaries of employee benefit plans – have rights, but no way of enforcing those rights that makes economic sense.

There is need for clarification and explanation of the scope of existing laws. Amendments or possibly new regulations may prove necessary. The only way to find out is through hearings – Congressional or Parliamentary – that focus specifically on shareholders' rights and ask the hard questions:

- Do shareholders/beneficiaries have adequate rights under current law?
- Do shareholders/beneficiaries have a cost-effective means of asserting these rights?
- Can fiduciary shareholders continue to subordinate their trust duties to the desires of their customers?
- Do government agencies – in particular, the Pension and Welfare Benefits Administration of the US Department of Labor – have an obligation

to bring cases in circumstances in which individual beneficiaries cannot or will not?[11]

Asking such questions in public hearings could lead to improvements in the law and to enforcement. It may also inspire a new level of awareness among investors about the need for greater activism.

Regulators will not stand in their way. The United States Department of Justice has long taken the position that there are no inherent antitrust problems in the cooperation between pension funds on ownership matters. When I started Institutional Shareholder Services some 15 years ago, I asked Assistant Attorney General Charles F. Rule whether our activities would encounter any legal difficulties. Rule responded:

> *"According to your letters, several employees benefit plan sponsors may be involved with ISS as owners or directors, and the services of ISS will be available to any firm, acting as a fiduciary to shareholders, that is willing to pay ISS's fees. You have stated, however, that ISS will offer advice only on matters relating to the exercise of voting rights on issues of corporate governance, and that ISS will not provide advice or engage in discussions with respect to the corporate operations or business activities, such as the purchase, production or sale of goods or services, of any company.*
>
> *"On the basis of the information provided in your letter, the Department of Justice has no current intention to bring action under the antitrust laws to enjoin the establishment and operation of ISS."*

The US President and the UK Prime Minister can instruct the principal law enforcement officials to identify companies that have not adequately considered the interests of pension beneficiaries, and to bring suit in appropriate situations. As government leaders, they are uniquely free from conflict of interest and especially empowered to take collective action. Their complaints will spark better legal reasoning in these matters. The likely result: coherent guidelines for fiduciaries and enforceable rights for beneficiaries.

Enabling technology

Not only do pensions have access to the information they need, but they can process it quickly using new technology. It is well within the capability of today's Internet for pension plans to be able to communicate directly, immediately, and inexpensively with all of their plan participants and for the participants to feed back questions and votes and elections. This electronic link is the last piece in the puzzle of legitimation.

The Department of Labor has for over ten years been issuing instructions to ERISA trustees as to their obligation to inform beneficiaries of voting and tendering alternatives. During this short period of time, technology has utterly transformed what was formally a burdensome and inefficient process. Today, one can contemplate trustees' maintaining e-mail addresses for all beneficiaries, transmitting information and receiving responses, all free and virtually instantaneous. What was theory in the past is now reality. It will be possible to move the ultimate authority to the beneficiaries who are the real Global Investors.

The trustees will continue to play an important role in the new world. The reality of concentration of ownership makes the "collective action" and "free rider" costs tolerable. Trustees can be held responsible for maintaining accurate rosters of beneficiaries, of assuring communication to them, of providing even-handed and clear information about alternatives. Trustees can be held responsible for the votes of beneficiaries from whom no response can be elicited. The legitimacy of corporate power will rest ultimately on the involvement of such a large percentage of the polity in the affected countries.

It is possible to require even a large institution to inform itself on the governance status of the many thousands of publicly owned companies in the world? There exist several professional organizations providing proxy and ownership services at a competitive price. Among them, Institutional Shareholder Services, Proxy Monitor, PIRC, ProxyInvest, and Deminor.

With no regulatory impediments before them, and with every justification to act, pension funds should move forward now. Whether they should act alone or together, whether they should act in unison or be segregated between public and private, and whether they should act through their own trustees or through money managers remain questions that do not have to be answered here.

The future of investment

The future of corporate investment lies squarely in the hands of every reader of this book. We must urge our governments to remove the obstacles they have created to the working of a free market in corporate governance. In doing so, governments must explicitly recognize who the real guardians of the corporate future are. They must hold to account the institutional trustees who have by their nature the primary responsibility for expressing the interests of the ultimate owners in the governance of the modern business corporation. The sustained vitality and integrity of the corporate system demand nothing less.

Endnotes

1 Max Farrand, *The Records of the Federal Convention of 1787* (Newhaven, CT: Yale University Press, 1911), Vol. 1, p. 301.

2 As the responsible federal official for the administration of ERISA on April 30, 1984, I wrote John Welch of the law firm of Latham & Watkins: "Situations where a procedure for obtaining instructions from participants could lawfully be put into effect would occur only when the trustee had determined that the participants had in fact rendered an independent decision in directing the trustee, without pressure from their employer as to how to vote their shares. Therefore, the trustees would remain responsible for such matters as assuring that the plan's provisions are fairly implemented, that clearly false or misleading information is not distributed to participants (or to correct any such false or misleading information that may have been distributed to participants by other parties) and would also remain responsible for determining whether following participant directions would result in a violation of title I of ERISA."

3 Henry Jacoby, *The Bureaucratization of the World* (Berkeley, CA: University of California Press, 1973), p. 222

4 For more on this topic, see my speech of 12/12/1997 to the American Bar Association's Fifth Annual Advanced ALI-ABA course of Study in Washington, DC, 1997.

5 For illumination of this concept, readers should consult the writings of the late James Willard Hurst.

6 This was the case with a contract between Wells Fargo Bank and the Federal Employees Retirement System Administration (FERSA) in 1988.

7   Note LENS, FOCUS, and the investments of Warren Buffett.

8   Yet the current official posture is acquiescence. Lulled into compla-cency by a decade of stock price advance that is bound to change, they say in effect, "If it ain't broke, don't fix it" or they say nothing at all. Not-withstanding more than ten years of effort, I have been unable to elicit from the SEC a reply to "my" letter requesting a statement of policy on the obligation of mutual fund trustees to vote shares of portfolio com-panies (along the lines of the Department of Labor's policy respecting pension plans, first articulated 15 years ago). Nicholas H.S. Higgins, November 9, 1988, letter to Thomas Harman, Chief Counsel, SEC re-questing advice re responsibility of mutual funds. The UK has been presented with a definitive battery of policy suggestions from Allen Sykes, a noted UK industrialist and governance scholar. It is not yet clear what, if anything, will emerge.

9   If this is indeed the case, then perhaps "active shareholders" could be paid by or at least reimbursed by the corporation, as suggested in a reso-lution I proposed at Exxon two decades ago.

10   Alfred F. Conard, "Beyond Managerialism: Investor Capitalism?," 22 *Michigan Law Review* 1, pp. 117, 178 (Fall 1988).

11   See Appendix II.

Appendix I

Brightline®

The purpose of the Brightline® simulation is to create a simplified, accurate model of a market economy in which businesses compete against each other for a fixed pool of consumers. Brightline® currently models five companies that can be customized by the user. Additionally, the shareowners (owners) of one of the five companies are given the potential to become actively involved in running the company, should the company's performance fall below their expectations. The company assigned to have potentially active shareholders will be called the "Focus" company.

Scope

The Brightline® simulation encompasses five companies from any given industry competing against each other for a fixed pool of consumers. All parameters in the simulation are created to operate on a random basis. The user then adds certain "influences" to the basic random nature of the program to entice the companies and consumers to act in a manner consistent with a certain market. The time span for the market competition can be determined by the user, but 10–15 years is suggested for purposes of simulating the long-term investing typically used by institutional investors.

The five companies must compete in the presence of potential government regulation and shareowner "moderation" of their externalization practices. The fixed pool of consumers represents the total market for the industry. The fraction of the total customer pool using a given company as its supplier therefore represents that company's market share in the industry. Highlights of the simulation are described below:

> *"**Principles of Customer Movement:** Consumers, or customers, are directly correlated to earnings in Brightline®. Companies therefore compete to gain and retain the largest customer base possible. Consumers are attracted to companies with the lowest price product, also known as the best value supplier. Companies can only make their product more attractive by increasing their externalization and, therefore, lowering the price of their product. In the Brightline® simulation, customers will remain with their current supplier until they notice a lower price supplier. Once "seen," through a survey of the market, they will consider moving to the new supplier according to predefined Brand Loyalty levels.*
>
> *"**Government and Shareowner Intervention:** When a company is externalizing beyond the government-defined legal limit, the government can impose a fine and bring the company's externalization back down below the legal limit for a set amount of time. Fining therefore makes the illegally operating company less competitive for a set amount of time. Shareholders of the Focus company have the potential to become active managers in their company, should two conditions be met: 1) their company's market share must fall below a specified level, and 2) the company must be externalizing beyond the legal limit. Once activated, the Focus company shareholders prevent their company from externalizing over the legal limit for the remainder of the simulation.*

Statistical analysis of Brightline®

A statistical analysis of the Brightline® program was performed to ensure the integrity and non-biased performance of the program. To demonstrate the validity of simulation results in Brightline®, we began by analyzing the functioning of all input parameters for the simulation independently and in relation to each other. We began by demonstrating that, with all companies set to function according to the same rules, the basic random movement of consumers does function properly. We then determined that with each company set, one at a time, to have a differential market advantage or disadvantage, the other four companies would win randomly. Such tests were conducted for each parameter that can be set by the user.

Extensive efforts were taken to ensure that the Focus company was modeled in an impartial, unbiased way with the exception of the intended functions of the active shareowners. Indeed, testing demonstrated that the only additional inputs into the Focus company are active shareowner effects.

We have begun testing to determine the potential advantages of Eco-friendly companies and of active shareholder intervention in long-term investment demonstrated by most institutional investors. Analyses presented in this book, while still in their early stages, clearly demonstrate these proposed advantages. We have seen that, in the short-term, the most aggressive, externalizing and Eco-unfriendly companies gain a market advantage. However, we can reliably demonstrate that, with a 12-year investment horizon, a discount rate of 6%, and all companies operating with the same management strategy, the Focus company "wins" the market 17 out of 20 times ($p < 0.01$).

Oil industry analysis

For our Brightline® analysis of the oil industry, we were fortunate to have the expert input of Dr Martin Whittaker, principal author of the 2000 Global Integrated Oil and Gas Survey for Innovest. Dr Whittaker took the lead role in defining how to accurately represent the oil industry in the Brightline® parameters. With Dr Whittaker's assistance, we were able to pit British Petroleum, ExxonMobil, Total Fina, Imperial Oil, and Occidental against each other for 12 years of simulated industry competition. Detailed and described below are explanations of the Brightline® parameters used as inputs in this simulation.

- *Interest rate used for discounting.* Because of the 12-year time span of the simulation, we needed to provide the asset managers with a consistent language with which to evaluate and justify alternatives. We applied a 6% discount rate to all earnings to account for inflation.
- *Run time.* In this analysis, we sought to simulate the long-term investing of most institutional investors. We chose 12 years in order to represent investments longer then the average tenure of senior executives, and yet be short enough to be realistic in terms of projection.
- *(Cycle length).* Although not a parameter to be set in Brightline®, it merits description here. Each year in a Brightline® simulation is broken down

into 24 two-week cycles (for a total of 288 cycles). In the simulation, customers, companies and shareholders are given the option to make decisions and changes in their business once every cycle. This two-week time span for a cycle is intended to be short enough to allow consumers and customers to react quickly to a changing environment, yet be long enough to stabilize the potentially frenetic movement of customers allowed by the speed of computer modeling.

- *Customer brand loyalty.* In every industry there is a notion of loyalty to the brand, or reluctance to change suppliers for whatever reasons. In the oil industry, there are two main types of customers: industrial customers (large corporations) and customers who pay at the pump. Brand loyalty at the pump tends to be low, as customers can willingly and easily, say, drive a block further to buy gas at 2 cents less per gallon. We chose a 30% brand loyalty for this portion of the market. Industrial customers are more reluctant or unable to change suppliers than individuals. We estimated 80% brand loyalty for them. We then estimated that 2/3 of industry revenues are ultimately due to individuals and 1/3 to industrial customers. Using these numbers to average the loyalty, we arrived at a 60% overall brand loyalty which we used in the simulation.

- *Shareholder reactivity.* Shareholder reactivity determines the likelihood that shareholders of the Focus company will become "angry," and thus actively involved in the management of a company, should certain conditions in the Shareholder Anger Mode (described below) be met. This parameter was not used in these analyses because, in the baseline simulation, no shareholders were allowed to become actively involved, and in the Focus company simulations, shareholders were set to be active from the start.

- *Government vigilance.* Different industries are more or less scrutinized by regulators, public interest groups, and the general public eye. The Government Vigilance parameter is intended to represent this scrutiny that keeps companies in an industry from externalizing their costs beyond reason. In Brightline®, this parameter functions by determining the probability that the government will fine a company if it has exceeded the legal limit. We decided that a 60% probability of fining, in each cycle, would best represent the world environment within which the oil industry operates.

- *Vigilance mode.* This parameter determines how the government selects a company to fine, should it choose to fine one in a given cycle. We have used what we call the "weighted-exceed mode." In this mode, one company among those that have exceeded the Legal Externalization Limit (described below) is selected to be fined at a probability proportional to its externalization over the legal limit in that cycle. Using this setting, the company that is operating most illegally has the highest probability of being fined, but all illegally operating companies are vulnerable.

- *Brightline®*. Brightline® is a parameter which represents the "operating freedom" that a new industry enjoys before they externalize their costs on the world to an excessive level. It is in essence a period of time when companies are operating within reasonable bounds on their own accord, and are thus not moderated by the government or shareholders. In the Brightline® simulator, this parameter functions by allowing a set "pool" of total externalization that is allowed to an industry before the government is activated to control externalization via fining. Because the oil industry is quite mature and well monitored, we did not use this parameter in our simulation.

- *Legal externalization limit*. This parameter is used to set the total "units" of externalization that are allowed for a given company before they risk fining. Although it will be described in more detail below (in Management Aggressiveness), suffice it to say that a unit of externalization is equal to a unit of competitiveness. The more a company externalizes its costs, the lower the price of its product. However, externalizing costs are placed on society (for example, higher toxic gas emissions due to outdated equipment), and society will only absorb a finite amount of "waste." This parameter defines that limit which society (the government) determines is allowable.

- *Cycle shareowners may become active*. This parameter allows us to keep shareowners of the Focus company from becoming active shareholders for a specified amount of time. For our baseline analysis, where no company was allowed to have active shareholders, we set this to the 289th cycle (after the simulation had already ended), to prevent shareholders from activating. For our analyses with different Focus companies, we set all shareowners to be active from the beginning, so as to show the current potential of active shareholders.

- *Number of votes needed for shareowners to become active*. Brightline® assumes that there are five significant shareowners in each company. If the company is a Focus company, their shareholders have the potential to become active, should the performance of a company fall below defined standards (established in Shareholder Anger Mode, below). This parameter defines the number of votes, out of five, needed to activate the shareowners and force the company into compliance with the Legal Externalization Limit. This parameter was not needed in our analyses.

- *Supplier selection mode.* This parameter determines how customers potentially choose a new supplier (company) for their services. We used what we call a "random mode." Using this mode, in each cycle, customers will look at one other company, chosen at random, as a potential supplier. If the price of their product is lower, and their Brand Loyalty allows, they will move to the new company. If the other company's price is higher, they will stay with their current company. Consumers therefore do not survey the whole market place every two weeks for a new supplier. Use of this mode in particular reflects Brightline's® roots as an agent-based, complexity theory model. A former member of the SWARM programming team at the Santa Fe Institute created the core simulation classes used in Brightline®. Experimentation with SWARM suggests this approach to be more realistic than a completely random mode.

- *Shareholder anger mode.* This parameter sets the conditions that make the shareholders angry, thus involving them in the running of their company. We used a mode that causes the shareholders to become angry if their company's share price falls below half of the market leader's share price.

- *Penalty hold time.* This parameter determines how long the effect of a fine imposed on a company will last (fining will be described in more detail below in Constraint Level). We estimated that in the oil industry, 6 months would best represent the real world. This estimation is based on observations that results even as tragic as the Exxon Valdez incident are real, but not long lasting in the public market.

- *Constraint mode.* This parameter gives a number of options for how a company is penalized when they are fined. We selected a mode (mode 4) that holds the company's externalization at a pre-defined level (to be defined in Constraint Level, below).

- *Constraint level.* This parameter defines the externalization limit at which a company is held for the duration of the Penalty Hold Time if they are fined. This parameter is only used if Constraint Mode is set to 4. We estimated that in the oil industry, a 25% reduction in competitiveness would be most appropriate. This estimate is based on observations that companies can be hit fairly hard in the short term for certain acts. Take, for example, Shell attempting to dump the Brent Spar platform in the

North Sea. Although this is not illegal, Shell lost 20% of its market share in Germany in one week. We set this parameter to 3, or 25% below the legal limit of 4.

- *Company management aggressiveness.* This parameter is the crux of the oil industry analysis, and the data for which we are most indebted to Innovest. This parameter sets the willingness of the management of each of the five companies to externalize their costs. Recall that externalizing costs makes a company more competitive in price, but unloads the company's internal burdens on society. Therefore, the more aggressive a company, the more they unload their costs on society. We used the Innovest EcoValue 21 scores from their 2000 Global Integrated Oil and Gas Survey. We picked our five companies based on their international presence and their broad range of EcoValue scores. Dr Whittaker was kind enough to provide us with preliminary scores before the actual publication was released. EcoValue scores go from best to worst as follows: AAA, AA, A, BBB, BB, B, CCC. BP received an AAA, ExxonMobil an A, Total Fina a BBB, Imperial a B, and Occidental a CCC. To these scores we attached the following Management Aggressiveness numbers (significance to be explained later). BP was a 20, ExxonMobil a 16, Total Fina a 14, Imperial a 12, and Occidental an 8. These numbers determine the likelihood that a company will increase their externalization in a given cycle. A 20 means that there is a 1 in 20 chance in each cycle that a company will increase externalization. An 8 means that there is a 1 in 8 chance (more likely) that they will increase, and so on in between.

The results presented in the main text of the book use the Brightline® settings we have described above. The Brightline® simulator and the parameter file used for the baseline Oil Industry analysis can be seen at **http://www.ragm.com/brightline/index.html**. The version currently available online is slightly older than the one we have used here. However, Brightline® is a work-in-progress and new versions will be updated regularly. Indeed, we encourage any interested parties to use Brightline® and give us feedback on the program. We consider Brightline® to be an ongoing project and value users' suggestions.

Appendix II

Stone & Webster
Employee/Beneficiary Remedies

Robert A.G. Monks
1200 G Street, NW, Suite 800
Washington, DC 20005

February 12, 2001

Honorable Edward M. Kennedy
Committee on Health, Education, Labor and Pensions
United States Senate
315 Senate Russell Office Bldg
Washington, DC 20510

Re: Rights and Remedies of Employee/Investors Under the Employee
Retirement Income Security Act of 1974 ("ERISA") – Stone & Webster –
Proof of Claim, US Bankruptcy Court, US Department of Labor – Case
Number 00–02142 (RRM)

Dear Ted,

Certain recent developments have confirmed my concern that ERISA
protection against trustee negligence and misconduct is not available to
employee/investors under certain circumstances. This situation has caused
and continues to cause substantial damage to working people who have
been encouraged by the statute to invest; it is plainly contrary to the intention of the drafters of the statute. The situation needs administrative review

within the Department of Labor (DOL) and Hearings by the appropriate legislative committees.

I served as the federal official responsible for the administration of ERISA* from 1984 to 1985 and have for the last twenty years been actively involved in the questions of shareholder rights. ERISA is one of the great legislative accomplishments of recent decades. Encouraged by its precise articulation of right and obligations, American employees and employers have created the largest pool of investment capital in the history of the world. This is a hugely important national asset. More Americans have a beneficial ownership of business today than in any other country or at any other time.

One of the important elements of ERISA is the creation of structure and rules by which employee benefit plans are able to invest in the securities of the employer. The employer retains the power to choose the trustee of employee benefit plans. Since the decisions of the Delaware Chancery and Supreme Counts in the Polaroid case in early 1989, many employee benefit plans have become the dominant shareholder in their employer company. An utterly unintended consequence of the interpretation of ERISA by the courts and administrative practices of PWBA is the practical inability of employee/beneficial owners to hold trustees accountable for losses in cases of conflict of interest and negligence in the investment and management of employer securities. This is a grotesque result.

I have asked my long time counselor and friend, Peter Murray, Esq., a professor of law and practitioner knowledgeable in this field, to review a current situation involving massive losses to employee/beneficial owners. A copy of his opinion concluding that employees have no practical remedy is attached to this letter. Congress plainly did not intend to discriminate against employee benefit plan beneficiaries – and that is the current situation. The law should either be amended; its administration by DOL modified; or the legislative intent should be made unmistakably clear through Hearings so that essential rights can henceforth be protected by the courts.

Respectfully yours,

Robert A.G. Monks
Enc.

*The position is now styled Assistant Secretary of Labor, Pension Welfare Benefits Administration ("PWBA").

Law Office of
Peter L. Murray
89 West Street
Portland, Maine 04102
Phone: 207 879-1533
Fax 207 879-9073
January 25, 2001

Mr Robert A. G. Monks
Lens, Inc.
45 Exchange Street
Portland, ME 04101

Re: Employee ERISA Remedies for Fiduciary Investment Mismanagement

Dear Mr Monks,
You have asked my opinion whether employee participants in employee benefit plans maintained by Stone & Webster, Inc., have a reasonable avenue of legal recourse against Putnam Fiduciary Trust ("Putnam"), the ERISA Trustee of Stone & Webster's employee benefit plans, for 1) Putnam's improvident investment of plan funds in common stock of Stone & Webster only a few months before that firm declared bankruptcy, and 2) Putnam's failure to take any affirmative action as Stone & Webster's single largest shareholder to avert the firm's financial collapse. Based on the facts as related to me, and based on my own legal research and that of Barbara T. Schneider, Esq. of Murray, Plumb & Murray, Portland, Maine, it is my opinion that the Employees Retirement Security Act of 1974 as it is currently construed by the courts does not as a practical matter provide the Stone & Webster employees with a viable legal remedy for the above cited actions and inaction on the part of Putnam and the employees' resulting financial loss.

Material facts

You have advised me of the following material facts, on which this opinion is based.

Stone & Webster, Inc., a Delaware corporation with a principal place of business in Boston, Massachusetts, has been primarily an engineering and construction company, although it has been engaged in other businesses, including at one time securities underwriting and, more recently, cold storage. It has sponsored various employee benefit plans, including a pension plan and various employee thrift and stock ownership plans. These employee plans have invested substantially in Stone & Webster stock and have been for a long time collectively the Company's largest shareholder, holding nearly 33.9% of the Company's outstanding common stock. Putnam Fiduciary Trust, of Quincy, Massachusetts, serves as Trustee of these plans and is responsible for investment of plans' funds and administration of the plans' portfolios. Putnam is a "named fiduciary" within the meaning of the Employee Retirement Income Security Act of 1974. *See* 29 U.S.C. §§ 1102(21)(A) & 1102(a) (ERISA).

Several years ago as the result of shareholder initiatives spearheaded by Lens, Inc. the Company's Board of Directors adopted certain governance reforms including election of at least one truly independent director. The Board also resolved to focus the Company's activities on its core engineering business and divest itself of extraneous assets and investments, including the Company's cold-storage properties.

In 1998 the Company experienced a cash shortage as a result of cancellation of major construction projects abroad. At the same time Company management inexplicably abandoned its earlier efforts to sell the cold storage properties and instead made a major new investment in cold storage warehouses. The cash crisis intensified.

Late in 1999 Company management and Putnam entered into an arrangement to generate needed cash by the sale of additional shares of Stone & Webster common stock to the Stone & Webster employee benefit plans. On December 14, 1999 Putnam purchased with plan funds one million shares of Stone & Webster common stock at a price of $15.35 per share.

Within four months the stock price had tumbled, and on June 2, 2000, a scarce six months after Putnam had bought the stock the Company declared bankruptcy. The employee benefit plans had lost a total of approximately $75,000,000 on their Stone & Webster stock, including nearly $14 Million in this most recent investment.

You have suggested that Putnam's conduct in connection with this investment may give rise to fiduciary liability in at least two senses:

1   The decision to buy more Stone & Webster stock was a very bad one at the time it was made. There were abundant indications that the Company was in trouble. Its engineering business was floundering. The 180% shift on the cold storage business was inexplicable. The independent director had resigned. These circumstances were such as to lead a prudent trustee to use extreme caution in considering a further investment of fiduciary funds. Under these circumstances Putnam's decision to invest $15 Million in plan funds in Stone & Webster stock, possibly without sufficient analysis and due diligence, may well not have been the action of a prudent person in the management of plan funds.

2   Putnam took no action in its position as Stone & Webster's largest single shareholder, owning more than one-third of the company, to investigate the Company's circumstances, to work with other large shareholders to effect positive change, or to challenge management or to hold it accountable. While one cannot expect much pro-active behavior from small shareholders, a shareholder with the relative voting power of Putnam as fiduciary of all the employee plans has real options to protect its investment and can exercise a strong positive influence on management and the state of affairs at the company. Moreover, the proportion of its portfolio invested in Stone & Webster stock meant that the consequences of Putnam's failure properly to manage, monitor and exercise the ownership rights inherent in this investment would be particularly catastrophic. Putnam took no action to exercise its rights as Stone & Webster's largest single shareholder but let management continue in a counter-productive and ultimately self-destructive downward spiral. It can be persuasively argued that such inaction by a plan fiduciary (whose sole duty is to the employee participants of the plans) can smack of conflict of interest and rise to a breach of fiduciary duty in the administration of the plan's invested assets.

At least the first basis for liability finds support not only in reported decisions under ERISA, but also in the Regulations issued by the Labor Department under ERISA.

Section 404(a)(1) of ERISA requires, in part, that plan fiduciaries must act solely in the interest of participants and beneficiaries of a plan and with the care, skill, prudence, and diligence under the circumstances then prevailing that a prudent person acting in like capacity and familiar with such matters would use in the conduct of an enterprise of a like character and with like aims. A Plan may be permitted to acquire qualifying employer securities under section 408(3); however, if the acquisition is not prudent (because, for example, of the poor financial condition of the employer) or is not for the exclusive purpose of benefiting participants and beneficiaries (such as an acquisition that is made primarily to finance the employer), the responsible plan fiduciaries will remain liable for any loss resulting from a breach of fiduciary responsibility.

Department of Labor, Opinion of the Office of Regulations and Interpretations, 96-08A (1996).

If the foregoing facts were asserted and proven in court one would expect that Putnam would be held liable to reimburse the Stone & Webster employee plans for the losses sustained by reason of this most recent investment in Stone & Webster stock. *The question, though, is who is in a position to bring Putnam to court and hold it accountable to provide redress to the employee plans which it harmed?*[1]

Question presented

Does ERISA give Stone & Webster employees who are participants in the employee benefit plans administered by Putnam practical ability to obtain redress from Putnam for the harm suffered by the employee benefit plans and themselves as plan beneficiaries? As stated above and for the reasons hereafter set forth, the provisions of ERISA as construed by the courts do not give adequate support or incentives for employee participants to seek and obtain redress for Trustee malfeasance under the circumstances posed, even assuming that the Trustee is guilty of either or both of the breaches of fiduciary duty described above.

Reasons for opinion

The Employee Retirement Income Security Act of 1974 (ERISA) was hailed at its enactment as legislation giving important rights to employee beneficiaries of private pension and employee benefit plans. For the first time, the entire group of obligations and relationships involved in the nation's private pension system were brought under one regulatory scheme. The obligations of sponsors and administrators of employee benefit plans were federalized and clarified. The "prudent man rule" was adopted to govern the responsibilities of plan fiduciaries with respect to investment of plan funds. All of these measures, although creating some added complexity in employee benefit administration, have tended to rationalize and improve the administration of employee benefit plans. On the other hand, it is now evident, if it was not evident at the time ERISA was enacted, that the portions of ERISA which provide remedies for breach of ERISA-created fiduciary obligations seriously limit the practical ability of employee participants in ERISA plans to obtain legal redress either for themselves or for the plans of which they are members.

1. Employee claims for fiduciary liability under ERISA

The provisions of ERISA that provide remedies for breaches of fiduciary duty by trustees are found in 29 U.S.C. § 1109 and 1132. Read together, the statutory sections of ERISA that provide the remedy for breach of fiduciary duty give both individual plan participants, beneficiaries, and fiduciaries, as well as the Department of Labor standing to enforce ERISA's fiduciary requirements by suit in court.

Individual employees or beneficiaries may bring claims against fiduciaries both in their individual capacities, *see* 29 U.S.C. § 1132(a)(3) (allowing generalized relief) and on behalf of the plan as a whole, *see* 29 U.S.C. § 1132 (a)(2) (allowing specific relief under section 1109). *See Varity Corp. v. Howe*, 516 U.S. 489 (1996) (recognizing right of individual plan members in breach of fiduciary duty case to bring claims pursuant to 29 U.S.C. § 1132(a)(3) to seek reinstatement of benefits that were given up as a result of fiduciary's breach). ERISA does not, however, give individual employees or beneficiaries the right to bring breach of fiduciary duty cases seeking their own compensatory damages. Although individual employees or beneficiaries may bring actions on behalf of a plan against a trustee for breach of fiduciary duty and obtain in such actions restitutionary remedies to reimburse the plan for its losses, the structure of ERISA as it now exists deters such actions and makes them a practical improbability.

The only circumstances under which a plan participant, fiduciary, or beneficiary can complain in her own name of actions of the trustee are those cases in which the individual can establish some sort of individualized harm. For example, in *Varity,* after a company that sponsored a self-funded employee welfare benefit plan decided to transfer the assets of all of its failing divisions to a new company, the employees were induced by the company in its capacity as plan administrator to release it from its obligations under its plan and "sign up" for benefits in the new company's plan. The new company failed and the employees successfully brought suit to be "reinstated" into the plan of the original employer. In the case of *Varity*, the employees were able to show some sort of individualized harm to their own benefit packages, which the Supreme Court enabled them to pursue under 29 U.S.C. § 1132(a)(3).

Under this doctrine, the most common category of cases brought under ERISA are claims by employees for withheld or terminated benefits. Such claims involve individualized harm to the employees. They also produce individual economic recoveries which will support the employment of counsel and contingent fee arrangements.

In cases where a fiduciary has mismanaged plan investments, the harm is to the plan as a whole rather than individual employees, and will not support individual actions. Although employees clearly have the right to bring suit for such harms, the proceeds of such suits go directly to the benefit of the plans. There is nothing which goes to the employee or employees who go to the trouble to bring the suits.

There is also no money available from which to pay contingent fees to the employees' lawyers. Employees, although authorized to bring suit for the benefit of employee plans, do not have the authority to dedicate plan assets (including amounts recovered for the benefit of the plan) to the payment of the employees' lawyers' fees. There is thus very little incentive for employees to bring such suits and no means by which to finance them.

This does not mean that there are no cases in which employees have complained of breaches of fiduciary duty by trustees and other fiduciaries. There have even been cases where employees have been able to maintain breach of fiduciary claims against trustees that have invested in employer stock, when the employees have been able to demonstrate that the trustees abused their discretion. *E.g. Moench v. Roberston*, 62 F.3d 553, 571 (3rd Cir. 1995) (reversing summary judgment in favor of trustee and remanding for factual determination of whether trustee had divided loyalties and made an impartial investigation of all options). The difficulty is that there is very little practical incentive for most employees, particularly non-management employees of large corporations, to bring such actions, where there is no direct economic return to the employee and no direct economic recovery to support a contingent fee to the employees' lawyer.

While claims in behalf of numerous employees against a single wrongdoer would seem to be well suited to class action treatment, ERISA effectively displaces the class action by authorizing any employee to bring suit in behalf of the plan, and limits the opportunity of employees to bring claims in their own interests by limiting employees' ability to obtain compensatory damages. *See McLeod v. Oregon Lithopring, Inc.*, 102 F.3d 376 (9th Cir. 1996) (holding that while individuals may bring breach of fiduciary duty claims against a plan administrator as a result of the Supreme Court's holding in *Varity*, such claims are limited to equitable relief and employees may not pursue compensatory damages); *see also Hoeberling v. Nolan*, 49 F.Supp. 575 E.D. Mich. 1999).

It is unlikely that even a group of employees will wish to bring a suit which will only redound indirectly and in small part to their benefit. The indirect per-employee effect of even egregious losses such as those sustained by the Stone & Webster plans in this case is unlikely to provide enough incentive to cause employees to initiate a David-and-Goliath battle with a multi-million dollar adversary such as Putnam Fiduciary Trust, to recover funds which will only ultimately redound in tiny proportion to their individual benefits.

2. Actions by the Department of Labor for the benefit of employees harmed by fiduciary misconduct

One option for the Stone & Webster employees might be to try to convince the U.S. Department of Labor (DOL) to bring suit and obtain redress in their behalf. An aggressive program of public enforcement of ERISA fiduciary standards by DOL-instituted litigation could in part make up for the lack of resources and incentives for private enforcement by employees and their lawyers. While the DOL has occasionally brought a case raising issues of fiduciary liability for poor investment decisions, the relative rarity of reported cases of this kind suggests that such actions may be more the exception than the rule. One would expect that the Department of Labor's limited resources must be allocated to those programs it considers most important for the nation as a whole, and may not suffice to provide redress to individual groups of employees harmed by investment mismanagement by their plan fiduciaries. Indeed, the policy of the DOL in recent years has been to emphasize bringing erring fiduciaries into "voluntary compliance" rather than holding them financially responsible for the effects of their lapses on the plans in their trust. *See, e.g.* U.S. Department of Labor, Fact Sheet: Voluntary Fiduciary Correction Program, www.dol.dol/pwba/public/pubs/vfcpfs.htm. Although an enterprising employee might attempt to convince the DOL to litigate the issues in this case, given the relative novelty of at least the second issue, one could have no confidence that the DOL would make this one of the relatively few fiduciary enforcement actions that it would bring in court.

3. Attorneys' fees in ERISA claims

ERISA does attempt to mitigate the burden of litigation on successful parties by authorizing awards of attorneys' fees in the discretion of the court. However these provisions, as construed to date, tend to exacerbate rather than mitigate the disincentive to plaintiffs to undertake claims of the kind involved in the Stone & Webster case.

The terms of 29 U.S.C. §1132(g) provide that "the court in its discretion may allow a reasonable attorney's fee and costs of action to either party." For potential employee plaintiffs the message of this section is clear. Any compensation from the defendant for the employees' counsel will be only at the discretion of the court:

> *"Unlike other fee-shifting statutes … ERISA does not provide for a virtually automatic award of attorneys' fees to prevailing plaintiffs. Instead, fee awards under ERISA are wholly discretionary."*

See Cottrill v. Sparrow, Johnson & Ursillo, Inc., 100 F.3d 220, 225 (1st Cir. 1996).

Most circuits that have addressed the question have refused to adopt any "mandatory presumption that attorneys' fees will be awarded to prevailing plaintiffs in ERISA cases absent special circumstances. " *Id.* Instead, attorneys' fees are awarded after consideration of five factors, namely:

> *"(1) the degree of the opposing parties' culpability or bad faith; (2) the ability of the opposing parties to personally satisfy an award of attorney's fees; (3) whether*

*an award of attorney's fees against the opposing party would deter others from
acting under similar circumstances; (4) whether the parties requesting fees sought
to benefit all participants and beneficiaries of an ERISA plan or to resolve a
significant legal question regarding ERISA: and (5) the relative merits of the
parties' positions."*

Sage v. Automation, Inc, Pension Plan and Trust, 931 F.2d 900 (10th Cir. 1991)
(attorneys' fees denied to successful plaintiffs on remand at 777 F. Supp. 876
(D. Kansas 1991).

Thus, a plaintiff seeking to establish a fiduciary's liability to a plan for
breach of duty will have to reckon with the possibility that even if successful, payment of attorneys fees by the other party is not guaranteed. And
awards of fees have tended to be relatively modest, computed on an hourly
basis without multipliers to reflect the actually contingent nature of such
compensation. *See, e.g. Bruner v. Boatmen's Trust Company*, 918 F. Supp. 1347
(E.D. Mo. 1996) (award of attorneys fees equal to about 10% of amount recovered for the fund based on hourly rate of $100 without enhancement).

Moreover, the provisions of ERISA permitting awards of attorneys' fees
go both ways. An unsuccessful plaintiff may be ordered to pay the fees incurred by the defendant. Although the five factors that most courts use to
determine whether or not attorney's fees should be awarded tend to discourage awards to prevailing defendants, *see Salovaara v. Eckert,* 222 F.3d
19, 28 (2nd Cir. 2000), there are instances where losing plaintiffs have been
required to pay attorney's fees incurred by the other side, *Operating Engineers
Pension Trust v. Gilliam,* 737 F.2d 1501 (9th Cir. 1984).

The effect of ERISA'S fee-shifting provisions in the area of claims for
fiduciary liability is to deter all but the most cut-and-dried "slam-dunk"
cases of trustee malfeasance. Without some guarantee of reasonable compensation, or at least a good chance for a real contingency fee, plaintiffs' attorneys can scarcely be expected to undertake complex litigation against
corporate trustees. And the risk of being required to pay the adversary's fees
will screen out all but the most obvious and routine claims, certainly any
cases that raise new theories or attempt to cut new ground.

While it might occasionally be possible to find a lawyer willing to pros-
ecute a simple and relatively obvious case of fiduciary negligence or incompetence, for the reasons above stated, more serious cases such as the Stone &
Webster case, are very likely to go begging. This is particularly the case if

the claim is somewhat novel, as would be the case with the second potential claim described above. While it is perfectly logical to hold that a trustee who neglects the prudent management of an investment once bought is as negligent as one who carelessly makes the investment in the first place, the fact that this claim is not specifically established by statute and is not well known in the case law would make it extremely unlikely that a plaintiff would assert it if it had to pay its own attorney's fees or, potentially, pay its opponent's attorney's fees.

Conclusion

This statutory scheme, as construed to date by the courts, means that at least some of the obligations ERISA imposes on plan fiduciaries may be illusory in that there is no effective means for the employee beneficiaries to hold the plan fiduciaries accountable. This state of affairs is not in accord with the stated purposes of ERISA, but it appears to be an undeniable practical reality.

What would be needed to "even the playing field" would be:

1   Better standards for the award of attorneys' fees in ERISA cases, including a "risk factor" to compensate successful plaintiffs' counsel for the practically contingent nature of such engagements, and standards limiting awards of fees to defendants to egregious cases of plaintiff bad faith.
2   More clearly defined standards of fiduciary responsibility, especially in the area of the fiduciary's exercise of its governance rights and options as a shareholder. This is particularly important where the fiduciary is a major shareholder of the employer, and not only has the ability to exercise shareholder power in the interest of plan participants and beneficiaries, but also is subject to potential conflicts of interest which might impede it in the exercise of this power.

In the absence of either or both of these reforms, not only the Stone & Webster employees, but many others like them, will continue to go without effective practical remedy for serious breaches of fiduciary duty by employee plan administrators and trustees.

My qualifications to render this opinion include several decades of practice experience with employee benefit plans, before and under ERISA, my experience as a litigator in cases involving ERISA issues, and my ongoing work in law academics as Braucher Visiting Professor of Law from Practice at Harvard Law School.

Very truly yours,

Peter L. Murray

Endnote

1   It has been decided that other shareholders of Stone & Webster do not have standing to enforce the ERISA fiduciary obligations of Putnam. *Lens, Inc. et al. v. Stone & Webster, Inc. et al.*, Civil Action No. 94-10787-REK, U.S. District Court, D. Massachusetts, June 29, 1994.

Index

ABP 102–3
AccountAbility 1000 (1999) 152
accounting
    environment 153, 156
    global reporting initiative *154–5*
    holistic reporting system 151
        eliminate concept of waste 151
        insist on accountability of nations 152
        make conservation profitable 151
        make prices reflect costs 151
        promote diversity 151
        restore the guardian 152
        restore accountability 151
    impact of new 159–60
    nonfinancial criteria 156–7
    presentation 150–51
    problems with 148–50
    socially responsible 157–8
    traditional/supplementary balance 152–3
    training/R&D costs 150, 157
Acher, Gerry 170
Advisory Committee on Business in the Environment 170
Alger, Dean 64
American Depository Receipts (ADRs) 80, 91

American Federation of International Labor-Congress of Industrial Organizations (AFL-CIO) 48, 127
American Oil 73, 74
American Tobacco 59–60
Anti-corporate movement
    points of friction
        artistic control 51
        brands 51
        commercialism in schools 51
        consumerism 51
        frankenfoods 51
        globalization 51
        politics 51
        sweatshops 52
        urban sprawl 52
        wages 52
Arthur Andersen LLP 97
AT&T 162
Atlantic Richfield 73

Baladi, Andre 167
Bank of America 130
Bankers Trust 74
Barzun, Jacques 53
Belotti case 54–5, 63
Berle, Adolphe 111, 114, 128, 181

Binns, Gordon 125
Bismarck, Otto von 33
Blackstone, Sir William 33
Boards of Directors 160–62
Boston Foundation 100
Bower, Marvin 17
BP Amoco 73, 74, 161–2
Brancato, Carolyn 92
Brandeis, Louis D. 50–51
Brent Spar 69
Brightline program 171–2, 184
    oil industry analysis 193–7
    purpose 191
    scope 191–2
    statistical analysis 192–3
British Nuclear Fuel Laboratories (BNFL)
    16
British Petroleum (BP) 73, 74, 166, 193, 197
British Telephone and Postal System
    (BTPS) 182
Browne, Sir John 161, 162
Brundtland Commission 166
Buckley case 54
Buffett, Warren 121, 184
Burger, Warren 54, 63
Bush, George W. 164
Business Roundtable (BRT) 72, 115
Butler, Peter 134
Byers, Stephen 159
BZ group 121

Cadbury, Sir Adrian 46
CalPERS *see* Public Employees'
    Retirement System of California
Calvert Group 147
Carter Hawley Hale 130
CBS 16–17, 68, 175
CDI company 85
Cede & Co 116
Centre for Tomorrow's Company 157
CEO (chief executive officer)
    abuse of power 159
    incentives 161–2
    level/rate of pay increase 69–70

pay reviews 113–14
performance measures 160
as philosopher king 112–14
power over government 72–4
process of setting pay for 70–71
as real corporate directors 160–62
charitable investment 99–100
Charkham, Jonathan 120
Chase Manhattan Bank 131
Choudhuri, K.N. 27
Christianity 31–3
Chrysler 74
Chute, Carolyn 52–3, 54, 62
City of London 33, 88
City Watch 88, 89
Clowes, Michael 86, 90
Coalition for Environmentally
        Responsible Economies
        (CERES) 6, 153
Coca Cola 165
Columbus Foundation 99
Committee on Investment of Employee
        Benefit Assets (CIEBA) 125
community foundations 99–100
Companies Act (UK) 88
Complex Adaptive Systems 107
Conard, Alfred F. 185
Conference Board (New York) 106
Constitutional Convention 177–8
Corporate Democracy Act (1980) 46
corporate governance
    global standards
        equitable treatment of shareholders
            137
        protection of shareholders rights
            136–7
        recognize rights of stakeholders 137
        strategic guidance/effective
            management/board
            accountability 138–40
        timely/accurate disclosure on all
            material matters 137–8
Corporate Governance Forum of Japan
    103

corporate value 145, 168
  buy stocks in businesses disapproved by
      fund managers 148
  impact of new accounting 159–60
  optimized long-term 146–7
  problem with GAAP 148–58
corporations
  adaptivity of 10
  antisocial behavior 74–5
  Brandeis' warning 50–51
  centralized management 24
  difference between political/corporate
      modes 180
  direct participation 179
  encouragement of genius 20–22, 29, 35
  evolutionary phases 34–5
  externalizers 167–9
  fallacy of citizenship 54–6
  historical change 44
    cyclical patterns 46
    globalisation 45–6
    government reform 45
    legislation 44–6
    power 45
    royal issuance of charters 44
  lessons from the Founding Fathers
      177–9
  managerial compensation/employee
      satisfaction 162–4
  media companies 63–5
  multinational concerns 47–9
    aggression invites corrective action
        50
    distant externalities permit
        antisocial behaviour 49
    limited liability encourages
        investment 49
    opportunity for profit encourages
        externalization of
        risk/responsibility 49
  performance codes 160–62
  performance criteria 163, 164–5
    Long-Term Performance Plan 161
    Reward Philosophy 161

  share options 161
  privatization 116–19
  problem of legitimacy 176
  problems of hegemony 47
  public/private 9–10
  relationship with society 67–8
  social responsibility 111
  threats
    lifespan 42–3
    power 43
    size 43
    unlimited license 43–4
  tobacco industry example 56–62
  unlimited license 175–6
  values 63
  voices of protest 51–4
Country Music Television 16
Cromwell Charter (1657) 26, 27
Crystal, Graef (Bud) 71
Cummins Engine 167

Daimler Benz 74
Danforth, Douglas 12
democracy 181–2
Department of Labor (DOL) 91, 92
Deutsche Bank 80, 91
Dingman, Michael D. 163
Dirlam, John 97
Dodd, Chris 72
Dole, Robert 58, 64
Domini Social Investment 147
Dow Chemical 68, 122
Drucker, Peter 39, 92, 119, 160
Dupont 149

East India Company 22–3, 44, 49, 79
  lasting energy of 27–8
  legacy of 28–9
  as long-term investment 26–7
  particular genius of 24
  as popular investment target 25–6
  significance of monopoly rights 24–5
Ebner, Martin 121
Edkins, Michelle 134

Edvinsson, Leif 152
Eisner, Michael 65
Employee Retirement Income Security
      Act (ERISA) (1974) 91, 122, 129,
      130, 133, 147, 182, 184, 187,
      199–211
environment 161, 162
  sustainable 166, 170
ERISA *see* Employee Retirement Income
      Security Act
Ernst & Young 153
Estes, Ralph 149
Evergreen 147
Exxon Corporation 43, 153
Exxon Mobil 166, 193, 197

Fidelity Investments 101
Financial Accounting Standards Board
      (FASB) 6, 72–3
Firestone, Karen 101
Focus 184
Forbes, Malcolm 55
Ford Foundation 124, 126
Ford Motor Company 117, 163, 164
Foreign Corrupt Practices Act 167
foreign direct investment (FDI) 81, 119
Frank, Reuven 119
free society 50–51
Freedom of Information Act (FOIA) 91
Friedman, Milton 145

Gates, Bill 28
Gauguin, Paul 35
General Electric (GE) 11, 74, 95, 162
General Motors (GM) 67, 117, 125, 167
Generally Accepted Accounting Principles
      (GAAP) 148–58
Georgeson & Company 84
Gerry, Elbridge 178
Gerstner, Lou 17
Gingrich, Newt 58
Global 147
global corporations 107
global investors

background 79
basis for activism 171–2
charitable investor 99–100
constitution
  full disclosure of information 169
  obey the law 170
  restraint in government dealings
    169–70
convergence of behavior 106–7
fiduciary duty of involvement 159
as ideal arbiter of corporate action
    180–81
identification challenges
  overcoming 90–92
  UK style 88–9
  US style 84–8
importance of 101–2
indexation 100–102
leadership 170–71
modern investment process 81, 84
numbers 80–81
origins 183
ownership mystery 89–90
retirement funds
  defined benefit/contribution plans
    96–9
  major constituent 92–5
  overfunding 95–6
standards for action 105–6
worldwide movement 102–4
Global Reporting Initiative (GRI) 6, 153,
    154–5
globalization 9, 51, 62
Goldstone, Steve 56–7, 59
Goobey, Alastair Ross 134
government
  denationalization of companies 116–19
  inaction 130–31, 133–4
  initiating change 184–6
  regulation of corporations 45
Goyder, Mark 157
Gray, Rob 150
Greenwich Associates 91
Grilles, Joe 125

Gulf Oil 167

Hancock, John 148
Hanratty, Judith 89
Harding, Raymond 60
Harvard University 122, 126
Hawken, Paul 151
Hayek, Frederick 145
Hermes 121, 125, 167
Hermes Investment Management Ltd 134
Hermes Lens Asset Management 88
Hopkins, Michael 167
Houlihan, Lokey, Howard & Zukin 132
How do we stand? People, Plant & Profits
(Shell Report 2000) 165
Hurst, James Willard 113
wisdom from 67–8

IBM 125
Icahn, Carl 61–2, 184
Imperial Oil 193, 197
incentive systems 5
INFACT 6
Infinity Broadcasting 16
Innovest 156–7
Institute of Social and Ethical
AccountAbility (ISEA) 152
Institutional Shareholder Services (ISS) 70,
186
Internal Revenue Service (IRS) 91
International Corporate Governance
Network (ICGN) 105, 126
International Finance Corporation 114
International Monetary Fund (IMF) 48
Intersec Research Group (Deutsche Bank)
80, 91
investment
active 21–2
change in 4
conflicts of interest 4–5
crossroads 177
described 1
direct 84
energy 38–9

framework for fiduciaries 5–6
future 187–8
governing principles 6–7
green (social) 146–7
historical perspective 1–2, 4
large owners of corporations 5
long-term 26–7
modern notions 38
nature of 36–9
origins 28–9
program-related 124
religious origins 29–33
splitting of corporate atom 2–3
ultimate meaning of 35–6
Investment Company Act (1940) 85
Investment Company Institute (ICI) 86,
93
Investor Responsibility Research Center
(Washington, DC) 122
Islam 30–31, 32
ITT 167

Jacobs Engineering 132
Japan 103, 106, 129
Jensen, Michael 168
Jessie Smith Noyes Foundation 122
JETRO 103
John Paul II, Pope 31
joint stock companies 26, 42
Jordan, Michael H. 13–18
Jubilee 2000 Coalition 48
Judaism 29–30, 32

Kamm, Thomas 146
Karmazin, Mel 16, 17
Keay, John 23
Keeton, Judge 131
Kessler, Dr 58
Kiernan, Matthew 156
Kluger, Richard 58
Knowledge Capital Scoreboard 149
Kohlburg Kravis Roberts 43

LeBaron, Dean 115

Lego, Paul 12
Lens Inc 121, 125, 131, 166–7, 171, 184
Lev, Baruch 149, 157
limited liability companies 24, 111
Lodge, George Cabot 115
Lublin, Joann 113
Lund, Peter 16–17
Luther, Martin 32

McCain, John 64
McConnell, Mitch 58–9
McDonough, W. 151
McKinsey & Company 15, 17–18, 106
Mandela, Nelson 124
Mannesmann 43, 127
Manning, Bayless 112, 116, 117
Marks & Spencer 66
Marous, John 12
Marron, Donald 74
Martin, James 156
Means, Gardiner 111
media companies 63–5
Merck 149, 162
Merrill, John P. 132
Metzenbam, Howard 46
Meyer, Jane 65
Meyer, Pearl 162
Microsoft 45, 67, 68, 69, 74
Milken 45
Millstein, Ira M. 104
Minow, Nell 113
Mintz, Cy 149
Mitchell, George 58
Mitsubishi Corporation 147
Mobil 43
Mobilization for Global Justice group 48
Monitor Group Corporate Finance Practice 69
Moody-Stuart, Mark 158
Moore, Stephen 36
Morgan Stanley Capital International World Index 91
Morrison Knudsen Corporation 16

Multilateral Agreement on Investments (MAI) 146
Murninghan, Marcy 31, 99, 122
Murphy, David 163–4
Myners' Commission 185

Nader, Ralph 167
Nashville Network cable TV station 16
National Bureau of Economic Research (US) 159
Newman, Frank 74
nonprofit foundations 122, 124–6
Nulty, Peter 11

Occidental Petroleum 68, 167, 193, 197
oil industry 193–7
O'Neill, Paul 164
option-based compensation 7
Organization for Economic Cooperation and Development (OECD) 45, 81, 84, 104, 126, 146
ownership 111
    creative tension 115–16
    legal/beneficial 121
    legislation 130
    nobody's concern 129
    obligation 120–21
    voting rights 115
    without power 112

Paine Webber 74
Parable of the Talents 20–22, 39–40
Parnassus 147
pension funds 5, 9, 119, 125, 132, 183–4
    activist 127
    benefit/contribution plans 96–7
        age/service-weighted/profit-sharing 98
        cash balance 97
        combination 98
        cost savings 98–9
        employee benchmarks 98
        equity 97
        target 98

major investment force 92–5
new power base 95–6
nonactivist excuses 128–34
ominous significance of indexing
        182–3
overfunding 95–6
worldwide holdings *82–3*
Pension and Welfare Benefits Program 130
Perot, Ross 55
perpetuities, medieval law against 33–4
Philip Morris company 57–8
Phillips & Drew 89, 92
Pohle, Klaus 101
portfolio investment 84, 119
    company guidelines
        board 134
        policies, procedures, verification
            135
Powell, Lewis Jr 54
private companies 116–19
Protection of Shareholders' Rights Act
        (1980) 46
Prototype PLC Core Company Report (2000)
        157
public companies 65–74, 87
Public Employees' Retirement System of
        California (CalPERS) 87–8, 89,
        100–101, 134, 182
publicly owned corporation
    adapting to change 68–9
    CEO power over government/rule
        setters 72–4
    characteristics 65–6
    Hurst's views 67–8
    level/rate of increase of CEO pay 69–70
    process of setting pay 70–71
    self-financing 66–7
Pujo Committee (1913) 111–12
Purcell, Phil 17
Putin, Vladimir V. 104
Putnam (company) 131, 132, 133
Putnam, Samuel 133

Records Retention Program 47

Rehnquist, Chief Justice 55
Reichardt, Carl E. 163
Relational Investors 121, 184
The Report of the Committee of Experts on
        Tobacco Industry Documents (2000)
        61
Revolutionary Abby *see* Chute
Reynolds, Fred 14, 16
RJ Reynolds 43, 165
RJR Nabisco 56
Rockefeller, Nelson 55
Rohatyn, Felix 94
Rosenthal, Benjamin 46
Royal Dutch Shell 68, 106, 158, 165–6
Royal Society of Arts 157
Rubin, Robert E. 163
Rueda-Sabater, Enrique 104
Rule, Charles F. 186

Sarah Lee company 62
Schellhardt, Timothy D. 162
Schering AG 101
Schlesinger, Arthur Jr 46
Sears Roebuck 84
Securities Exchange Act (1933) 85–6
Securities and Exchange Commission
        (SEC) 91
shareholders 111
    activist 127–8, 165–7
    exit of 116–19
    involvement/accountability 120–21
    passive 114–16
    votes 129–30
Simon, Julian 36
Simpson, Anne 120
Skandia Group *Navigator* 152
Sleasman, Barbara 92
Smith, Adam 42, 175, 179
Stone & Webster 9, 131–3
    employee/beneficiary remedies
        199–211
Sullivan Principles 124
Summers, Lawrence 102
Sykes, Allen 128

technology 186–7
Thompson Financial 85
TIAA/CREF 127
Timms, Stephen 38
tobacco industry 56–7
  legal battles 60–62
  legislative background 57–62
  strategic mistakes 59–60
Total Fina 193, 197
Transparency 167
trustees 121–2, 129, 130
  clear responsibility 127–8
  misconduct 131
Turow, Scott 55

Value Creation Index 153
venture capital 36
Verner-Lipfert, Bernhard, McPherson and
    Hand 58
Viacom 18, 66, 68, 175
  see also Westinghouse
Viederman, Stephen 122
Vivian, Jay 125
Vlvisaker, Dr Paul N. 124
Vodafone 43, 127

Voloshin, Aleksandr 104

Walden 147
Walker, Sir David 118
Weil Gotshal and Manges 104
Wells Fargo 100–101
Westinghouse Corporation 66, 68, 175
  acquisitions 15–17
  history 10–11
  merged with CBS 17
  mismanagement in 11–15
  threats to 11
Westinghouse Credit Corporation 11
Westinghouse Electric Company 16
Westinghouse, George 10–11
Wharton School (University of
    Pennsylvania) 153
White, Byron 54
Whittaker, Martin 193, 197
Wilcox, John 84
World Bank 45, 48, 89, 101, 104, 106, 114,
    126, 146
World Health Organization (WHO) 61
World Trade Organization (WTO) 47, 114
WX see Westinghouse Corporation